Green + Productive Workplace

The Office of the Future … Today

Simone Skopek & Bob Best

Jones Lang LaSalle

Cover and text design by Tania Craan

ISBN 978-0-692-29485-7

Printed in the United States of America

Acknowledgements

Our profound thanks to all who helped us research, write, edit, proof and produce this book:

Meirav Even-Har Recycling Council of Ontario (RCO) for her time and insights on waste management

Alissa Tritman of Cambridge Sound Management for reviewing the chapter on Acoustics

Ken Leedham and **Carey Guerin** for their eagle eyed proof-reading

Dan Probst, for his support

John Schinter who started us on this journey six years ago

Jiri Skopek and **Linda Tate (Best)**, for their support and advice (as only spouses can provide)

Table of Contents
. . . .

PART 2

CREATING A PRODUCTIVE WORKPLACE

Introduction

Despite their good intentions, today's businesses are missing an opportunity to integrate social responsibility and day-to-day business objectives — to do good and make money simultaneously.

— Cindy Gallop, Founder of US branch of advertising firm Bartle Bogle Hegarty

We'd like to help you to make your offices more green and more productive.

This book is a distillation of best practices, guiding principles and findings from books, studies, white papers and great articles by some of the most knowledgeable minds in the field. It's also the result of having spent five years working in the "trenches," greening offices for all types of organizations, and discovering that they can be more productive environments as well.

There's a wealth of literature on improving sustainability and productivity in the workplace. Some concepts have been repeated so often that they have gone unchallenged until some lesser-known study emerges that puts them into question. Are green buildings always more productive? Do slides, a climbing wall and beanbags necessarily foster loyalty and creativity?

This book is our effort to summarize the really good stuff, avoid dwelling on the obvious, and provide practical information that's likely to actually help you move the needle. We also want to separate the wheat from the chaff with respect to the many trends, pop-psychology and marketing hyperbole — with arguments that are based on scientific research and common sense.

Greening offices — how we got to where we are

The following, in a nutshell, describes the evolution of greening real estate over the past 20 years, leading to the current interest in greening tenant spaces, and exploring how certain features in the office can help with productivity.

Until quite recently, the focus was almost entirely on **base buildings** and on integrating **green features and technologies** such as energy-efficient HVAC components, green roofs, water-efficient toilets and the like.

Over time, it became apparent that **management practices** such as energy monitoring and verification, preventive maintenance and ongoing commissioning are as important as having all the latest green bells and whistles, if not more so.

The next step in the evolution of greening buildings has been the realization by the owners and operators that a building is only as green and energy-efficient as its **occupants**. Building systems and their operation only get you so far. After all, it's the occupants who use most of the plug load, turn on lights, generate waste and so forth.

This is not just a concern of building owners; there is a growing interest by the occupants themselves to *be* green and to be *seen* as green. This is being driven by a need to **reduce costs**, for example by reducing the amount of space per occupant that needs to be heated and cooled, and a desire to brag about policies and practices that contribute to **corporate social responsibility**, for example, by choosing LEED-certified buildings or commercial interiors.

Base building systems and their operation only get you so far. After all, it's the occupants who use most of the plug load, turn on lights, generate waste and so forth.

And yet, because many organizations don't own the buildings that they occupy, there may be minimal interest by the tenants in spending money to make them green. For example, in buildings where utility costs are buried in the rent, there's little financial incentive for tenants to practice energy conservation. Sub-metering has helped to address this to some extent by allowing tenants to pay for just the energy that they use. As a result, tenants may put pressure on the landlord to make their building more energy efficient. However, in this situation, there's little incentive for landlord to make improvements since it's the tenants who reap the benefits. Another approach is to incentivize *both* the landlord and the tenants, such that whoever undertakes an upgrade gets the benefit of the savings. This complex issue can be largely addressed by certain clauses in a "green lease," which we discuss in Chapter 5.

What about productivity?

While facility managers have been trying to determine the best financial model to make their leased offices more energy-efficient and green, on a different front, human resource (HR) departments have come to realize the importance of creating office environments that **attract** and retain the best talent and support **employee productivity**.

Until quite recently, "greening the office" and creating an office environment where employees were more likely to do their best work were seen as different activities. Now, there is growing interest in finding the link between green offices and improved productivity.

Meanwhile, there are major developments in information technology (IT) resulting in many employees working from home, and a growing realization that open offices need to better support tasks that require concentration, collaboration, connection and confidentiality. With improved communications technology and increased employee mobility, HR, IT and real estate professionals must work together, employing thoughtful office design to develop solutions which are also green.

This book outlines some interesting studies linking green offices and productivity, and discusses key physical characteristics and management practices that contribute to both.

Link between greening the workplace and improved productivity

A recent headline in a trade journal said *"Want to improve productivity? Simple. Go Green!"*[1] This begs the question, "What is it about green buildings that improves productivity? Is it possible to have a non-green building that is productive?"

People have come to associate green buildings with improved productivity as a result of many studies that claim that certain improvements to the workplace have improved productivity. Here are just a few examples of the type of claims, which we present here — not as "facts," but simply to illustrate the connections being made between workplace practices and features and improved employee performance:

Improved acoustics	+ 6% productivity
Improved lighting, daylighting & views	+ 5.5% productivity
Improved thermal comfort & ventilation	+ 5% productivity
Reduced commuting	+ 11.5 days/FTE/year
Improved ergonomics and privacy	+ 6% productivity
Green workplaces vs. non-green	+ 16% productivity
Green bank branches vs. non-green	+ $460K revenue/FTE

If we consider payroll costs, which can run into the millions, just think how much money these productivity gains potentially represent. Based on these results, surely every organization should be bending over backwards to improve conditions in their workplace! But they're not. Why? It would appear that there is a lot of skepticism.

The question that immediately jumps to mind is: "How is productivity being measured?" All these studies have different methodologies, controls and ways of measuring productivity — and besides, you may think, "My organization has its own way of measuring productivity, so what assurance is there that these results can be replicated here?"

That said, even doubters will generally acknowledge that very likely *some* gains in productivity can be expected from upgrading a workplace environment. Clearly, productivity suffers when employees are too hot or cold, sleepy from lack of oxygen, distracted and irritated by noises around them, headachy from glare, exhausted from a tiresome commute, feeling isolated in the workplace and depressed by drab surroundings. Obviously, over time, employees working in these conditions will be less concentrated on their work than those who enjoy a healthy, comfortable, dynamic and engaging environment.

What is it about green buildings that improves productivity? Is it possible to have a non-green building that is productive?

The burning question is, how much productivity gain can an organization *realistically* expect from modifying the workplace environment — and are those changes, lighting, acoustics and thermal comfort and so on, necessarily green?

Notwithstanding the extraordinary claims that some studies make, if we scale down the productivity improvements cited to just a fraction of what is claimed, the financial impacts of even tiny productivity improvements are immense. Take one tenth of these percentages and multiply them against payroll costs, and it's easy to see why organizations are starting to take a closer look at the financial benefit of making certain positive changes to the work environment.

Need to better define terms like "productivity," "employee satisfaction," and "employee engagement"

The problem with a headline like *Want to improve productivity? Simple. Go Green!* is that "productivity" and "green" are fuzzy terms.

In the world of human resources, terms like "productivity," "employee satisfaction" and "employee engagement" have clear definitions. By contrast, the real estate sector has a muddled definition of productivity. Not only that, we're not even consistent in our definitions of "sustainability" and "green." The International Institute of Sustainable Development defines sustainability as "development that meets the needs of the present without compromising the ability of future generations to meet their own needs." Sustainability generally refers to environmental impacts on the planet. For buildings, these relate to energy and greenhouse gas (GHG) emissions, water, use of non-renewable resources, waste management and pollution.

At some time early in the evolution of green building certifications, following the 70's energy crisis, someone came to the wise realization that a building that's tightly sealed and uses almost no energy could be rather uncomfortably stuffy, dim and chilly (or warm). And so naturally, it was decided to incorporate into these green assessments, a section called "Indoor Environment," which gave a nod to ventilation, thermal comfort, daylighting and acoustics. These indoor comfort criteria had little to do with reducing the environmental impact on the planet. They were added to make sure that we wouldn't get so carried away with energy savings to the point that people would be uncomfortable.

Sustainability: Development that meets the needs of the present without compromising the ability of future generations to meet their own needs.

Now, more than thirty years later, as the real estate industry is becoming increasingly interested in the idea of productivity, we find ourselves somewhat muddled in our definitions of "green" and "productive." We're also beginning to realize that there are many ways that an office environment can contribute to occupant wellness, well-being and happiness — for example, providing ergonomic chairs and a juicer on every floor — which, just like ventilation, temperature, lighting and acoustics don't reduce our environmental impact on the planet!

The reason that definitions matter is that if terms such as "green," "productivity," "employee satisfaction" and "employee engagement" are not well-understood, the result can be misdirected effort and expense, and unmet expectations. For example, when an organization believes that switching to an ultra-green building is going to solve employee engagement issues without defining what "green" means, it will be impossible to connect green improvements to employee engagement — or to anything else, for that matter.

It is possible to have a green office that is not productive and vice versa
· ·

All this is just to say that we need better working definitions. If by "green" we mean lowering energy, recycling and that sort of thing, then greening an office does *not* necessarily lead to increased productivity.

Performance & Perceptions of Green Buildings, a study of the experiences of working in Green Star certified buildings in Australia by the Institute of Sustainable Development & Architecture and Bond University, in association with the Green Building Council, found that while a green workplace is a great place to be, there is often a discrepancy between the views of management, who often see greater benefits of the green workplace, and the experiences of their employees.[2] The study found, for example, that almost two thirds of employees in green offices are *not* convinced that they are healthier or more productive.

This should not be entirely surprising. For example, reducing the amount of space that is heated, cooled and lighted can produce energy savings, but it won't improve productivity if employees are packed together without attention to noise, visual comfort, privacy and amenities.

Reducing heating and cooling saves energy but can hamper workplace productivity if people are too hot or too cold. Figure 3 shows the most and least favorite features identified in the *Performance & Perceptions of Green Buildings* study.

Conversely, some highly productive offices may not be green nor efficient with respect to their use of energy and resources, waste management and space utilization. Some buildings that epitomize wellness in the workplace have 13 foot ceilings, and floor to ceiling glazing that offers wonderful daylight and views, but is far from being energy-efficient.

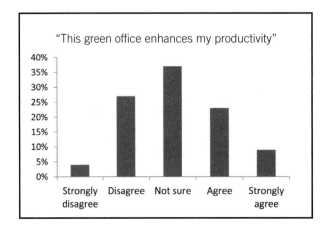

Figure 1

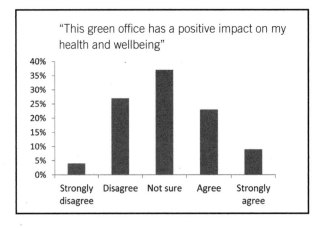

Figure 2

And so the time has come for the real estate industry to tear a page out of the human resources book and be clear on a few working definitions relating to employee satisfaction, engagement and productivity.

If we wish to evaluate a workplace in terms of how environmentally sustainable it is and how well it supports productivity, then we need to draw an arbitrary line between the working definitions of "green" on the one hand, and "occupant wellness and productivity" on the other. This will also make it easier to see where the two overlap.

> **Most and least favorite features in green buildings**
> **'In your opinion, what is *the best thing* about this office?'**
> 1. Natural light
> 2. Open plan
> 3. View
>
> **'Please describe *your biggest complaint* about your office'**
> 1. Air temperature
> 2. Lack of privacy
> 3. Noise

Figure 3

Overview of this book

· · · · · · · · · · · · · · · · ·

In this book, the working definition of a "green" workplace is one that has a low environmental impact. A "productive" workplace is one that has the features and management practices that help to attract and retain the best talent and contribute to employee satisfaction, leading to greater work output.

The aim of a *green + productive workplace* is to achieve a balance: an office that is not only sustainable and energy-efficient, but also provides a healthy and comfortable physical environment, where employees can do their best work, better support business goals and are more inclined to remain as valued employees.

This book outlines how a green workplace environment can be an effective way to embed environmental sustainability deep into the organization. It also addresses how a healthy, comfortable, dynamic and engaging environment can contribute to employee satisfaction, leading to improved productivity.

Following this introduction, Chapter 1 addresses the question "Why Go Green?" So much has been written about the advantages of greening the workplace that it almost seems a redundant topic. Yet despite widespread acceptance of the green imperative, progress remains surprisingly slow. There must be good reasons that not all companies are embracing this. Or are there?

Chapter 2 talks about corporate policies, guidelines and directives. No one wants more rules and "thou shalts." And yet, if one wishes to green a portfolio of offices, then there are certain directives that need to be applied consistently. These should be few, simple, well-communicated, and their value proposition should be clear. Each employee should know what is expected of them.

Chapter 3 is about Green Teams. Where would we be without them?! After all, they are the ones who started this whole business of greening the workplace, and they still represent the "grassroots" that can most effectively change a culture, particularly if they are given some direction and support.

Until recently, Green Teams were usually self-organized, voluntary groups of enthusiasts — with minimal direct involvement of senior management. There is recognition now that grassroots involvement has the potential and power to alter an entire culture. However, this can only happen if management is also genuinely engaged and supportive of Green Teams.

Chapters 4-9 describe certain industry trends with respect to GHG reporting, energy, water and waste management, which have operational and economic implications for greening offices. These chapters also describe ways to future-proof facilities with an eye on the bottom line. For example:

- What is happening in the world of GHG reporting? Is there a business reason that our firm should be reporting the GHGs of our leased assets? And if so, what's the correct way to do this?
- America risks severe water shortages in 11 major cities and is facing rising infrastructure costs across the continent. What impact is this likely to have in terms of future-proofing our portfolio of offices? Is there a business case for retrofitting the washroom fixtures in our offices now?

- How do global recycling markets impact the waste management programs in our office facilities? Is there an economic benefit from recycling? An independent waste audit can cost quite a lot; so why do it?
- As tenant or landlord, how do we derive financial benefit from making energy efficiency upgrades to a leased space? Where are the best energy savings to be found in an office environment?

In Chapter 10, we examine the difference between "employee satisfaction" and "employee engagement," and how these relate to one another and contribute to "productivity."

Chapter 11 discusses the use of employee surveys as a means to help an organization to find ways to increase productivity. No one enjoys filling out surveys and many managers are skeptical that they can help make meaningful changes. We look at the "dos and don'ts" of employee surveys in relation to workplace employee satisfaction and how to relate these to productivity.

In Chapter 12, we talk about how the workplace helps an organization to define itself as a culture, manage and motivate employees and conduct its operations effectively. Workplace conditions can also be a source of satisfaction or dissatisfaction, which in turn have an impact on productivity.

Chapters 13-15 look at the implications of open office environments. On the one hand, there are tremendous economic benefits, but do these come at a cost in terms of productivity? One advantage of open offices that is often mentioned is that they support collaboration. Some employees love working in an open office. Others simply hate it, and their concerns appear to be justified based on the data from many studies that report a negative impact on productivity. How can we design an open office environment to overcome these challenges?

Chapters 16-19 address some of the key conditions in the work environment that can make a difference in terms of employee satisfaction. These chapters describe the various aspects of the workplace that can support or detract from productivity: noise, lighting, thermal comfort, indoor air quality, visual comfort, and amenities that support human connections and a work-life balance.

Chapter 20 concludes this book by addressing these many concepts and issues with a tool to define and measure the greenness and productivity of a workplace. We believe the tangibility of this approach will help to move the discussion beyond ideas into definitive actions with measurable results.

GREENING THE WORKPLACE

PART 1

CHAPTER 1

Why Go Green?

If you are clever, you make sustainability the first factor for your growth.

This gives you years of advantage over other economies.

— Philippe Joubert, Chair of the EU Corporate Leaders Group (2013)

"Going Green is good for the bottom line." Okay — so you've heard that one before. So many arguments have been raised about the advantages of greening the workplace that it almost seems a redundant topic. Unless they've been hiding under a rock, organizations know that they should be practicing sustainability because it's been drummed into them that it's good for business, not to mention the planet.

Yet despite widespread acceptance of the green imperative, progress remains surprisingly slow. That's because greening a large organization is not just about making some big decisions at the top. It's also about establishing a culture that promotes thousands of small actions practiced by many people — like turning off lights or pulling down a blind at the end of the day.

> "I don't see sustainability as something that's in the full front of my mind on a daily basis. I don't see it as being that important when I've got a million other things going on."

"We just purchased recycled photocopy paper. I think it's nearly twice the price, which is a bit scandalous."

"I certainly don't mind doing double-sided, but my printer doesn't do double-sided printing."

As these quotes in a study[3] of employees at City University, London, show, the barrier to "going green" is largely a human one — most people *say* that they would like to live and work sustainably, but for some reason, they're not doing it very much. In the workplace, it may be that systems aren't aligned with the green vision because middle managers are not on board. Employees, for their part, may view environmental or social programs as unwelcome additions to an already-full workload. The reality is that changing to a green culture doesn't happen overnight.

A useful way to understand the benefits of going green is to see what positive impacts this can have for different players in the organization in terms of their roles.

Green initiatives often relate more to an organization's operations than the workplace. That said, greening requires a fundamental shift in culture, and the place where employees experience the corporate culture each and every day is in the roles they play and the offices where they work — the "workplace."

The reality is that changing to a green culture doesn't happen overnight.

For the CEOs and shareholders of the company, greening is necessary to remain competitive

Until a few years ago, green practices were primarily associated with "tree-huggers." Large, thriving corporations, it seemed, could get away with spewing greenhouse gases into the atmosphere, pumping pollutants into the air, land and water, guzzling vast amounts of energy to power their production, and draining off natural resources — with relative impunity and minimal regard for the health of their workforce or the communities in which they operated. As *Green Biz* writer and contributor to Fortune magazine, Marc Gunther once noted, "Big business and environmentalists used to be sworn enemies — and for good reason. General Electric dumped toxins into the Hudson River. Wal-Mart bulldozed its way across America, and DuPont was named the nation's worst polluter."[4] In those days, being big was often synonymous with being bad to the environment.

But the corporate world has changed. Companies that were once considered environmental villains now want to *be* green — and be *seen* as green. In 2011, GE Appliances & Lighting became the first appliance manufacturer to partner with the U.S. EPA in their Responsible Appliance Disposal (RAD) Program to help protect the ozone layer and reduce GHG emissions.[5] Dupont reports that it reduced its environmental footprint since 2004 through 25% less greenhouse gas emissions, 65% less air carcinogen emissions, and 21% less water consumption.[6] Walmart aims to be the number one corporate solar user in America, diverts more than 50% of operational waste from landfill in China and Brazil and 80% from its US operations, and aims to eliminate landfill waste entirely from US stores and Sam's Club locations by 2025.[7]

The competitive arena for all businesses, large and small, is now largely determined by the way that they use — or misuse the environment. As Scott Lawson, a leader in safety, health and environmental programs puts it, "Being green has become one of the most highly sought-after competitive advantages, making it clear to see why so many businesses are coming down with 'green fever'."[8] As a result, corporate executives, small business owners, and employees alike compete to have the latest green technologies, facilities, and products in their industry. In the words of Niall Fitzgerald, former CEO of Unilever, "Sustainability is here to stay or we may not be."

For marketing, greening provides rich data for CSR reporting (if it's done right)

In addition to the obvious, everyday brand value that sustainability can bring, it can also constitute a rich source of material for the company's Corporate Social Responsibility (CSR) report. For example, at UPS, sustainability education is part of employee training. Their United Way campaigns have raised $1.2 billion and supported humanitarian relief including 250 shipments across 46 countries worth US$7.5 million.[9] This kind of data packs a punch with their stakeholders — stockholders, customers, employees and suppliers.

CSR reporting is now a norm. Just about every major company does it. Unfortunately, many do it badly! Increasingly, these glossy reports are criticized as superficial PR "green wash" or thinly disguised advertising, designed to appease investors.

Advertising and marketing veteran and digital marketing pioneer Jim Nail has developed a diagnostic scorecard with 15 criteria to evaluate CSR reports. He finds that fewer than 10% of CSR reports meet a passing grade.[10]

For example, every PR person loves to say that their company is a "leader." Whereas ten years ago, any organization that reduced its carbon and waste and had "vendor relationships" could claim to be a leader, today that's not sufficient. The hallmark of real leadership is when a company puts a sincere and concentrated effort into understanding the issues that concern stakeholders, then presents steps to integrate solutions throughout its business operations, and measures the impact of those solutions.

A good example of this can be found in UK retailer Marks and Spencer's (M&S) CSR report.[11] It shows how M&S is really reinventing its business by trying new approaches — admittedly, with varying degrees of success — but most importantly, learning lessons along the journey. Its aim? To be among the world's most socially and environmentally responsible retailers.

The M&S CSR report is devoid of tree-hugging language. Instead, it outlines 100 ambitious commitments with Key Performance Indicators (KPIs). In addition to community and human resources initiatives, the list ranges from responsible sourcing of products and raw materials (e.g. leather, cotton, wool, food and fish), to energy efficient, low pollution manufacturing, as well as rethinking packaging and in-store operations. Tying this to their bottom line, the report points to £50 million savings in a year as a result of initiatives such as electricity, fuel and waste reduction — money which is being reinvested back into the business. Most importantly, the report does not hesitate to note where the company could do better and states its commitment to improve.

Jim Nail notes also that companies can effectively demonstrate true leadership by using their influence to attack problems bigger than they can solve alone. An example can be found, once again, in a M&S 2014 report, where CEO Mark Bolland writes in the introduction:

> We know we can't deliver "Plan A 2020" alone. That's why we're stepping up our efforts to 'lead with others' by participating in broader coalitions to deliver sector-wide change. Networks of like-minded businesses, working with society and government can make a bigger difference. As our business becomes more international, so too does our ability grow to lead with others on a global scale. Our work with the Consumer Goods Forum and the World Economic Forum are good examples. Closer to home, we've helped create the *Movement to Work* scheme to help thousands of UK businesses deliver 100,000 youth employment opportunities. I'm incredibly proud to see how our plan has motivated colleagues, suppliers, customers and their communities to work together. I want to thank them all for helping us get this far, and I look forward to continuing the journey with them. I also want to thank our remarkable external Advisory Board for continually challenging us to be bold in our ambitions and in our actions.

For public relations and risk managers, greening is a form of 'reputation insurance'

A green reputation and a strong corporate social responsibility commitment can also have a powerful effect on consumers' brand perceptions in the unfortunate event of a major product-failure crisis. Headline news such as the BP oil spill into the Gulf of Mexico, the Red Cross tainted blood scandal, or the cyanide laced Tylenol have the potential to destroy organizations. With news-churning scandals such as these, the reaction by media and the public will be largely influenced by the company's corporate social responsibility track record.

This was the finding in a study[12] by Jill Klein of INSEAD and Niraj Dawar of the Ivey Business School (Western University), which showed that a company's environmental and corporate social responsibility track record has such a powerful effect on brand perception during a product-failure crisis that it can actually serve as a kind of "reputation insurance."

In the study, consumers were given background information about a fictitious oil company, "OilCo." One group of participants was told that OilCo was one of the most environmentally-responsible oil companies. Other subjects were not given this positive information. Study participants then learned that an OilCo lubricant had caused severe engine damage to several hundred vehicles. However, they were also told that this was partly the fault of retailers who had sold the lubricant past its expiration date.

Subjects who thought that OilCo had a poor environmental track record tended to blame OilCo for the product failure, whereas those who believed OilCo had a strong environmental record were more likely to blame the retailers who had not complied with the expiration date.

Dr. Remi Trudel, of Boston University School of Management, whose research focuses on consumer decision-making around social issues, says "Implementing positive environmental practices and cultivating a good CSR image serves as a form of 'insurance' in a product failure situation."[13]

For financial officers, 'Going Green' saves money

As we have said, going green saves money. But have you wondered *how much*?

In 2012, Walmart announced to its shareholders that it had saved $231 million from waste reduction and recycling.[14] DuPont reduced its global energy use by 7% and saved $3 billion over a decade by using cleaner technologies to make chemicals and textiles.[15] In 2005, FedEx Express activated California's then-largest corporate solar power installation at its Oakland facility.[16] FedEx now has 9 solar installations.[17] Director of Environmental Programs, Mitch Jackson said, "We have a clean renewable supply of power at a consistent price, free, from the sun, for 30 years."

"Implementing positive environmental practices and cultivating a good CSR image serves as a form of 'insurance' in a product failure situation."

But saving money isn't just for the big corporations. Try EPA's *Savings Calculator for ENERGY STAR Qualified Office Equipment* at **http://energy. gov/eere/femp/energy-and-cost-savings-calculators-energy-efficient-products**, and you'll be amazed at the potential savings that are right at your fingertips. For example, replacing an old desktop computer with an ENERGY STAR model saves $13 in energy per year or $51 over the life cycle of the machine. Using an ENERGY STAR laptop would save even more.

Another example of easy energy savings is lighting. Here's a simple math exercise[18] that shows how much money could be saved by shutting off lights in a small meeting room. Suppose there are four fixtures, each having three 32-watt bulbs operating 24 hours a day including weekends. Over 365 days (or 8,760 hours per year) and assuming $0.08 per kWh, the cost would be $269.11. Now install an automatic timer to switch off the lights at the end of the day and on weekends. Assuming that office hours are from 8 a.m. to 5 p.m. five days a week (2,340 hours per year), the cost would be $71.88, which represents a saving of $197.23 Now suppose that the office is empty on average 3 hours per day and employees adopt the habit of switching lights off when the last person leaves. Over 260 days, this would save an additional 780 hours per year or $23.96. While $221.19 might not seem like a lot of money, consider that it is accomplished with no investment and can be multiplied across all the meeting rooms in one location. Then, consider applying it throughout the organization's portfolio.

Chapters 5 and 6 examine several inexpensive measures and savings related to lighting, heating and cooling, plug load, server rooms and energy management practices.

For human resources, greening attracts the best, breaks down silos, and harnesses the power of networks

For sustainability professionals, having an engaged human resources department is essential because it's the employees who make greening in the workplace happen. Elaine Cohen, a veteran HR executive and the author of *CSR for HR*,[19] says "HR can help convert the sustainability impacts of an organization *on* employees into positive sustainability impacts *of* employees. Involving employees can have ripple effects given the impact of their work and their multiple daily interactions with internal and external stakeholders, which have the potential to advance an organization's sustainability goals."

But what direct advantage can there be for HR to be involved in greening the organization?

In fact, sustainability initiatives can greatly support many of the objectives of human resources, including being an "employer of choice," a phrase that has become an accepted objective of leading organizations. As contributing writer to *Workforce Management*,[20] Charlotte Huff says, "In the race to attract the most talented employees, many companies are painting themselves a rich, environmental green."

David Jones of the University of Vermont's School of Business Administration and Chelsea Willness of the University of Saskatchewan's Edwards School of Business suggest three reasons that companies' sustainability initiatives help to draw the best employees.[21] The first is that sustainability can really boost a company's reputation and status. Many job seekers

"In the race to attract the most talented employees, many companies are painting themselves a rich, environmental green."

feel that they would be proud to work for a prestigious organization. The second reason is that sustainability implies that a prospective employer cares about its employees. If a company genuinely cares about the well-being of society, it would seem therefore probable that it also treats its own people — its employees — well. Many companies reinforce this belief by communicating how their sustainability practices are connected to their people practices through messages such as, "We care about how we treat the planet, just as we care about how we treat our people." Reason number three is that job seekers who value sustainability want an employer whose values fit with their own.

Companies are leveraging this "green advantage" for recruitment by integrating sustainability with their brand, products and services, and by seeking recognition from reputable third party organizations. They highlight their commitment to sustainability through company websites, career pages, employee testimonials, and recruitment handouts that show how sustainability is infused in daily work activities.

And they use reward systems. GE was doing this even as long ago as 2007, when it launched a contest for university students with a prize of $25,000 in grant money for the best environmental project on their campus.[22] The aim was to boost GE's profile among college consumers, but it was also to attract and recruit the most innovative students.

Perhaps one of the greatest contributions to human resources is that sustainability initiatives can help to break down silos and create rich networks that can have a transformative effect. In *Harnessing the Power of Informal Employee Networks,*[23] authors Lowell L. Bryan, Eric Matson, and Leigh M. Weiss describe how most organizations have dozens of informal networks — whether we call them "peer groups," "communities of practice," or "functional councils" — which can mobilize talent and knowledge across the enterprise, resulting in greater engagement, collaboration and overall superior performance. This is because more information and knowledge often flows through these types of networks than through official hierarchical and matrix structures.

"Green Teams" are one of the best opportunities to harness the power of networks and bring together natural professional communities. By involving many departments with a common goal of integrating sustainability thinking into the very DNA of the organization, teams can affect all operations, paving the way for the future — from how employees are managed, to the overall structure of the organization, and how work is designed.

Conclusion
· · · · · · · · · ·

"Deep-greening" an organization can produce broad benefits, beginning with the numerous savings — from leaner utility bills to less money feeding the photocopier. Consumers want eco-friendly products from earth-loving businesses. So do investors. Reducing your environmental footprint can also make your company more efficient. Reducing corporate travel and implementing telework saves money and can improve efficiency. Finally, working for a "company with heart" is a powerful motivator for your employees. It can boost productivity, loyalty, and innovation.

So, there is a "green advantage." Really.

CHAPTER 2

Green Policies, Directives and Guidelines

To succeed today, you have to set priorities and decide what you stand for. Start with good people, lay out the rules, communicate with your employees, motivate them and reward them. If you do all those things effectively, you can't miss.

— Lee Iacoca

For those of us who call ourselves individualists or "voluntaryists," the idea of more rules and policies is irksome. However, when we envisage the kind of world we want to live in or think of organizations that are most effective, most of us recognize that policies do have their place. As individuals, all we ask, quite simply, is that they should make sense to *us*!

In this chapter we explore some *sensible* policies that, in the right circumstances, can make our office portfolios more energy efficient and sustainable.

Environmental policies help a portfolio to have consistent procedures

The purpose of a policy is to give clear direction on what is to be done by an organization or a group of people.

When it comes to sustainability, it has become a normal practice for companies to have an environmental policy statement. This is a written statement of a fairly general nature by senior management that outlines the organization's aims and principles in relation to managing the environmental effects and aspects of *all* of its operations.

In this chapter, we examine policies and guidelines that apply specifically to greening a portfolio of workplaces, and certain key roles in implementing the policies. In this context, when we use the word "policy" we are not referring to the organization's general environmental principles. Instead, we mean a fairly detailed directive that will ensure that a certain procedure is implemented where feasible, in every workplace of an organization.

Challenges of greening an entire portfolio

In life and at work, we often don't accomplish all that we set out to do. That's because our ability to plan and imagine things ahead of time deceives us into believing that we are able to accomplish more than we actually can. It explains why, despite the best intentions, many Green Workplace Guidelines lie pristine on a shelf, with barely a fingerprint or smudge from actual use.

People in an organization may not feel much ownership when faced with someone else's checklist.

There are countless checklists, guidelines, principles, techniques, and protocols for greening an office that attempt to turn what may appear to be a fairly complex process into so-called "best practices."

However, as we know, the mere existence of these kinds of tools doesn't guarantee success. This may be because people in an organization do not feel much **ownership** when faced with someone else's checklist. A second challenge may be the uncertainty about **implementation** — particularly across a portfolio of diverse offices.

Green policy — make sure it is simple, has a credible value proposition and can be personalized
• •

First is the question of "ownership". People generally hate policies and processes when they've had no input. It's human nature to resist mindless obedience, or even engage in mindful disobedience when someone tries to force us to do something where we see little value. To gain widespread acceptance of an organization's green policies, make sure that they are well-communicated and that the value proposition makes sense to those involved.

It's also important to establish clear ownership, so that each individual understands the part they play. Because greening a portfolio of workplaces involves many people and cross functions, it's easy for individuals to lose sight of the big picture and of their place in it. One way to address this is to break out the great long list of best practices into smaller chunks by role, and make sure that everyone understands their specific responsibilities. In most cases, these personal responsibilities consist of just a few simple habits that are not onerous to implement, but which are important to achieving the organization's goals.

As with any program that requires full participation, breaking out the list into roles and responsibilities can help each individual to understand and take ownership of what is expected.

Also, personalized messages make it easier to take ownership. The closer the message is to a person, the more it resonates. For example finding out about a new drop-off location for recycling eyeglasses to *Vision Aid* is more interesting than reading dry statistics about the company's recycling results.

Messages can be personalized by providing common content for local leaders to customize. Derek Wong, who sits on the advisory board of

Sustainable Business Forum recommends providing a steady drumbeat of "did you know" quizzes, contests, reminders, internal articles, polls, rewards and recognition.[24]

Implementation should take into account the diversity of a portfolio

One of the particular challenges of turning green theory into practice across a portfolio of facilities has to do with the process of establishing communications and implementing action plans that may be quite diverse in terms of size, location, type of operations and work culture in each facility. A large head office with a thousand employees doing a wide variety of jobs is very different from a call center or a small bank branch.

Implementation requires commitment, communications, training, and allocation of resources. It's also necessary to monitor progress to make sure that everyone is doing what they're supposed to, and to catch policies that aren't practicable or don't make sense — and correct them. In short, all of the actions one associates with any effective program management.

Greening a portfolio takes willingness, common sense and good project management

In our long experience of greening client portfolios, we've learned that comprehensive checklists and best practice guidelines tell us *what* to do, but they don't tell us *how*. The truth is that 90% of the "how" is a matter of willingness, ordinary common sense and good project management — with one or two twists.

For example, we've discovered that greening a portfolio is best done using a systematic "top-down meets bottom-up" approach. This means that there are roles for everyone, and a two-way sharing of information and ideas along channels that include the CEO at the top, senior management, middle management and grass roots Green Teams.

The difference between directives and guidelines
· ·

Sustainability directives play a crucial role in the green performance of organizations. These are often developed by fairly senior management, especially where there are implications with respect to time or resources. Examples of this are waste audits and reporting of carbon or water consumption, which may entail certain costs, operational changes or training.

Some companies prefer to use the term "guideline" rather than "policy." The difference is that a guideline is more like a suggestion and is voluntary, whereas a policy is enforceable and is clearly defined. The problem with policies, say some, is that they do not allow enough freedom and autonomy for Green Teams.

In our experience, there is room for both, but it is important to be clear on whether a certain green practice being proposed is a requirement or merely a guideline.

For example, the Sustainability Director of a Fortune 500 company was able to describe many of the company's green initiatives but couldn't say for sure whether there was a requirement for each facility to do an annual waste audit. In the absence of a clear directive, some facility managers were doing waste audits, and some weren't. Consequently, the data for the portfolio was incomplete and was being reported in an inconsistent manner. Diligent facility managers were going to the trouble of doing waste audits, but their data wasn't being used to best effect.

Once an organization has determined which of certain practices should be standardized across the portfolio, then these should be written down and clearly communicated as "must-haves" (i.e. policies). For example, a company may require the following:

- "Every facility greater than 10,000 SF or having more than 25 employees shall appoint a Sustainability Coordinator to serve as advisor and departmental contact for the central environmental team and to organize events and initiatives."
- "Our target is to reduce consumption of paper by 10%. Henceforth, all printers shall be set to double-sided printing. All business units shall track and report the amount of paper that is used."
- "All office renovations shall comply with our company's green construction guidelines to reduce our environmental impact, reduce costs by incorporating more efficient systems and alternatives, and create a healthy environment for our employees."

By conducting a review of a company's corporate green policies and directives, we can better understand what the expectations are and explore the gaps.

The good news is that green office policies can be simple

As the old saying goes, "too much of a good thing is not good." This is very true when it comes to having too many rules and procedures. Sometimes the more policies there are, the less employees feel accountable for tasks. Some businesses have bookshelves filled with three inch binders describing the procedures for hundreds of possible events, or fully developed online databases of policies and procedures which employees can reference through the corporate intranet (but seldom do).

When it comes to greening workplaces, the good news is that there aren't hundreds of policies to choose from and for the most part, the choices are pretty simple. We either dispose of our e-waste responsibly, or not. We either report our carbon emissions, or not. We either switch off lights when we leave a conference room, or we don't. Our choice of normative rules defines our actions collectively, which soon translate to habits and norms that shape and define the green culture of an organization.

Implementation can vary greatly depending on the region and the facility and that's why employees should be empowered to point out where a certain policy just doesn't apply in a given situation.

Need good data
· · · · · · · · · · · · ·

No one likes to have to do another survey — especially not a facility manager who is stretched to the max. However, baselining the performance of a portfolio is important, and necessarily involves collecting *some* data. For this reason, it is essential to make this as painless as possible by streamlining the time needed for data collection, avoiding unnecessary questions that take a lot effort to research, and avoiding duplication. A good "rule of thumb" is to carefully ensure that every piece of data collected is absolutely relevant. In our experience, "the more you ask for, the less you get."

At JLL, we have refined, honed and carefully timed our *Green + Productive Workplace* data gathering so that a facility manager can easily do it in just one sitting, and in less than hour. Quantitative data such as energy intensity, carbon, exact square footage and population, which the facility manager may not have at his or her fingertips, is pre-populated from centralized corporate databases.

There is also an art to analyzing the data. In our experience, the most efficient way to deal with a vast amount of data is to view portfolio performance as a whole, harvest all the strengths (so that they can be disclosed in a CSR report) — and then zoom in on problem areas. This begins at a high level by first reviewing corporate policies and directives and then seeing to what extent these are being implemented in each office.

Greening an entire portfolio is an exercise in prioritization.

We've also learned from experience that trying to do everything at once is like drinking from a fire hose. Greening an entire portfolio is an exercise in prioritization, which assigns more importance to certain tasks and helps to determine what will take chronological priority.

Senior management and the environmental coordinator set policies
· · · · · · · · · · · · · · · · · · · ·

In the end, however, the decision to pursue certain actions across the board rests with senior management and the firm's environmental coordinator — particularly when there are resource implications. The Dow Jones Sustainability Index (DJSI) criteria illustrate the kind of decisions that must be taken at the corporate level. The following are examples of corporate decisions and actions, including but not limited to Dow Jones Sustainability Index (DJSI) criteria for corporate facilities:

- Produce a comprehensive, written Environmental Policy that addresses the company's real estate including leased assets. (DJSI requirement)
- Report the ENERGY CONSUMPTION of all leased assets where tenant energy consumption is metered. (DJSI requirement)
- Report the SCOPE 1 and SCOPE 2 GREENHOUSE GAS EMISSIONS associated with leased spaces that meter tenant fuel and/or electricity consumption. (DJSI requirement)
- Report the quantity of WATER that is consumed annually in leased assets that have metering. (DJSI requirement)
- Report the quantity of WASTE generated annually that is directed to landfill. (DJSI requirement)
- Conduct audits of the reported values for energy, carbon, water and waste. (DJSI requirement)
- Document a green procurement policy for office maintenance supplies equipment and housekeeping products. All new appliance purchases must be ENERGY STAR. Computers should be laptops except for tasks that require a high level of computing power and fast processors, which are best provided by desktops. (not a DJSI requirement)
- Establish criteria and protocols for partial work from home that would reduce commuting. (not a DJSI requirement)
- Document a green construction standard for office fit-outs. (not a DJSI requirement)
- Institute awards or a recognition program that acknowledges contributions and offers opportunities for increased participation. (not a DJSI requirement)

Middle management champions the policies within their sphere of oversight

. . . .

We have already mentioned the important role of senior management in setting the tone for an organization to be green. This responsibility also extends to middle managers and supervisors. Each workplace has its own internal sets of rules and norms. Within this "mini society," managers have an important role in actively championing the organization's values. This includes ensuring that green policies are being implemented within their sphere of oversight and by the employees who report to them.

Many organizations delegate the responsibility of greening the workplace to the human resources department. A study by the Society for Human Resource Management[25] found that the greatest barriers to having effective green workplace programs were i) cost of setting them up and maintaining them; and ii) **lack of support by management**. It is clear that without the engagement by the management in each business unit, green programs have little chance of taking hold.

The following are some suggested examples of the responsibilities of business unit managers.

- Appoint an Environmental Coordinator/Green Team for your business unit (over a certain size), or seek volunteers.
- Actively support the Green Team and green workplace campaigns and encourage employees to participate.
- Encourage participation in the landlord's building-wide green committee.
- Work with the Green Team and facility manager to identify environmental goals, recommend capital upgrades and operational measures, monitor progress through the year, and review the annual green report for the facility.
- Establish criteria and protocols for partial work from home that would reduce commuting; support efforts to report the organization's carbon footprint for commuting.

As Management Consultant Francisca Quinn noted in an address to the hotel industry in the *Toronto Speaks* series, "Stand-alone sustainability programs that is to say, those that are not integrated with business operations, don't do an organization much good. Managers may claim to support them, but if in reality, they know little about them, then the organization will fail to fully capitalize on the benefits of going green."[26]

Facility Managers

"I oversee 50 plus bank branches in the Houston, TX metropolitan area. I take care of all FM issues at all of the branches, as well as putting out bids for jobs, working with vendors, coordinating projects, etc. I have only two employees working for me, and they are on the trucks taking care of daily branch issues. I am the most understaffed facilities manager in the entire southeast system. How do I learn to make the best of this situation, knowing I will not be hiring any new staff in the near future?"

— A facility manager

For this facility manager, greening a portfolio is very likely not going to be a priority!

There's no doubt that greening the workplace has an impact on the work of facility managers. Also, just as business unit managers have an important role to champion the work of the Green Team, facility managers need to advise and work closely with the Green Team.

But there can also be an advantage for the facility manager, for where there's a close relationship, a Green Team can help to take some of the burden from the facility manager's shoulders with respect to energy and sustainability. That said, there are certain tasks which can only be done by the facility manager, for example:

- Actively support the Green Team and green workplace campaigns.
- Participate on the landlord's Green Tenants' Committee and any building-wide green initiatives.
- Review monthly/quarterly energy and water reports to identify and investigate unexpected spikes.
- Arrange for an energy review of the server room HVAC. Monitor temperature set points.

- Arrange for a waste audit. Report waste diversion rates annually.
- Calibrate temperature set-points. Train occupants on office temperature controls.
- Ensure that fit-outs and renovations comply with green construction guidelines.
- Sell, donate or recycle used furniture.
- Adhere to the firm's green purchasing policy for materials and equipment.
- Track concerns (formal or informal) about lighting, acoustics, thermal comfort and indoor air quality.
- Recommend capital improvements for energy savings and workplace productivity.

Without employee involvement, greening the workplace is impossible

We have said that one of the roles of senior management is to establish the "must-have" directives for the portfolio, that middle management has a responsibility to actively champion greening initiatives, and that facility managers must make certain adjustments to the operations and maintenance of the facility. So what are the responsibilities of Green Teams and employees?

Green Teams drive progress by providing awareness and coordinating office campaigns, a topic that is further discussed in the next chapter.

As for employees, their responsibility is simply to be mindful and responsible in their use of energy and resources. These are not just abstract concepts. Being mindful means, for example, reporting a toilet that keeps flushing or removing the food wrapper from the left-over sandwich before tossing it into the organic waste bin, properly disposing of used batteries, and participating in green office campaigns.

Being responsible in the use of energy and resources means small actions such as switching off lights and equipment, avoiding printing when possible, washing a cup instead of a tossing out a polystyrene cup and plastic cover, and pulling down a blind on a cold winter evening.

The many small everyday actions such as these by employees constitute a more responsible lifestyle and add up in immeasurable ways for the organization. The role of employees is not onerous, but it is essential, for without their involvement, greening the office simply won't happen.

Here is our suggested list of employee actions:

- Switch off lights when your area of the office is unoccupied.
- Switch off desk equipment and office appliances when not in use. Check that your computer and monitor have enhanced energy settings. Get help from IT.
- Remove personal fridges, fans and printers to reduce plug load.
- (IT employees only) Decommission un-used servers.
- Pull down blinds near your workstation in summer to keep out excess solar heat, and in winter, before leaving the office to retain heat in the building during the night.
- Bring a sweater to work.
- Keep air grilles and returns unobstructed by papers, furniture etc.
- Recycle paper, glass, plastic, cans and organic waste.
- Safely dispose of electronic waste, batteries, compact light bulbs, printer cartridges in the containers provided.
- Print double-sided. Keep printing to a minimum.
- Use unscented personal care products.
- Participate in green workplace campaigns and employee surveys including commuting surveys and occupant satisfaction surveys.

Policies provide the authority for facility managers and Green Teams to carry out their mandate

Greening an office puts an additional burden of responsibility on the facility managers. They are the ones who ensure that certain directives are followed, for example, by participating on a landlord's Green Tenants' Committee and engaging in building-wide green initiatives, monitoring temperature set points, adhering to the firm's green purchasing policy for materials and equipment, and removing redundant equipment such as personal fridges or printers.

Similarly, Green Team coordinators have their specific responsibilities, including promoting certain initiatives such as a carpooling program, monitoring paper and other resources, encouraging their fellow employees to participate in employee satisfaction surveys or commuting surveys, using window blinds effectively to reduce excess heat loss or unwanted solar gain and so on.

The role of employees is not onerous, but it is essential, for without their involvement, greening the office simply won't happen.

Facility managers and Green Office coordinators need senior management to grant them the authority to carry out these tasks and to expect their colleagues to respect and comply with established protocols. That authority comes from corporate policies that are broadly and clearly communicated, preferably in an employee handbook or by posting them in public employee areas.

Conclusion

Many of us don't care for the idea of having *more* corporate policies and directives, so the bottom line is that they must make sense. Well-thought-out policies provide instructions and delegate the authority to make decisions and take action. They guide the use of limited resources and serve as a standard to analyze performance. Sound policies also help to develop a good public image.

For successful greening throughout a portfolio of workplaces, certain policies need to be applied consistently. These should be simple, well communicated, with a clear value proposition. Each employee should know what is expected of them.

CHAPTER 3

Green Teams

Team player: One who unites others toward a shared destiny through sharing information and ideas, empowering others and developing trust

— Author unknown

Until recently, organizations were content to leave sustainability initiatives to employee-driven Green Teams — voluntary groups of enthusiasts with a personal mission to "green" operations. These Green Teams typically consisted of self-organized, grassroots, cross-functional groups of employees who were passionate about environmental matters and who voluntarily came together to educate, inspire and empower employees around sustainability.

Initiated by a few committed employees, they essentially organized themselves without any direct involvement by senior management. Their efforts generally revolved around recycling, composting food waste, reducing the use of disposable take-out containers, eliminating plastic water bottles and that sort of thing. At the heart of their efforts was (and still is) employee education and awareness-building, with a lot of human interest thrown into the process.

Green Teams are the grassroots that can alter an entire culture

These pioneers of greening the workplace often had a challenge to convince senior management of the financial benefits of greening. In time though, organizations have come to recognize the positive power of Green Teams to achieve broader objectives such as operational efficiency, risk management, cost savings, corporate citizenship, quality of work life, ability to attract talent and reduce turnover, and a culture of innovation and cross-functional collaboration. As a result, Green Teams have evolved from being loosely organized to officially sanctioned entities that can be instrumental in changing the culture of an organization. The most successful organizations embrace Green Teams and actually integrate their activities into their job descriptions and/or performance criteria.

Empowering Green Teams

By their nature, "grassroots" organizations are often made up of people who don't necessarily hold positions of power or wield authority. In fact, grassroots often work outside established structures and prefer not to be centrally managed. Unlike many bureaucratic committees that happily spend more time thinking and planning than actually doing, grassroots groups are "doers." This is great, but it also means that they can easily lose momentum when things don't happen fast enough, a point that is well illustrated in an article in *Green Steps* called *Green Teams that Work*.[27]

Is this a familiar story? Your organization wants to address its environmental footprint, so it sets up a Green Team filled with passionate volunteers from across the organization. The team meets for the first time. Lots of ideas fly around. There is great enthusiasm... and muffins of course.

People leave trembling with excitement. A month later at the next meeting, still lots of good ideas, but not much has happened. And the same again the next month. You realize this is starting to become a pattern — lots of talk during the meetings, but no action beyond this. Slowly, Green Team members stop showing up for meetings, the actions list stays long and onerous, and the gap between meetings gets longer and longer as other priorities take over, while senior management wonders where the time and muffins have gone.

We hear this story all too often. Set up with the best of intentions, and expected to fulfill the bulk of many organizations' sustainability efforts, these teams often stagnate after a year or so due to lack of support, skills and focus. As a result, their effectiveness and contribution to an organization's sustainability performance becomes very limited.

Green organizations have come to realize that consistent and measurable sustainability achievements require a strategic approach that includes genuine top-down support, made visible at every opportunity, as well as efforts to fully integrate sustainability across all business operations.

As a result, Green Teams in many organizations have become more formalized. In some large corporations, Green Teams connect with a Chief Sustainability Officer. This is a management position, often supported by a steering committee comprised of managers from various company functions or locations. The value of having this connection is that it provides a two-way communication path: the Green Team educates management on new ways to make the business more sustainable; management informs the Green Team on necessary business values that must be present in their proposals.

CEO support of Green Teams includes providing the necessary tools and resources

CEO support of Green Teams is essential and should be easy to obtain. After all, their work will benefit the company, not just financially but also in terms of staff satisfaction, image and branding. In return, senior management champions have a responsibility to provide the necessary tools and resources. And as with any effective program management, there should be some structure — a chairperson, a process to bring new members into the team, roles, responsibilities, timeframes and so forth.

Recognition also goes a long way to ensure continued engagement of the members of a Green Team, for example, by acknowledging in employee performance reviews the Green Team hours and activities.

Properly understood and respected, grassroots have the potential and power to alter an entire culture thanks to their deep engagement. However, this can only happen if management is also genuinely engaged and involves those in lower echelons to actively participate in advisory or leadership roles.

CEO support of Green Teams is essential and should be easy to obtain. After all, their work will benefit the company, not just financially but also in terms of staff satisfaction, image and branding.

Green Team tasks

The following are some of the tasks of a Green Team:

- Communicate with and support employees to help them to meet their responsibilities, (for example ensuring that the person in charge of procurement is aware of the firm's green procurement policy)
- Initiate green workplace campaigns with measurable performance metrics. For example, monitor and report on the amount of paper and other resources that are being used. Monitor samples of waste streams for signs of contamination; communicate results and continue to monitor regularly until acceptable levels are achieved. Promote www.free-cycle.com or another platform for employees to sell, donate or recycle used furniture and/or household belongings. Investigate the feasibility of carpooling and promote office or regional carpooling platforms.
- Participate in landlord-driven, building-wide green initiatives.
- Establish and report annually on measurable environmental goals for the office.

Make green 'normal'

We've talked a great deal about the need for corporate directives and senior management support. While these top-down approaches are often needed to kick-start a program, provide support for Green Teams and steer the organization towards a greener culture, the real objective is to make green normal and mainstream.

The outcome should be that green becomes the default choice, not an option — something everyone does, not just the granola-loving "tree huggers." "Lose the crunch!" says Derek Wong, who serves on the Advisory Board of *Sustainable Business Forum*. "The message should focus on the personal benefits rather than the altruism angle — that it's healthier and more fun to be in a sustainable world — rather than a 'charitable' contribution that just benefits the planet or future generations."

Finally, don't be shy about using rewards. "Green Teams should be allowed to bribe shamelessly and punish wisely," says Wong. "Treats, prizes and kudos are effective to reward behavioral change. Conversely, small doses of guilt and shame can also motivate behavioral changes, especially if one is also reminded of the green options that are available."[28]

Conclusion

Deep-greening the organization requires the involvement of everyone. When companies have a senior management that is committed to sustainability in every aspect of operations, a middle management that is engaged in the process, and dynamic Green Teams doing cool workplace campaigns, this can have a powerful halo effect that boosts morale and employee engagement — even among those who normally don't care very much about the environment. In the next chapters, we will turn our attention to some of the green measures in an office setting.

CHAPTER 4

Greenhouse Gas Emissions

There is a time for weighing evidence and a time for acting. And if there's one thing I've learned throughout my work in finance, government and conservation, it is to act before problems become too big to manage. When the credit bubble burst in 2008, the damage was devastating. Millions suffered. Many still do. We're making the same mistake today with climate change. We're staring down a climate bubble that poses enormous risks to both our environment and economy. This is a crisis we can't afford to ignore. I feel as if I'm watching as we fly in slow motion on a collision course toward a giant mountain. We can see the crash coming, and yet we're sitting on our hands rather than altering course. We need to act now. We can do this by putting a price on emissions of carbon dioxide — a carbon tax.[29]

— Henry M. Paulson Jr., Former United States Secretary of the Treasury

Although climate change can be caused by both natural processes and human activities, scientific studies show that recent changes can be largely attributed to human activity, primarily the release of carbon dioxide and other greenhouse gases to the atmosphere. The impacts of climate change are significant for the environment and species, the economy, coastal cities, infrastructure, health, food and water.

In this chapter, we look at an important corporate decision that needs to be made in any organization that wants to *be* green and be *seen* as green: whether or not to report greenhouse gas (GHG) emissions. We also examine some trends in the industry and discuss the correct way for offices to report GHG emissions, as described in the World Resources Institute *Greenhouse Gas Protocol*.

The extent to which an organization reports its energy consumption and GHG emissions is a question that must be decided at a senior level. This is necessary so that everyone involved understands what activities should be included in the GHG inventory and to establish a process for consistent measuring and accounting. This is a complex issue that cannot be approached casually. It requires commitment and will take careful thought and organizational resources to do properly.

Before we launch into a description of GHG reporting, (also known as "carbon reporting") as it applies to offices, first a bit of background context on where the business world is at in terms of GHG reporting.

Greenhouse gas reporting has not gained as much traction as had been expected
. . . .

One reason that carbon reporting has not gained as much traction as might have been expected is that many national carbon emission credit markets have faltered. The US federal policy on trading carbon emission credits has stalled, the European Union's Emission Trading System (EU-ETS) has seen its prices fluctuate and fall, and Australia's carbon tax has been repealed.[30]

Governments face the challenge of finding the right balance — collecting meaningful information without putting an excessive burden on companies, as well as creating the right incentives to motivate companies to reduce emissions. Governments also worry that businesses may be driven away if their country or region has more stringent programs. To make it as simple as possible, most GHG reporting schemes (in particular those linked to emission trading schemes) just ask companies to disclose GHG emissions, although some also invite companies to report on emission reduction targets and other climate change related information.

Jurisdictional boundaries can also make it problematic to coordinate GHG reporting schemes with other pieces of legislation. Not surprisingly, meshing various programs into some sort of global framework can be a significant hurdle. Duke University researchers, Richard Newell, William Pizer and Daniel Raimi, in a study in *Science Magazine*,[31] published by the American Association for the Advancement of Science, note some of the difficulties, including uncertainty over carbon market prices, as well as the challenge of managing financial flows and policies across programs that have different structures and reporting periods. For example, in the UK, the reporting periodicity is annual, in line with financial reporting, whereas France allows a three-year period between inventories to leave time for companies to achieve emission reductions.

GHG reporting — compared to financial reporting, few companies do it well

Broadly speaking, companies fall into three categories.

First, there are those that measure and report their greenhouse gas emissions correctly, either with third party verification or not. These companies are in a minority. Notable among the top large corporations that are showing leadership are BMW, Daimler, Philips Electronics, Nestlé, BNY Mellon, Cisco Systems, Gas Natural SDG, Honda Motor, Nissan Motor, Volkswagen, Hewlett -Packard and Samsung.[32] It is interesting to note that companies that integrate successful climate strategies also perform better financially, according to the CDP (formerly known as the Global Carbon Disclosure Project).[33]

Next are those that measure but do not report externally. This could be because their GHG emissions don't quite measure up to their targeted reductions or perhaps they don't feel confident in the accuracy of their numbers.

Finally, there are companies — the vast majority — that neither measure nor report their GHGs in a consistent way.

There's no doubt that reporting GHG emissions can be complex, which is perhaps why globally, so few companies do it well. Also, compared to mainstream financial reporting, GHG accounting has certainly not been a priority for organizations. As a result, there has been less oversight and quality assurance, which makes it more prone to error. While this is changing, it has been a slow process.

As the saying goes, "If you don't measure it, you can't manage it." A baseline that is not credible is not very useful. It should come as no surprise then that the 2013 CDP Global report, which informs institutional investors representing over US$90 trillion in invested capital, shows that carbon emissions from 389 of the world's largest companies listed on the FTSE Global 500 Equity Index have not improved much in the past five years, and in several cases have actually increased.

The good news is that there is now more quality assurance. Nearly three-quarters of responding companies verified their emissions in 2013, a 29% increase from 2012 and almost double the percentage in 2011. Joe Cofino, executive editor of the *Guardian* and editorial director of *Guardian Sustainable Business* comments that investors and shareholders have always demanded accuracy in a company's financial information. Increasingly, they are demanding accuracy in non-financial information as well. This should increase trust in the data and therefore its use.[34]

Compared to mainstream financial reporting, GHG accounting has certainly not been a priority for organizations. As a result, there has been less oversight and quality assurance, which makes it more prone to error.

Why greenhouse gas reporting
is likely to become mainstream
· ·

Notwithstanding all of the challenges, GHG reporting is likely to become mainstream, driven by shareholder demand, government requirements and carbon markets.

Already a basic component of most organizations' corporate social responsibility (CSR) reporting, GHG reporting and third party verification are two of the criteria of the Dow Jones Sustainability Index. Paul Dickinson, founder of the CDP says, "There is a problem with climate change. Corporations are the principle agents of greenhouse gas emissions, and their shareholders will hold them to account." As more companies offer monetary rewards for their board, executive team or employees to encourage energy or emissions reductions, the result is that more are likely to report improvements.

There is also growing pressure from governments. Malcolm Preston, global lead for sustainability and climate change at Price Waterhouse Cooper, comments that the continuing lack of action means that tougher regulation will almost certainly occur. Some jurisdictions are already making it a requirement to report greenhouse gas emissions. For example, in the UK, all businesses listed on the main market of the London Stock Exchange must report their GHG emissions in their annual reports, and as of 2014, all companies listed on FTSE 350 must publicly disclose all of their GHG emissions. Meanwhile, many cities in North America have mandatory energy disclosure for buildings, which is then translated into GHG emissions.

Meanwhile, several local carbon markets have emerged or are being piloted. For example, China has a number of these, which have nearly doubled the volume of emissions being reported; Quebec and California have linked their carbon markets; and South Korea is piloting a program. Local carbon markets such as these are poised to become key components of an emerging global policy framework that includes trading programs, renewable energy incentives, carbon taxes, and regulations.[35]

More companies are reporting GHG emissions
· ·

As governments and investors increasingly cast an eagle eye on the GHG bottom line, companies are strengthening their GHG accounting processes as well as their quality assurance, to ensure that their information is accurate. There also seems to be a correlation between how well companies measure their GHG emissions and how well they publicize their performance.

Public reporting systems are designed to incentivize organizations to voluntarily disclose their performance, enabling investors to make decisions that will protect their long-term investments against environmental risks. As such, the performance reporting is of organizations — not individual properties.

The *CDP*[36] (formerly known as Global Carbon Disclosure Project) offers the most widely used global platform for organizations to report their GHG emissions. Two other reporting platforms are the *Global Reporting Initiative (GRI)* , which is similar to the *CDP* in many respects, and the *Dow Jones Sustainability Index (DJSI)* , both of which also address social and economic issues as well as environmental ones. Figure 4 shows responses by 277 GreenBiz members to the question: Which sustainability framework does your organization use?[37]

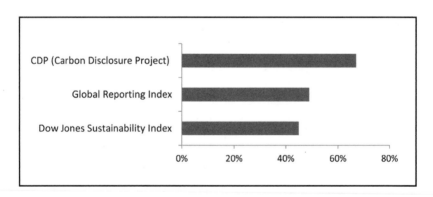

Figure 4 — "Which sustainability framework does your organization use?"

The *CDP* includes standardized year-by-year data on companies' greenhouse gas emissions, water usage and strategies for managing climate change, water and deforestation. This data is viewed by more than 750 institutional investors representing an excess of US$92 trillion in assets.

Since its founding in 2000, the number of *CDP* respondents has steadily grown, as shown in Figure 5, and now includes most FTSE 100, Global 500 and Europe's 300 largest companies. The *CDP* is also helping to promote a multi-million dollar auditing industry, resulting in nearly half of the companies that reported in 2013 having had their figures officially verified.

The way it works is that *CDP* sends an annual questionnaire to the world's largest companies on behalf of their institutional investors, who endorse them as '*CDP* signatories'. These investor requests for information encourage companies to account for and be transparent about their environmental performance. The growing expectation of shareholders and lenders to be able to see this information is triggering an increase in sustainably-responsible corporate behavior, including supply chain management, which in turn is helping to drive a low-carbon, more sustainable economy. [38]

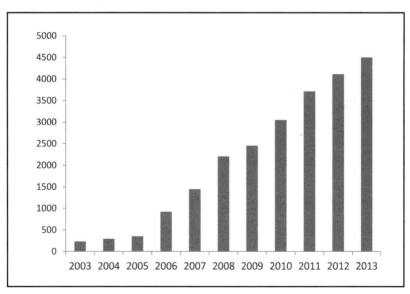

Figure 5 — Number of CDP respondents by year

The *GRI* and the *CDP* questionnaires both invite reporting on climate change, and have a common core module of questions. *GRI* and *CDP* have therefore agreed to collaborate in the development of Sector Supplements and to provide feedback on each other's guidelines/questionnaires. They have also created tables which show how their questions are aligned, leading to more and better quality reporting, and enabling reporters to use or adapt the same data in both reporting processes.[39]

The *Dow Jones Sustainability Index (DJSI)* evaluates the sustainability performance of the largest 2,500 companies listed on the Dow Jones Global Total Stock Market Index with respect to three dimensions: Economic (e.g. codes of conduct, anti-corruption, risk management), Social (e.g. labor practices, philanthropy), and Environmental. The Environmental dimension focuses primarily on environmental reporting of carbon, water and waste as well as some industry-specific criteria.

To participate in the *DJSI*, companies are assessed and selected based on their long-term economic, social and environmental asset management plans. Selection criteria evolve each year and companies must continue to make improvements to their long-term sustainability plans in order to remain on the Index. Indices are updated yearly and companies are monitored throughout the year.[40]

How to report GHG's for offices
· ·

Large companies, particularly those involved in manufacturing, or financial institutions that have lots of investments in various industries face a significant challenge in accounting for the carbon emissions associated with **all** of their activities particularly where there are extensive supply chains.

Although there are many reporting platforms, the GHG accounting framework that most of them use is the *Greenhouse Gas Protocol (GHG Protocol)* , jointly convened by the World Business Council for Sustainable Development (WBCSD) and the World Resources Institute (WRI) in 1998.

The good news for real estate professionals is that carbon accounting for buildings and leased office space is relatively simple.

That said, one of the challenges in a leased office is to discern which carbon emissions belong to the Landlord and which belong to the Tenant. This is important in order to avoid double counting. To decide which of the emissions should be included in the carbon inventory of a leased space, it is necessary to understand the concept of "direct" emissions and "indirect" emissions.

In our view, one of the simplest explanations is given by Pankaj Bhatia and Samantha Putt del Pino in a document that they produced for the World Resources Institute called *Working 9 to 5 on Climate Change: An Office Guide*.[41] It includes guidance on how to address the emissions for activities associated with an office — from heating and cooling the space, to using the photocopier and traveling to meetings.

Direct Emissions are emissions from GHG sources that your organization owns — or controls as if it owned them. For example, if you, as a **tenant**, operate the furnace and pay the fuel bills in an office building that you lease, then the emissions from the furnace should be reported as direct emissions of your organization. However, if the **landlord** operates the furnace and pays the fuel bills, embedding the cost in your rent, then the GHGs emitted would be direct emissions of the Landlord. If business travel takes place in your organization's company car, then these are your direct emissions. If your organization leases vehicles or equipment but pays for the fuel used, these emissions also are counted as direct emissions for your organization, because your company is controlling the type and amount of emissions by the type of car you choose, and whether you have a heavy foot on the pedal. Other typical examples are listed in Table 1. **The GHG Protocol requires an organization to report its direct emissions, also known as Scope 1 emissions.**

Indirect Emissions result from your organization's activities but they occur from GHG sources that are owned or controlled by another organization. For example, although your organization may own its photocopier, the source of the emissions is located and controlled at the power plant, not the photocopier and depends on how the plant generates electricity. Consequently, the photocopier emissions are indirect. In fact, any purchased electricity is considered an indirect emission because some other organization is controlling the actual process by which the emissions are being released. If you are renting an office space and the heating fuel is part of the landlord's operations and costs, then this too would be an indirect source. Where your organization is leasing the office space, most emissions related to that office will very likely be indirect. That said, although as a tenant you do not control many of the sources of the emissions, nevertheless you can reduce the amount of indirect emissions that you are producing, for example, by installing energy-efficient lighting, switching off appliances reducing air travel, and so on.

Typical Office Emission Sources	
SCOPE 1 Direct Emissions from…	• Combustion of fuel in boilers/furnaces that are owned by the reporting organization • Generation of electricity, steam or heat in equipment that is owned by the reporting organization • Business travel or employee commuting in company owned vehicles, corporate jets, etc.
SCOPE 2 Indirect emissions from…	• Generation of purchased electricity, steam or heat
SCOPE 3 Indirect emissions from…..	• Business travel and commuting in non-company owned vehicles (e.g. employee cars, rental cars, trains, commercial jets) • Combustion of fuel in boilers or furnaces not owed by the reporting organization • Out-sourced activities such as shipping, courier services

Table 1 — How to report GHG emissions for an office

For reporting purposes, indirect emissions are divided into **"Scope 2"** emissions — those from the generation of purchased electricity, steam, or heat; and **"Scope 3"** emissions — which cover everything else.

The GHG Protocol requires an organization to report its Scope 2 emissions because these are likely to make up a significant percentage of any organization's inventory and are relatively easy to quantify. Naturally, to report their Scope 2 emissions, there need to be utility meters for each office. The energy value is then multiplied by the correct coefficient, depending on the energy source. For example, electricity derived from coal generates a lot of GHGs, and therefore has a high coefficient value, whereas hydro power generates no carbon emissions and therefore has a zero coefficient.

Reporting all Scope 3 emissions is encouraged but not mandatory in the GHG Protocol. For some companies, Scope 3 emissions related to their corporate facilities may be difficult to measure, and may be relatively small compared to the magnitude of emissions from certain other business and industrial operations.

Some manufacturing companies have enormous Scope 3 emissions in their supply chain such as those related to energy intensive third world operations.[42] It's interesting to note that many organizations selectively measure and report only certain indirect Scope 3 emissions such as corporate travel, while neglecting the far larger emissions from their supply chain manufacturing operations. Indeed, only 6% of finance companies report the emissions associated with their most carbon-intensive industrial investments.[43] This resonates with a United Nations Global Compact's survey of members, which showed that while companies are generally perfectly capable of identifying these supply chain emissions, they are doing a bad job of quantifying them, or choosing not to quantify them at all, which is misleading as to the full carbon impact of a company.

For offices, the most commonly reported Scope 3 emissions relate to combustion of fuel in boilers or furnaces not owned by the reporting organization, as well as air business travel and employee commuting. Many travel service providers are now reporting the carbon emissions for their corporate clients and show the data on the traveler's itinerary records.

As for commuting, some employees feel that this is a matter of personal privacy and fear they'll be pressured to give up their SUV, ride the bus, or join a carpool. However, some organizations, in an effort to reduce their emissions, adopt measures that actually benefit employees — for example, attractive incentive programs to encourage them to use mass transit or carpooling, relocation of the office closer to public transportation, or the possibility of telework.

An organization's carbon reporting policy and procedure need to be communicated to the person(s) who monitor the utility bills. Once a baseline has been established, GHG reduction targets can be set. Facility managers and Green Teams should be actively involved to ensure that measures will be implemented to achieve the targets — for example by reducing the energy needed for lighting, heating and cooling, plug load, server rooms, travel, and possibly also commuting.

Conclusion

Whether for the purpose of carbon trading or to meet regulations, it is likely that there will be an increase in reporting of GHG emissions. For organizations that have large portfolios of offices, GHG disclosure has become a key part of corporate social responsibility reporting. Currently, very few portfolios do a good job of reporting their GHG emissions. And yet this should not be a complicated process, provided there is metering of electricity for a facility.

Climate change has been called "the greatest challenge of our time." For most people, the link between climate change and carbon emissions is still somewhat abstract. However, the threat of rising sea levels, increased wildfires, dangerous heat events, extreme storms and widespread droughts is a reality that with each passing day is harder to deny.

CHAPTER 5

Energy Management

So how do commercial tenants know how efficient their spaces are compared to their peers? In many cases, they don't, which can make it challenging to optimize energy performance and energy savings.

— Yerina Mugica, Associate Director, Center for Market Innovation, New York City

As discussed earlier, whether and how to report GHG emissions is a decision that needs to be made at a senior level. In this chapter, we look at **other** corporate policies and management practices that can have an impact on a portfolio's energy performance.

Corporate policies related to energy

Having too many rules (aka policies) is as bad as having not enough. That said, we find that sustainability policies are especially useful in two situations.

The first is where an organization wishes to report on certain **key performance indicators (KPIs) at the portfolio** level. Whether it's GHG emissions, energy, waste, or paper consumption, consistent accounting and reporting are necessary for the data to have any value. And for this to happen, there needs to be some clear direction.

The second situation is where an organization wishes to establish certain **workplace standards and norms of behavior**. It's no accident that some offices have a green culture and others don't. Whether through written or unwritten rules, certain expectations have been made clear at some point in time: "In this office, we switch off lights; pull down blinds before leaving the place on cold winter evenings to retain heat within; decommission servers that are not being used and check temperature set points in our server room ..." and so on.

In our experience of some offices where no such expectations have been communicated, it always seems to be the same people who are doing the heavy lifting, which can soon lead to frustration, resentment or apathy. Having certain corporate policies that employees are *expected* to abide by can also make life easier for the facility manager, and also provides moral support for the Green Team.

The following are some other examples of corporate policies that set out clear and simple expectations aimed at reducing energy consumption. These measures can have a significant cumulative effect, if they are practiced throughout the portfolio:

- Post signage or send e-mail messages to remind employees to switch off their devices, and turn off lights in spaces that are unoccupied. (not applicable where there are plug load automatic switch-off devices or lighting occupancy sensors, or where there is already a well-established culture of switching off lights and desktop equipment)
- Purchase ENERGY STAR laptop computers and office equipment and appliances.
- Remove redundant devices such as personal fridges, heaters etc.
- Ensure that IT decommissions un-used servers, and that medium and large server rooms undergo a review by a qualified energy expert.
- Review energy bills monthly or quarterly to identify and investigate unexpected energy spikes.

Energy monitoring
· · · · · · · · · · · · · · · ·

Energy management in a leased space is largely a matter of keeping a close eye on the energy consumption, investigating unexpected spikes in energy use and taking corrective action. Naturally, this presupposes that there is energy metering in the tenant space. Much of the responsibility for monitoring energy falls squarely on the shoulders of Facility or Energy Managers, who should review monthly energy bills or monitor energy use using real time measurement tools.

In recent years, companies producing all manner of energy dashboard features, reports and gadgets, from the simple to the very complicated, have sprouted like toadstools after a rain. By "dashboards," we mean any type of software that lies on top of a building automation system and provides some type of energy reporting.

The true merit of dashboards and other real time monitoring tools is to show when bad things are happening so that corrective action can be taken. For example, some tools enable remote off-site controls to switch off devices as well as eliminate "vampire load", the energy that an appliance draws even when the power button is off. The American Council for an Energy Efficient Economy (ACEEE) claims that up to 12% energy savings can be achieved by way of real-time feedback devices. This reduction is almost double what is usually achieved using retroactive reporting (after consumption has occurred).[44]

Although many dashboards claim to achieve a rapid return on investment in terms of energy savings, it goes without saying that they are effective only to the extent that users are skilled at using them and are following up with appropriate action. In other words, they require a certain commitment in time and effort to take their full advantage. John Pitcher, often credited as the inventor of automated fault detection and diagnosis,

The American Council for an Energy Efficient Economy (ACEEE) claims that up to 12% energy savings can be achieved by way of real-time feedback devices.

and Rob Watson, widely known as the "Father of LEED" have compared some of the very glitzy and complicated dashboards to new toys at Christmas, which can soon lose their appeal!

> "Sure, facility managers may use their new dashboard for a while and some even 'forever,' but most of them are either like kids playing with their toys right after Christmas, or they use it because their boss is watching. In reality, most facility managers' time is spent having to triage which of the daily emergencies is the greatest threat to their job. Once people are looking the other way, typically these folks will go back to the way they have always done things, unless there is deep expertise behind the dashboard to support them. Unfortunately this expertise is not to be found within most dashboard companies, principally because they have failed to understand, or understand too late, that nothing scales in the building industry without good people. Only too late do they realize that they spent too much time and money developing overpriced bloatware that looks awesome in an investor's boardroom, but is too time-consuming, too complicated and ultimately not effective enough for facility people to use on an ongoing basis."[45]

Even where there is no sub-metering in an office, it is possible to monitor plug load including "vampire load" in individual workstations, using any one of the many user friendly and affordable feedback devices that are coming into the market. These can meter energy use at the plug and allow the data to be monitored wirelessly through a web browser on various platforms.

Although many dashboards claim to achieve a rapid return on investment in terms of energy savings, it goes without saying that they are effective only to the extent that users are skilled at using them and are following up with appropriate action.

Who pays for energy improvements in a building or tenant space — and who gets the benefit?
· ·

One of the challenges of energy conservation measures in leased offices relates to the question of who gets to benefit from the savings when certain capital improvements are made — the landlord or the tenant? There has been considerable progress in recent years to establish frameworks for landlords and tenants to collaborate to maximize the energy efficiency of their operations and benefit from investments.

An excellent *Energy Efficiency Lease Guidance*[46] document has been developed by Natural Resources Defense Council (NRDC) with input from green building academic institutions, public institutions and industry. It outlines three guiding principles, which now are fairly standard for the industry, as well as provides some simple amendments that can be added to an existing lease agreement. The three principles are stated as follows:

1. **The Landlord should operate the building — and the Tenant, the premises — as efficiently as possible.** The aim is to commit both the landlord and tenant to energy efficiency with respect to new installations, replacements and maintenance; limit any increase in electrical standby demand; and benchmark energy use. Clauses relating to this principle can be added in the lease sections typically labeled *"Landlord Services, Repair, Condition of Premises, Maintenance and Repairs, and/or Services and Utilities."*

2. **For any given system, installation, or piece of equipment, responsibility for capital expense and benefit of savings should reside with the same entity.** Clauses relating to this principle are typically found in lease sections labeled *"Additional Rent, Operating Expenses, or Operating Expense Escalation."*

3. **Consumption and demand for resources throughout the building should be measurable and transparent to the landlord and tenant.** This provision is principally intended to eliminate the practice of billing tenant electricity consumption on a flat annual $/sf basis — typically called Electric Rent Inclusion (ERI). This means that landlords should sub-meter tenant space utilities. Only by measuring electric usage is it possible to assess progress toward energy saving goals. Note that sub-metering of water, gas and steam may not be technically feasible.

A green lease need not be complicated, often requiring just a slight re-structuring of terms and agreements already in place. However, to maximize results, consider engaging a trusted independent advisor, who has expertise in commercial leasing and who is also knowledgeable about cost-saving sustainability measures.

For a tenant retrofit, be sure to model, quantify and measure savings

For tenants who want to energy-retrofit their space, the Natural Resources Defense Council's Center for Market Innovation (CMI) has been working with several industry leaders including Goldman Sachs, Johnson Controls, Jones Lang LaSalle (JLL), Empire State Realty Trust, SKANSKA, ULI/Greenprint and the Rockefeller Foundation to model, quantify and publish energy savings and ROI from some exemplary high efficiency tenant build-outs. The aim is to show the compounding value of owner/tenant collaboration, especially for tenants who value high performance spaces. These are tenants who often choose to locate or remain in buildings with highly efficient base building systems and transparent energy management practices.

The study has become the basis for CMI's *Energy Performance Optimization Guide*,[47] which shows how to quantify, implement, and measure energy performance solutions that are applicable across a broad spectrum of tenant conditions. The guide, which can be accessed online at **http://www.nrdc.org/business/cgi/guide.asp**, features three modules: i) Project Initiation; ii) Value Analysis; and iii) Implementation/Measurement and Verification, along with a set of supporting tools to map out an energy performance analysis. The Value Analysis helps to identify the highest-value set of energy-efficient measures to incorporate into the design of a tenant's new premises.

Tenant Star

· · · · · · · · · · ·

Although occupants (e.g. tenants) use much of the energy in office build-ings, most current green building certifications such as *ENERGY STAR®*, *LEED®* and *Green Globes®* are aimed at building owners, property man-agers and developers. These programs are effective at saving energy, and marketing buildings to prospective tenants and investors.

EPA's *ENERGY STAR®* is the best known way to benchmark energy use of buildings and certify top performers. Used by 40% of U.S. com-mercial building space, there are now more than 20,000 buildings that have been certified for being in the top quartile compared to buildings of similar type, location, size and use.

While you may be familiar with *ENERGY STAR®* for **buildings**, did you know that there is now *Tenant Star*?

In 2013, the Better Building Act (S. 1191), introduced *Tenant Star*, a certification to recognize tenants that operate energy-efficient leased spaces. *Tenant Star* is modeled on the *ENERGY STAR®* program for buildings.

To participate in *Tenant Star* will, of course, require metering for the tenant space being measured. At approximately $3,000 to install meter-ing, this cost is minimal, compared to the $25 to $100 per square foot to build out a space for a 5 or 10-year lease.

With metering in place, it is then possible for the tenant to benefit financially from having implemented efficient lighting, improved HVAC controls, reduced plug load and server room energy efficiency measures.

Thus *ENERGY STAR®* and *Tenant Star* will make it possible to address energy conservation at the base building level, where a building owner makes improvements, as well as by recognizing and rewarding ten-ants for their high-performance design and operations.

Conclusion

Energy reduction measures in offices are often represented merely as some simple "dos and don'ts" for occupiers. For a portfolio of leased office space, the reality is that there is another level of energy management that begins at the corporate level, which establishes some minimum expectations for employees and requires a certain level of energy monitoring, generally undertaken by the Facility (or Energy) Manager.

It's also important to recognize that energy management is a joint responsibility of the tenant and the landlord, which is best addressed by including certain terms in the lease.

Simply put, a green lease benefits both tenants and building owners/landlords by encouraging each to make certain key commitments, aligning financial incentives so that both parties benefit from adopting green measures, and by improving environmental reporting transparency to enable tenants and landlords to measure success against agreed-upon goals.

CHAPTER 6

Energy for Lighting, Plug load and Server Rooms

Miscellaneous electric loads are likely to be the biggest impediment to achieving high efficiency / net zero energy buildings.

— American Council for an Energy-Efficient Economy (ACEE), July 2013 Report[48]

So far, we have talked about corporate policies and energy management measures that can have an impact on a tenant portfolio's energy performance. In this chapter, we touch on the energy efficiency **features** related to some key energy demands: lighting, plug load and server rooms, and the **roles and responsibilities** of facility managers and employees in each of these areas.

Commercial and residential buildings consume about 41% of total energy in the USA. About 15% of this is used for lighting and about 20% is used for miscellaneous energy loads (MELs), which in offices, include — more or less in order of magnitude of their energy usage — personal computers, servers, monitors and vending machines.

This chapter describes three ways to reduce energy used for lighting in an office: use high efficiency bulbs, reduce lighting levels and improve lighting controls. We then turn our attention to plug load reduction measures and a brief discussion of server rooms and cloud computing.

Install high efficiency lighting

High efficiency bulbs include T8s, T5s and LEDs. The 'T', by the way, is a measure of the diameter of the tube. A T12 tube is **12**/8 (or 1.5 inch); a T8 tube is **8**/8 (or 1 inch); and a T5 is **5**/8 of an inch.

Until recently, most offices in America have been using a four-lamp fixture with 40 watt, T12 lamps on magnetic ballast, which consumes 172 watts of energy. The same fixture, retrofitted with 28 watt T8 lamps and electronic ballast uses 35% less energy and produces about 5% more light output.

To retrofit an existing T12 fixture is a simple process that requires elementary wiring knowledge. Simply remove the T12 ballasts, replace them with appropriate ballasts, and replace old lamps with new ones, using the same sockets.

T5s are only about 10% more efficient than T8s but cost significantly more than T8s. Also, in many cases, changing to T5s may require replacing or rewiring the whole light fixture, which adds significant cost and complexity.

LED technology has been growing so rapidly that it will soon also be the norm, not just for task lighting and displays but also for ambient lighting. Fluorescent T8 fixtures can be replaced with LED T8 tubes by removing the ballast and replacing the socket assembly. LED lights are 30% more efficient than T8s and have several other advantages, including longer life, and the fact that they contain no mercury.

Among the many free online energy saving calculators related to energy efficient lighting is **http://www.goodenergy.com/electricity_ consulting_products/lighting_retrofit_saving_calculator.aspx.**

Reduce lighting levels

The second measure to reduce energy needed for lighting is to reduce artificial light levels. Until the mid-nineties, no one talked much about over-illumination, as older lighting systems were designed for paper-based reading tasks, which needed light levels of 750-1000 lux. In fact, it was commonly believed that more light is always better. Health research indicates that this is not so. Now that most tasks are done on computers with back-lit screens, there's a recognition that over-illumination is not only expensive and energy-intensive, but is also annoying and can adversely affect health. Over-illumination, particularly when combined with the flicker of some fluorescent systems has been found to increase headache incidence, trigger migraines, cause fatigue, and increase medically defined stress and anxiety.

The Illuminating Engineering Society of North America (IESNA) recommends that overhead lighting can be reduced to between 300 and 500 lux in open offices, 400 lux in conference rooms, and 50 lux in corridors and stairs.

Over-illumination, particularly when combined with the flicker of some fluorescent systems has been found to increase headache incidence, trigger migraines, cause fatigue, and increase medically defined stress and anxiety.

Many people actually prefer lower lighting levels. Our JLL office in New York did an Earth Day exercise where we switched off all the lights in the office for one hour, leaving only daylighting. When the lights were turned back on, many of our colleagues complained that it felt like they were working under police spotlights.

For recommended lighting levels and lighting power as set out by the US General Services Administration (GSA), see **http://www.gsa.gov/portal/content/101308**.

To find out the light levels in your office, you need a simple light meter.

You can purchase one on the internet for under $50. There are now even light meter applications that can be downloaded on a cellphone. Measure at a time when there is no daylighting (i.e. in the evening). Turn on all ambient lights. Do not include task lighting. Readings will vary by location, so take 3 readings at a height of 1 meter or ~ 3 feet above floor and approximately 3 meters or ~ 10 feet apart: One of the readings should be in an area under the fixtures, one between the fixtures, and one reading away from the fixtures. Calculate an average of the readings.

One very simple way to reduce lighting levels is to "de-lamp."[49] The general lighting of most offices usually consists of fluorescent light fixtures in multiple lamp configurations of two, three or four. Where the levels of light are greater than required to perform the tasks, a simple way to reduce lighting levels (and energy) is to remove and possibly relocate some of the lighting fixtures, or remove some of the lamps within a fixture. This can be done uniformly in all areas, for example, by removing half of the lamps in each fixture or by disconnecting half of the fixtures; or it can be done just in those parts of the office where lighting levels are excessive.

If a complete fixture is to be removed, it is not enough to simply remove the lamps because the ballast will continue to draw power even when the lamps are not installed. For a situation where complete fixtures cannot be removed without affecting the lighting design, phantom tubes are a convenient and low cost solution. These are plain glass tubes that produce no light and draw no power, but allow the fixture wiring and ballasts to be untouched.

If lamps in a fixture are to be removed, some re-wiring may be necessary to reconnect ballasts to the remaining lamps. Alternatively, phantom tubes can be used.

Another way to reduce lighting levels is with lighting controls that can reduce the lighting load from full lighting, using either dual switching of alternate rows of luminaries, or switching off individual lamps independently of adjacent lamps within a luminaire. Dimmable controls also make it possible to reduce levels.

Install good lighting controls
. . . .

The third measure to reduce lighting energy is to install good **lighting controls**. One common myth about lighting is that it costs more to turn fluorescent lighting off and on again than to keep it running. According to the U.S. Department of Energy, the extra wear on the bulb caused by turning it off and on is negligible, and the amount of electricity consumed in lighting up a fluorescent lamp is equal to only a few seconds of normal operation.

Localized controls for each office or conference room and for different areas within a large open office make it possible to light up just certain areas that are being occupied.

Occupancy sensors ensure that lights turn off when a space is unoccupied. This is especially effective in areas that have intermittent traffic, for example, conference rooms, printing rooms, stairwells and washrooms. In the absence of occupancy sensors, employees must make it a habit to switch off lights when they are the last to leave a room or a lighting zone in a large open office. Where this is not yet part of the culture of the office, post prominent signage next to light switches.

Linking lighting to a building automation system (BAS) allows centralized control and scheduling, ensuring, for example, that all lights are shut off throughout the building at night, while still accommodating occupants' specific needs and operating profiles.

Today, wireless lighting controls allow simple and inexpensive connectivity to a BAS or central system.

Integrating the lighting controls with the BAS also makes it possible to report in real time the energy being used for lighting in different parts of the tenant space and to share data from the lighting controls such as whether the room is occupied. This in turn can allow the BAS to adjust the HVAC set points.

One common myth about lighting is that it costs more to turn fluorescent lighting off and on again than to keep it running

73

Photo-sensors can dim lights when there is good daylighting. These are typically installed to control lights that are within 15-20 ft. (4.5-6 m) of the perimeter, where there is adequate daylight for desired lighting levels.

Miscellaneous energy loads (MELs)

With the increase in communication devices, plug load — that is to say, from devices that plug into wall outlets — is the largest and fastest growing source of energy consumption, having increased by almost 50% since 2005. In California, it constitutes about 23% of total electricity consumption in commercial office buildings. Office equipment alone accounts for 74% of this plug load.[50]

The two main approaches to reducing plug load are to use energy efficient equipment and to make sure that equipment is switched off when it is not being used.

Office devices include, but are not limited to computer equipment, imaging equipment and lunchroom or break room appliances. The lifetime cost of most equipment consists primarily of operational cost rather than purchase price, which is why it is worth a few extra dollars up-front to achieve better energy savings over time.

Because offices have so many computers, phasing in energy-efficient models offers a good opportunity to reduce consumption. Laptops use significantly less energy than desktops. For example, a 30W notebook with LCD screen typically uses 80% less energy than a 120W desktop PC with an 80W CRT screen. Even with the addition of a larger screen (up to 16-17"), the savings of a laptop are still well over 50%. Naturally there are situations where only a desktop PC will do.

One reason that laptops are designed to be energy-efficient is that consumers want the batteries to last a long time before having to be recharged. This explains why laptops use the most energy-efficient displays, adapters, hard disks and CPUs that are available.

ENERGY STAR® labeled items meet strict specifications for electrical efficiency, so the symbol makes it possible to quickly identify equipment that will cost less over its life cycle.

The following are some examples of the magnitude of energy savings that are possible by replacing old equipment with *ENERGY STAR®* equipment:[51]

Computer equipment:
- Desktop — up to 32%
- Laptop — up to 31%
- Monitor — up to 21%
- Printer — up to 36%
- Enterprise servers — up to 30%

Small network equipment:
- Modems, routers, switches, optical devices, etc. — up to 20%

Uninterruptible power supplies:
- UPS — 30-55% (depending on the type)

Printers, copiers and imaging equipment:
- Inkjet multifunction device — up to 60%
- Color laser multifunction device — up to 40%
- Fax machine (injket or laser) — up to 50%
- Laser color copier — up to 7%

Lunch room or break room:
- Refrigerator — up to 15%
- Dishwasher — up to 10%
- Water coolers — up to 50%
- Vending machines — up to 50%
- Battery chargers — up to 30%

Switching off equipment is another way to reduce plug load. There are several ways to make sure that equipment is turned off when it is not being used.

Automated shut-off can produce far more energy savings than any amount of education on the importance of switching things off.

One approach is to simply ask employees to shut off their devices. Unfortunately, there is a psychological phenomenon called "single action bias," where a person who does just one or two things to address a problem tends to consider themselves off the hook. This may explain why many people feel it's okay to not switch things off when the appliances that they are using are energy-efficient.

Fortunately, there are other ways and means to ensure that things are turned off in workstations other than counting on behavioral changes. Automated shut-off can produce far more energy savings than any amount of education on the importance of switching things off. Aggressive power management settings on computers and imaging equipment provide a good energy savings opportunity at no cost. Alternatively, low-cost, network-based power-management software can allow IT managers to centrally control power to devices during nights and weekends. There may be challenges to this approach though, for example, users requesting remote access to their desktop computers.

So called "hardware control strategies" include load-sensing plug strips and occupancy sensor strips. Load-sensing plug strips use a master/slave approach, which can be set so that when an employee turns off a computer, everything else in the plug strip also turns off including task lighting and computer monitors. Occupancy-sensing strips detect the presence or absence of a user and automatically turn equipment off in response. These strips usually feature optional outlets for those devices a user does not want turned off. Savings of course depend on the energy consumption of the office equipment. This should be analyzed prior to making the investment for all the work stations.

There are numerous online energy saving calculators including ones developed by U.S. EPA and DOE to estimate the energy consumption and operating costs of office equipment and possible savings.

Server Rooms
· · · · · · · · · · · ·

Server rooms, depending on their size, can constitute a major energy draw, which is largely due to their cooling requirements. Therefore the most effective way to save energy is by reducing cooling demand. There are three ways to do this: by raising temperature set points, reducing the number of servers, and with features that optimize cold air distribution.

The simplest way to save energy is to **raise temperature set points** by one or two degrees. An energy saving of four percent for cooling can be achieved for every (Fahrenheit) degree of upward change in the set-points. ASHRAE 2008 recommends 18 - 27 degrees C (64 - 80F), and moisture from 5.5C DP (41.9F) to 60% RH & 15C DP (59F DP) — or follow instructions in equipment warranties.

While at first blush it may seem unfeasible to **reduce the number of servers** without affecting business, consider that up to 30% of energy in a large server room may be used by "comatose" servers — servers that run but do not perform a function. These idle servers waste energy. Also, quite often servers use only a fraction of their processing capabilities because it's common to dedicate each server to just one specific application. The reason for this is that one-task-per-server simplifies trouble-shooting. However, as a network gets more complex, the many servers use more physical space and power, and generate heat. Server virtualization software converts each physical server into multiple virtual machines. Each virtual server acts like a unique physical device. This saves space and energy.

A review of the server room by an energy expert can result in recommendations to **optimize the flow of hot and cold air**. Depending on the size of the server room and the heat that is being generated, cooling can take various configurations. For example, where heat density is relatively low, raised floors for conditioned air may be appropriate. Where more cooling is needed, the cold air may be fed directly to rows

An energy saving of four percent for cooling can be achieved for every (Fahrenheit) degree of upward change in the set-points.

of servers to create hot and cold aisles. Where the heat density is high, the coolant may be delivered directly to the servers.

Additionally, physical barriers used with hot aisle/cold aisles can further reduce the mixing of cold supply air and hot exhaust air. These may be PVC curtains or rigid enclosures with lightweight aisle roof panels and doors at each end of the aisle. Blanking panels can also help by sealing gaps and unused rack space between server rows within a server aisle.

Finally, there are grounding systems that diminish the probability of equipment damage from static electricity, decreasing the need for humidity control, another energy-consuming activity in server rooms.

Cloud computing
· · · · · · · · · · · · · · · ·

Data centers use 1-2% of the world's electricity and this is poised to surge further. Now that a growing number of organizations are turning to cloud computing, this begs the question of whether using the cloud saves energy and costs, and reduces GHG emissions. Although the word "cloud" evokes a clean, environmentally friendly process, these facilities are large industrial buildings, densely packed with processors and hard drives that devour energy by the megawatt.

To learn more about the environmental benefit of cloud computing, researchers at Lawrence Berkeley National Laboratory and Northwestern University developed a modeling tool called the *Cloud Energy and Emissions Research Model (CLEER)*.[52] It estimates the energy savings of moving local network software and computing into the server farms that make up the cloud.

One simulation using *CLEER* simulation showed that if all American businesses moved their email, spreadsheet applications and customer management software to centralized off-site servers, they would shrink their computing energy footprints by 87% — enough to satiate the 23 billion kilowatt-hour annual appetite for the city of Los Angeles. A study by *CDP* also showed how cloud computing could lead to $12.3 billion a year in energy savings by 2020.[53]

These energy savings are the result of the consolidation and economies of scale that cloud computing brings. Compared to many traditional businesses, whose inefficient and underused on-site servers soak up electricity while sitting more or less idle a good deal of the time, central locations ensure that every server is fully utilized. This in turn results in more efficient power use.

However, these energy savings do not always translate into significant **cost** savings for users. A study by CSC of 3,600 IT decision makers found that 64% of organizations cut their energy use as a result of a shift to cloud services. 47% said they witnessed lower operating costs after cloud adoption, although the savings were often small: 35% of the U.S. organizations reported savings of $20,000 or less, while 23% of U.S. organizations and 45% of U.S. small businesses (fewer than 50 employees) reported no savings.[54]

However, there are other cost benefits that include avoiding up-front capital costs of buying and setting up servers, and making better use of talented IT staff by redeploying them from the task of managing the in-house servers to areas that are more profitable for the organization. Finally, there can be a disaster-recovery advantage because clouds typically have several locations for their data centers to be able to mirror the data and applications of their clients.

Conclusion

Saving energy is good for the planet and the bottom line. The majority of the energy in North America comes from petroleum, coal and natural gas. Every 1,000 kilowatt-hours of electricity of energy from these types of non-renewable sources represents about 1,000 lbs. of carbon dioxide entering the atmosphere. Consider also that for a company that operates on a 10% profit margin, every extra dollar that is spent on energy requires $10 worth of revenue. Assuming that energy will become more expensive — and there is every reason to believe that it will — this means that an additional $10,000 must be raised for every $1,000 in increased energy costs.

CHAPTER 7

Energy for Heating, Cooling and Ventilation

Don't build a glass house if you're worried about saving money

on heating.

— Philip Johnson, Architect

Energy efficiency as it relates to heating and cooling in workplaces depends largely on features of the base building, and management by the base building operator. However, there *are* measures that can be taken in a leased space to reduce the energy demand for heating, cooling and ventilation.

For workplaces that have large expanses of window, reducing heat loss or unwanted solar heat gain through windows is one of the principle ways to reduce the energy needed for heating and cooling. Other strategies include temperature scheduling and temperature setback at night and weekends, localized temperature controls, and adhering to a range of temperatures.

Window U-factor, SHGC value

. . . .

According to the U.S. Department of Energy, up to 35% of energy wasted in buildings is due to inefficient windows. In California, around 40% of a typical building's cooling requirements are due to solar heat gain through windows.[55] During the summer months, ordinary glass lets the sun's heat penetrate easily. Also many buildings have a large window:wall ratio, far exceeding the recommended ratio of approximately 0.40 for optimal daylighting and heating/cooling.[56] As a result, HVAC systems must work harder to keep the interior cool in summer, and make up for heat lost through the glass in winter.

The degree to which a window allows heat loss or gain depends on many factors including their size, the type of glazing and frame, and how well sealed the window is. Two measures of performance are U-factor, which relates to the amount of energy that transfers through the window, resulting from the temperature difference between the inside and outside, and solar heat gain coefficient (SHGC), which is a measure of the solar radiation that flows through a window.

The **U-factor** of a window indicates how much heat transfers as a result of the temperature difference between the outdoors and indoors. Windows lose heat to the outside during the heating season and gain heat from the outside during the cooling season. The greater the U value, the more heat is lost or gained. In most of North America,

According to the U.S. Department of Energy, up to 35% of energy wasted in buildings is due to inefficient windows.

the increased energy load from this heat transfer is usually worse in winter than summer because indoor-outdoor temperature differences are generally greater in the winter. Glass, itself doesn't offer much resistance to heat flow, but double or triple glazing can significantly lower the U-factor because of the insulation from the still spaces between the panes, which are usually filled with low heat-conducting gases such as argon, krypton or carbon dioxide.

The **Solar Heat Gain Coefficient (SHGC)** is a measure of a window's ability to allow heat gain from direct solar radiation. A lower SHGC translates into less direct heat being pulled into the space resulting in lower cooling costs.

Reducing heat gain/loss with existing windows
. . . .

Factory installed low-e glass coatings are microscopically thin, transparent coatings that reflect heat and ultra violet light. When the interior heat energy tries to escape to the colder outside during the winter, the low-e coating reflects the heat back to the inside, reducing the radiant heat loss through the glass. The reverse happens during the summer time.

"Smart glass" in windows or skylights is glass that has the capability to block specific radiation wavelengths including light and/or solar heat when activated by light or heat or electrical controls. Smart glass can save costs for heating, air conditioning and lighting and avoid the cost of installing and maintaining motorized light screens or blinds or curtains.

Even though it may not be feasible to replace the windows or add coatings in a leased office space, it may still be possible to minimize the amount of **heat loss** through windows by ensuring that they are well-sealed around the perimeter and adding blinds, and to minimize **solar gain** by installing solar film and/or blinds.

Subtle drafts caused by **worn out seals** may be hard to detect just by placing your hand around the frame. A better way is to hold a lighter or candle near a window edge. If the flame flickers, this may indicate that the seal needs replacement. The caulking on most buildings should be inspected every five to ten years, depending on the type of caulking used.

Solar control window film applied to the interior of windows can reject up to 80% of solar heat gain without blocking visible light. Window film reduces the amount of solar heat transmission through window glass by increasing the solar reflection or solar absorption of the glass. Typical colored or dyed films work primarily through increased absorption. The color absorbs the solar energy at the glass, thus reducing the direct transmission into the room. These films are not as effective as reflective films, which are coated with metal molecules that increase the ability of the glass to reflect the solar heat so that it doesn't enter the building.

Some films also offer an increased performance against cold weather heat loss by reflecting more of the interior room heat back into the room where it is needed. This improves personal comfort by reducing cold spots near windows and can help save on fuel costs.

Simple payback from installing window film can be 2-5 years, depending upon the amount of sunlit glass exposure, the type of film, the type of glass, the cost of fuel, the cost of application, and other variables.

Installing **blinds** and using them correctly can keep unwanted solar gain out during the cooling season and also retain warmth within the building during cold winter nights.

If they are properly installed, that is to say, as close to the glass as possible, with the sides of the shade held close to the wall, blinds can provide a fairly good sealed air space which serves as insulation. On a cold or hot day, it is possible to detect a temperature difference on either side of the blind.

Solar shades are made from a synthetic mesh that significantly blocks the sun's radiant heat, glare and UV rays from entering the office space while still making it possible to see through them, depending on the "openness" factor, which relates to the percentage of light the solar shade allows in. This usually ranges from about 3-15%. For maximum protection, heat control and privacy, choose the smaller percentage. For better "view-through," choose a larger percentage.

Employees need greater awareness on the use of window blinds.
· ·

Most people understand the importance of switching off lights and plug load, but there is a general lack of awareness of the importance of using blinds correctly to reduce energy needed for heating and cooling.

In our experience, occupants use the blinds primarily for glare control. As long as the HVAC is working fine and they are feeling comfortable, it generally doesn't occur to them how hard the air conditioning must work to keep pace against all the solar heat gain that comes in through large expanses of glazing in the summer, nor that extra fuel is needed to make up for heat lost through those same windows during the cold season.

Given this general lack of awareness, clearly education and training and some simple house rules are in order. Those employees who are privileged to have work stations near windows should have the responsibility to close the blinds on hot summer days and on cold winter evenings before leaving the office.

This simple strategy can be surprisingly effective. In an office building that we managed, one of two chillers was being repaired during August. The building could barely meet the cooling load with one chiller, but we applied a number of practices that actually worked. First, we told the nighttime cleaning crew to close all the blinds at night, so that they were closed during the initial hours of the morning before people arrived. In many cases, the blinds we closed at night remained closed all day. Second, we shared the issue with tenants and asked them to keep their blinds closed as much as reasonable — for example, if space was unoccupied. We also asked that tenants on the east side keep their blinds closed in the morning and tenants on the west side to do the same in the afternoon. The entire strategy worked beautifully, and the tenants did not complain at all. In fact, many actually appreciated being involved in the effort.

Energy saving settings on thermostats

Another way to reduce energy for heating and cooling is to have energy-saving settings on thermostats, for example, 74 degrees F (23°C) or higher in the summer, and 70 degrees F (21°C) or lower in winter.

That said, for facility managers, keeping occupants comfortable usually trumps saving energy. Although smart buildings can turn down the heat or air-conditioning to energy saving settings, the problem is that occupants often just crank up the thermostats, plug in space heaters or open windows.

Underfloor ventilation provides some degree of individual control. Applications are also being developed that allow individual occupants to report on their cellphones whether they are too hot, too cold or feeling just right. These signals are sent to the BAS, which sets a temperature that will provide optimum satisfaction for the population. Thus buildings can "negotiate" energy saving measures with their occupants, factoring in the perceptions of all. These approaches are discussed further in Chapter 18 on thermal comfort.

Temperature set-back and scheduling

The goal of temperature set-back is to shut off systems whenever possible and refrain from starting them up for an occasional night-time user or weekend user. By implementing aggressive set-backs on nights and weekends, it should be possible to achieve a difference in consumption between the base load and the peak load of at least 30% or even much more.

Night set-back can lead to significant energy savings and is easy to implement. The weekend set-back strategy can be even more aggressive than weekday night set-back because there is so much more time when the building is unoccupied during the weekends. In extreme weather conditions, it will be necessary to maintain some preset limits, but for the majority of the year, the system can remain off on the weekends.

One challenge in commercial buildings is to provide the right amount of heating and cooling in spaces that have irregular occupancy patterns. One of the greatest energy inefficiencies occurs when only 5-10% of staff

By implementing aggressive set-backs on nights and weekends, it should be possible to achieve a difference in consumption between the base load and the peak load of at least 30% or even much more.

are working with all of the heating, ventilating, and air conditioning (HVAC) equipment running, all fresh air open and lights on.

At MIT, researchers have used their own campus to demonstrate a means of measuring this type of energy/occupancy mismatch, for example, where a lecture hall has 900 students for a couple of hours, followed by several hours during which the hall is empty — but is still being heated or cooled. Their research has focused on tracking occupancy via the WiFi network, which includes hotspots in most rooms and hallways.[57] With this data, it is possible to make operational and scheduling adjustments to optimize heating and cooling.

A simple concept that building managers are refining is called "energy coasting." At the end of the day, when a building is already cooled or heated to an acceptable level, building systems can be turned off or scaled back to allow that residual temperature in the building to hold during the last part of the day.

In an "energy coasting" program instituted by Beacon Capital, a test building gradually increased energy coasting periods from 15 minutes per day up to approximately 90 minutes per day. At this property, coasting load reduction averaged about 1,000 kWh/day five days a week and saved 260,000 kWh/yr. or $34,000 annually in marginal electricity cost.[58]

To cut ventilation costs, bring in outside air as needed

When outside air is brought into a space, energy must be used not only to heat or cool it, but also to push it around the building. Less air movement translates into less fan horsepower. Reducing the amount of ventilation air saves energy. But too little outside air can make for poor indoor air quality.

One way to modulate the amount of outdoor air required in response to the specific needs of each zone is with variable air volume (VAV). Variable air volume, in contrast to constant air volume (CAV) systems, regulates the amount of ventilation air targeted at a specific room or area by opening a valve to let more air through, or conversely, by constricting it. This is controlled by the Building Automation System (BAS). Small pressure sensors detect the pressure of air in the VAV box, and hinges open and close doors to manipulate airflow and volume in response to the BAS signals.

One way to determine just how much outside air is needed while saving energy is by sensing the amount of carbon dioxide (CO_2) in the indoor air. Unusually high carbon dioxide levels cause occupants to feel drowsy, get headaches, or function at lower activity levels. Carbon dioxide levels are usually greater inside a building than outside, even in buildings with few complaints about indoor air quality.

The CO_2 measurement is also an indicator of the effectiveness of the ventilation system, and of when the air needs to be changed. This is the principle of **demand ventilation**. As levels of carbon dioxide rise, the system increases the amount of conditioned outdoor air brought into that zone. As levels of carbon dioxide fall, the amount of outdoor air is reduced, reducing energy use.

Conclusion
. . . .

The energy needed for heating, cooling and ventilation depends on many factors, most of which are attributed to the base building. These include the building envelope and the energy efficiency of the HVAC, as well as base building operations. Energy conserving measures in the tenant space include reducing excessive solar gain in summer, or heat loss in winter through windows; implementing energy conserving set points; temperature set-back and scheduling; and monitoring the amount of ventilation. Energy conservation measures related to heating, cooling and ventilation need to take into account the effect on occupant comfort. This is discussed in Chapter 18.

The best approach, in our view, is that the tenant and building operator work together to develop an energy-efficient strategy. Once again, by getting all parties involved, a culture of energy efficiency can be developed that will have impacts far beyond just the immediate energy savings produced.

CHAPTER 8

Water

We never know the worth of water till the well is dry.

— Thomas Fuller, 17th century historian

Buildings use water primarily for HVAC, plant irrigation, kitchens, water fountains and washrooms. Many uses are controlled by the base building. In this chapter, we examine the most obvious area where tenants may have some control: washroom and kitchen fixtures. But first, a little background on the whole issue of sanitation.

Cities (and commercial buildings) can't exist without toilets, taps and sewers. Yet as we know, the water systems that we often take for granted are challenged, as some large populated areas experience drought while others try to cope with floods.

There are many reasons that water is often called "blue gold." Like gold, we have limited reserves of fresh water. Also, it costs a lot of money to expand networks to deliver water effectively, often from great distances, carry it away in sewers, maintain treatment plants, and meet the increasing cost of energy to pump and treat it.

Given the world's population explosion and the growth of third world mega-cities, our current global approach to city sanitation is certainly not sustainable. But this problem is not limited to third world countries.

According to the National Oceanic and Atmospheric Administration, nearly one in 10 watersheds in the U.S. is stressed due to water shortages combined with growing populations, resulting in demand for water exceeding natural supply. Cities that are threatened with water scarcity include Salt Lake City, Lincoln, Cleveland, Atlanta, Georgia, El Paso, San Antonio, San Francisco Bay Area, Houston and Los Angeles.

Compounding the problem is the fact that a lot of the blue gold is leaking out of North America's aging water infrastructure. Nearly six billion gallons of expensive, treated water are lost daily due to crumbling infrastructure and leaky, aging pipes. This adds up to 2.1 trillion gallons annually, or 16% of the nation's daily water use,[59] a problem which can be addressed with better leak detection monitoring, targeted repairs or upgrades, pressure management, and better metering technologies.

Nearly one in 10 watersheds in the U.S. is stressed due to water shortages.

Before we launch into a discussion of toilets and taps in office buildings, we should take a moment to remind ourselves that all great civilizations have had to develop a sanitation infrastructure. Other than the fact that we now have the capability to harness the energy needed to pump and pressurize water, our overall approach has, regrettably, not evolved greatly in over 2,000 years.

Toilets, taps and sewers — not much changed since Roman days

The Romans, like us, loved water and used a lot of it. To meet the needs of a city of almost a million people, water was conveyed from a distance of about 20 miles and taken away via underground sewers. Unlike our system, though, which uses pumps, Rome relied on sloped, gravity-fed aqueducts and canals that brought the water into the city. From the aqueducts, it was distributed to the population via lead pipes to approximately 600 delivery points, including a few homes of the rich and powerful, but primarily to local fountains and public baths, which also provided public toilets.

Waste water from the public baths, and toilet waste flowed continuously in small channels beneath the latrine seats to the branch sewers beneath the city, or into large cesspits — then into the main sewer to the Tiber and out to sea. The ancient Roman cesspools, like modern-day septic tanks, allowed heavy solids to settle to the bottom and the partially cleaned liquid to flow into a nearby body of water. Collected sludge was either used as fertilizer or simply buried. Where running water did not reach the poor tenements from the aqueducts and in multi-storey buildings, pots or commodes were used, which were then emptied into the cesspools throughout the city.[60]

Unlike the Roman toilets, our ability to pump water allows us to distribute it above ground floor level. Consequently, we use vast amounts of clean drinking water to flush sanitary waste and to push it all the way to treatment plants, where these great volumes must undergo extensive purification to remove high concentrations of bacteria.

Better things to do with clean water than flush it down the toilet
· ·

Assuming that the water content of feces could be removed, each person on average produces only about 25 pounds of **dried** fecal matter per year — an amount that would fit into a carry-on bag.[61] And yet we use 2,000 — 5,000 gallons (depending on the type of toilet) of **potable** water per person per year to flush this away. And that's not counting the additional volume of gray water from showers, taps and dishwashers, which is essential to keep things moving in our sewer system. The average person in the US uses around 80-100 gallons of drinking water daily, most of which ends up in the sewer. Surely we could be doing better things with clean water than flushing it down the toilet.

As large cities emerge all over the globe, there has to be a better way to deal with sanitary waste. It is likely that in the not distant future, there will be an increase in on-site solid waste incinerating toilets along with recycling and purification of liquid, which will allow us to re-use the cleaned toilet water for non-potable uses, or even — at some time in the more distant future, enable us to take the water from toilet to tap. Meanwhile, the mainstream solution is to reduce consumption by installing the most water efficient systems and fixtures.

Water usage in office buildings

Office buildings use water for heating and cooling systems, irrigation and washrooms and kitchens.[62] The common metric for water use is gallons per person per day. For water devices, the common metric is gallons per minute (gpm), per hour (gph), or per flush (gpf).

Throughout a building, water is distributed by a series of pressurized distribution pipes or lines. Unfortunately, sub-metering of water is generally not as advanced as it is for energy. In most buildings, it is metered upon entering the site but not at the distribution points or end use points. This lack of measurement makes it difficult to monitor users' water consumption, diagnose where water use is excessive and set reduction targets.

Despite the lack of water metering in most leased offices, there are prescriptive measures that can and should be taken to improve water conservation and efficiency. Washrooms of office buildings use about 30-40% of the water consumed in the building. This is one area over which tenants may have some control, primarily by using water-efficient fixtures.

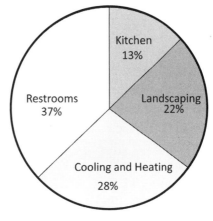

Figure 6 — Water usage in office buildings

Naturally, one must consider the effectiveness of devices. For example, a showerhead with a 50% lower flow rate that requires twice as long to rinse is no more efficient that the full flow-rate device. Nor is a water efficient toilet that has to be flushed twice to do the job, or automated controls that are not commissioned properly, resulting in phantom or continual flushing.

Toilets

· · · · · ·

Three common types of toilet are: the **traditional** model with a water cistern above and behind the toilet bowl, which uses gravity to send water into the bowl, and a siphon effect to drain the bowl; the **flushometer toilet**, which consists of no tank but instead, uses mains-pressurized line-water and a valve to flush away the waste; and finally, the **pressure-assisted tank toilet**, in which the pressurized line-water compresses air in a specially sealed tank (which looks very much like a regular tank behind the toilet), greatly increasing the flush water force.

Today's efficiency standard for new toilets requires them to use only 1.6 gallons or less per flush — a fraction of the consumption of those manufactured between 1977 and mid-1990s, which use about 3.5 gpf, and earlier ones (pre-1977 toilets), which use even more — as much as 4.5-7 gpf.

To find out whether your toilet is high efficiency, you may find a manufacturer's stamp showing the water usage per flush on the inside of the tank or on the "neck" of the toilet bowl. Where this does not appear, then a good indicator is probably the age of the toilet. Sometimes what appears to be a low-flush toilet actually consumes a lot of water. A rough indication of this is to count how many seconds it takes to flush.

Because a low-flow bowl can accommodate and work just as well with high flow flushing mechanisms, it's not uncommon to find a 3.5 gpf and 4.5 gpf mechanism mistakenly installed with a 1.6 gpf bowl. A simple way to determine whether the low-flow bowl is using more water than it needs is simply by timing the flush cycle. An average 1.6 gpf flushometer toilet should flush for only about 3 to 4 seconds, whereas a 3.5 gpf fixture would run for about 7 seconds, and a 4.5 gpf fixture would operate for about 9 to 10 seconds. If a supposedly low-flow flushometer toilet goes on for more than 4 seconds, then very likely there is an incorrectly-sized mechanism, which could be replaced with a lower flow. A longer flush cycle may also be a signal that the flushometer valves are worn and should be replaced.

Toilet retrofit or replacement?
. . . .

For many offices, savings of 25-30% are readily achievable by retrofitting toilets, urinals and taps. It's important to note, though, that for water efficient toilets and urinals to be effective, the shape of the bowl is as important as the flushing mechanism.

Old toilets with a water cistern on the back can be retrofitted by reducing the amount of water that goes into the bowl. It's unlikely that an old bowl can achieve the 1.6 gpf consumption of a newer water-efficient toilet. However, a simple upgrade to an older water-hogging toilet — one that uses more than 3.5 gpf — can still achieve significant water savings, take just a few minutes and cost as little as $20. For example, in an older toilet with a tank, it's possible to reduce each flush by up to 1 gallon or more by installing a displacement device or flexible insert (known as toilet dam) that reduces the amount of water that the tank holds. (Don't use a brick, because the particles from the brick can damage the flapper.) Alternatively, the existing flush valve in the tank can be replaced with an early closure flapper valve. Another option is a dual flush adapter that allows users to use a standard flush for solids removal or a smaller flush for liquid and paper.

For newer toilets that use less than 3.5 gpf but that are not as efficient as the 1.6 gpf models, retrofitting can be problematic. That's because a new low-flush mechanism may be unable to deliver enough water to empty an older model of bowl. In this case, it may be advisable to replace the toilet bowl and flushing mechanism.

Replacement rather than retrofit is especially advised where water and sewerage costs are high and/or where there are a high number of users per toilet. In these cases, replacing an older toilet with a 1.6 gpf model will provide the most water savings, with payback periods less than four years. The price to replace a toilet can range from $350-$500. Many water agencies offer rebates or incentives for upgrading toilet fixtures.

Most commercial/industrial facilities use flushometer toilets, easily identified by their distinctive chrome pipe-work and by the absence of a toilet tank or cistern. The water flows directly into the toilet for a pre-set period of time as a result of the water pressure in the line, which must be at least 30 pounds per square inch.

In addition to ensuring adequate mains line pressure to meet the minimum requirements of the fixture manufacturer, and making sure that the flushing mechanism is a high efficiency one, it's important to check the settings for automatic sensors to avoid double or phantom flushing, which if not corrected, can use significantly more water than manual flushing. Obviously, there are no savings, where a 1.6 gpf toilet is flushing twice for each use.

The most modern and effectively designed flush toilet currently on the market is the pressurized tank toilet, which includes what looks like a traditional ceramic flush tank. Unlike the traditional toilet tank though, the ceramic tank contains a plastic tank, which holds the flushing water as well as a sealed air-filled balloon-like rubber diaphragm. As the high-pressure main's water enters the tank, the rubber diaphragm comes under pressure and shrinks accordingly. During flushing, the compressed air inside the diaphragm greatly increases the flush water force. Pressurized tank toilets can provide a flush as low as 1.1 gpf. The disadvantage of pressurized tank toilets is that it takes a little while for the tank to refill, which can be problematic where there is high usage.

Replacement rather than retrofit is especially advised where water and sewerage costs are high and/or where there are a high number of users per toilet.

Where sewers or septic tanks are not available and where building inspection programs can approve such toilet systems, composting and incinerating toilets may be an option. However, these are still far from hitting the mainstream in office buildings.

Flushing urinals — avoiding continuous flushing

Traditional urinals use 2-3 gpf. Most public urinals have a flushing system to rinse urine from the bowl to prevent foul odors. Like toilets, these may use either a **tank gravity-fed system** that sends the water into the bowl, or they can have a **flushometer** valve, which has no tank but uses mains-line pressure. The flush can be triggered manually or automatically by sensors.

Manual flushing consists of a button or short lever, which users are expected to operate as they leave. Some urinals have water-saving "dual-flush" handles, which use half as much water when pushed upwards, and operate a standard full flush when pressed downwards.

The disadvantage with any manual system is that patrons may fail to use it to avoid touching the handle for sanitary reasons. An alternative is to provide a foot-activated flushing system, using a button set into the floor or a pedal on the wall at ankle height. However, this is often ineffective because many people are not used to it or choose not to use it.

The whole problem of people not flushing is often avoided by having a system of automated flushing at regular intervals using a timing mechanism. Where several urinals are connected to a single overhead cistern, a constant drip-feed of water slowly fills the cistern until a tipping point is reached, at which time

Check the settings for automatic sensors to avoid double or phantom flushing, which if not corrected, can use significantly more water than manual flushing.

the valve opens (or a siphon begins to drain the cistern), and all the urinals in the group are flushed.

Although this system doesn't require any action from its users, it is wasteful for urinals in offices to flush every few minutes 24/7 even during periods when there are no users, including night-time.

To reduce the frequency of flushing, it's possible to add a device that regulates the rate of water flow to the cistern according to the overall activity detected in the room. This is simple and inexpensive because only one device is required for the whole system. One way to avoid flushing when there are no users is to link the flushing action to the restroom lights or restroom door. When lights go on or after the door opens, a certain number of times, this triggers flushing. For example, during the day, when there's a lot of traffic, lights are on and the door is opening frequently, the timed flush operates normally. At night when the building is closed, the lights are turned off and doors never open, the flushing action never occurs.

Electronic automatic flushing consists of an infrared sensor that activates the flush only after someone has stood in front of the urinal for a few seconds and then moved away from the sensor range. There usually is also a small override button to allow optional manual flushing. The handle-operated valves of a manual system can be upgraded with a suitably designed, self-contained, electronic, battery-powered sensor control.

Retrofitting urinals

· · · · · · · · · · · · · · · · ·

Traditional urinals use as much as 3 gpf. Many options exist to improve the water efficiency of urinals. High-efficiency urinals (HEUs) include 0.5 gpf, one-quart (0.25 gpf) and one-pint (0.125 gpf) as well as waterless models.

Where there are flushometers, one option is to replace the urinal flushometer valve with a lower gpf model — providing the bowl can function at the lower flush volume setting of the high-efficiency valve. Since many older urinal bowls fail to empty properly at these reduced flows, what typically happens is that the maintenance person then adjusts the low-flush mechanism to its maximum flush volume setting, which doesn't really save much water. Obviously, in this situation, it would be better to replace the entire urinal and flush valve with an HEU.

As with toilets, there should be a regular inspection (annually, at a minimum) of the flushing mechanism and replacement of any worn parts as well as on-going checking and adjusting of automatic sensors to avoid double or phantom flushing. This simple solution, which requires a bit of coordination with the building staff, is a very low-cost activity that can have a significant impact on water use.

And, as with toilets, studies in office buildings show that water use tends to increase when manual valves are replaced with sensor-activated valves because of the double or phantom flushing. Note also, that override switches on automatic flush sensors often also release a larger volume of water than is typical for the standard flush.

Urinal replacement — Consider waterless urinals

Notwithstanding much initial protest by the plumbing industry, waterless urinals are becoming popular. Since waterless urinals literally use no water, they can save 1-3 gallons (3.7 to 11.3 liters) for each use. This certainly adds up if you consider that a single urinal in a workplace with just a dozen employees can use 20,000 gallons of water per year!

A waterless urinal consists of a vertical cartridge in the drain. Within the cartridge is a trap that contains a vegetable oil-based blue sealant liquid that is much lighter than urine. The urine flows down through the floating liquid sealant into a central reservoir connected to the bathroom's waste pipe. The urine from several users slowly fills up the reservoir, and when the level of liquid gets higher than the rim of the pipe, the excess drains out.

A single urinal in a workplace with a dozen employees can use 20,000 gallons of water per year!

The small amount of urine that remains in the reservoir is sealed by a head of the lighter blue sealant liquid floating on top, which also prevents any odors or bacteria from escaping.

Waterless urinals are actually more sanitary than flush models because no contaminants are sprayed during flushing. Also, there is less bacterial growth in general, compared to a regular urinal. Urine, when it leaves the body is pretty sterile — that is, until it mixes with water, upon which the minerals in urine react with those in the water, creating conditions for bacteria to thrive. Since there is no water in a waterless urinal, there is less bacteria growth.

In waterless urinals, the sealant liquid must be replaced every 1,500 uses (two to four times a year) because small amounts of it seep down the drain with the urine, eventually depleting it over time. In some urinals, the entire cartridge can be replaced (and recycled). In others, the trap is re-used. First it is removed, and any mineral build-up from urine is scrubbed away. Then it is refilled with fresh sealant liquid. Some traps cannot be removed. These need to be cleaned using a plumbing snake to remove the mineral sediment build-up, which otherwise will clog the trap.

Waterless urinals are not more expensive; in fact, they are often less expensive because they have fewer plumbing components. As a result of reduced water and sewer charges, their payback is very rapid — in most cases, 1-2 years. Also, some drought-prone municipalities offer an attractive rebate for replacing old urinals with waterless models as an incentive to decrease demands on the local water supply.

To replace a regular urinal with a waterless model, the unused water supply line needs to be capped. In the absence of flushing power, it may also be necessary to modify the pipe leading from the bottom of the urinal to the main waste line to provide enough slope (about 0.25 inch per foot) so that waste can drain out easily.

Faucets and showers

· · · · · · · · · · · · · · · · · · ·

Reducing water consumption at the tap or shower is easy and inexpensive — either by reducing the rate of flow and/or the time of flow. This not only saves water but also the energy to produce hot water. Reducing the **rate** of flow can be done by installing an aerator in an existing office faucet or, in the case of a shower, a low-flow (1.5 gpm) showerhead. This not only reduces water consumption by up to half but also saves on energy to heat water. Reducing the **flow-time** is done by automatic shut-off controls, either spring activated type or occupancy sensors.

Reducing the rate of flow or time of flow, in turn reduces the amount of water that needs to be heated, making it possible to reduce the size of the hot water tank. Many small offices have a 50-gallon water heater that is far greater than what is needed. Smaller tanks reduce the "stand-by" energy needed to keep the water hot. Tankless water heaters cut standby losses even further.

Drips and leaks

Leaky or dripping faucets can waste thousands of gallons a year. A faucet that drips once every second can waste more than 3,000 gallons per year — equivalent to more than 180 showers! In the case of hot water, it also wastes the energy to heat it. Heating water can account for more than 5% of energy use in a building.

A leaking faucet is often the result of a bad washer or seal, which is very simple to replace. Similarly, toilet leaks, if unchecked, can be very costly in terms of water and sewer costs. Toilet repairs depend on the type of toilet, but in any case, will always save money.

Conclusion

Water is essential for our survival. 98% of the water on the planet is in the oceans as saline, and therefore is unusable for drinking. Only 2% of the planet's water is fresh, but most of it is locked in polar icecaps and glaciers, leaving less than 1% of the fresh water available to us in lakes, rivers and underground aquifers. Meanwhile, parts of North America are now facing water crises. For example, the Colorado River basin, which supplies 40 million people, is being sucked dry and ground water is being depleted at a shocking rate. In California, it is now considered a criminal act to waste water following the State Water Resources Control Board declaration that certain types of water waste constitute a criminal infraction similar to a speeding violation. Accordingly, such practices as allowing landscape watering to spill into streets, or hosing off sidewalks and driveways — can be subject to fines of $500 per day.

There is no doubt that globally and nationally, we are recognizing the need to completely re-think how we manage our water. From a purely financial perspective, water shortages are leading to huge increases in the cost of water. This, as well as the increasing cost of energy to heat water, means that implementing water-efficiency measures is a no-brainer.

Office buildings use almost 10% of water in commercial and institutional facilities in the USA. Office tenants may have some control over bathroom and kitchen plumbing fixtures, which account for a significant portion of water use in office buildings. Upgrades and replacement of water fixtures, and proper maintenance to ensure that the controls are operating properly can save money and have short payback periods.

Now that you have learned more than you ever hoped to know about office plumbing, let's look beyond the obvious connection to sustainability and consider water management from a productivity perspective. The way an organization manages its water says a lot about its corporate culture.

Proactive water management practices by an organization communicate a commitment to several ideas that have growing appeal to today's workforce and help advertise the organization's values to its employees. The first is that the organization values sustainability. The second is that the organization seeks efficiency by trying to control wasteful practices, such as careless water use. The third is that the organization realizes a responsibility to the community of which it is a part — where its employees live. As we discuss in the chapter "Health, Work-Life Balance & Productivity," the most productive workplaces have clear connections that extend beyond their walls. Workplace water management is one way to make those important connections.

CHAPTER 9

Waste Management

To know our refuse is to know ourselves. We mark our own trail

from past to present with what we've used and consumed, fondled,

rejected, outgrown.

— Jane Avrich, *The Winter Without Milk: Stories*

Everyone is familiar with the 3Rs of waste management. The concept of "Reduce, Re-use, Recycle" seems quite straightforward — and perhaps even somewhat boring, until we discover that there's a lot more to it than meets the eye. The reason that waste management may seem simple is that most of us don't see what goes on beyond the waste bins at work or the weekly curbside garbage collection outside our homes and offices. What we don't realize in the course of our everyday lives is that this is just the tip of the iceberg.

In this chapter, we take a glimpse behind the scenes at the massive global industry of waste management and the indirect impact it has on how we manage our own workplace waste — now and in the future. We also outline some best practices in offices to reduce the use of non-renewable resources and minimize pollution and impact on landfill — while keeping an eye on the wallet.

Waste management is a vast, complex, highly interconnected global industry

The world of waste management includes global market forces of supply and demand, private and public infrastructure, and regulations that vary significantly from region to region and around the globe. It is an industry that is driven by global transactions worth an estimated $443 billion a year — and growing, thanks to increasing export volumes and rising prices.

Most recyclables go to Asian manufacturing nations. Their container ships deliver consumer goods to North America, and return with bales of compressed plastic, textiles, rubber and recovered paper, the size of houses, not to mention mountains of electronic waste. In fact, scrap was the top US export to China, worth $11.3 billion in 2011![63]

Scrap was the top US export to China, worth $11.3 billion in 2011!

This trading cycle is also being driven by domestic legislation and other pressures that encourage us to recycle more, which, in turn are being fueled by increasing landfill charges that make it cheaper to send the waste abroad.

Global networks shift

As interconnected as they are, these global networks are fragile, evolving, and can easily become disjointed. For example, in 2013, China's *Operation Green Fence* set a strict limit of 1.5% of allowable contaminant for each bale of imported plastic, putting an end to the import of plastic that isn't cleaned or thoroughly sorted. This initiative came about because contaminated plastic has become a huge problem for China's landfills.

The rigorous standard set by *Operation Green Fence* sent business shockwaves to both sides of the Pacific as thousands of North American shipments were rejected at Chinese ports, resulting in bankruptcy of many North American exporters. American recycling facilities, who found themselves drowning in plastic, stopped accepting certain plastics because they had no market for them. Meanwhile, in China, the price of clean recyclable materials rocketed, which resulted in widespread bankruptcy among Chinese manufacturers, who depended on inexpensive materials.

This incident has served as a warning to North America that we must do more to boost our domestic recycling industries and economies, rather than rely entirely on fragile markets in foreign developing countries to buy our waste. "*Operation Green Fence* has sent an alarming signal regarding the sustainability of an export-based recycling system," says David Newman, president of the International Solid Waste Association (ISWA). "We must think twice about the costs and benefits of exporting recyclables to developing countries and identify the consequences along the value chain of a monopoly market player like China."

Another example that illustrates change in the export of waste is the massive trade in electronics product waste, also known as "e-waste." In 2012, nearly 50 million metric tons of e-waste were generated worldwide — or about 7 kg (~15.5 lbs.) for every person on the planet, an amount that is expected to grow by 33% in the next four years.[64] These electronic goods contain toxic substances such as lead, mercury, cadmium, arsenic and flame retardants. For example, an old-style CRT computer screen can contain up to 3 kg of lead. For a long time, North American recyclers of electronic equipment found that they could earn far more by exporting e-waste than they could by recycling it at home. While we have assumed that our e-waste was being dealt with in an environmentally-responsible way, it was, in fact, ending up in countries such as China, India, and Nigeria, where gold, silver lead and copper were being extracted as part of a huge, unregulated, dangerous and polluting cottage industry.

Following the *Basel Convention on the Control of Transboundary Movements of Hazardous Wastes and Their Disposal*, aimed at reducing the transfer of hazardous waste from developed to less-developed countries, many countries have now banned the shipping of hazardous waste and used electrical products.

Notwithstanding regulations to prevent the export of hazardous products, these materials still continue to flood West Africa and Asia — often under the guise of "used goods" or "charitable donations," allowing traders, often enabled by criminal networks, to elude these laws. According to the UN Environment Program and the Green Customs Initiative, there are indications that crime syndicates earn $20 to $30 billion a year from hazardous waste violations. Even in 2005, when standards were less rigorous, inspections of 18 European seaports in 2005 found as much as 47% of waste destined for export was illegal hazardous waste.

Given the difficulties in estimating the volume, value and destination of e-waste in these countries, it is almost impossible to determine exactly how much of our e-waste is now being refurbished, but undoubtedly, a large proportion is still being dismantled by unprotected workers, including children, who remove small pieces of metal to be sold, the remaining plastics and cables often being dumped or burned.

The good news is that developed countries are starting to build clean e-waste and refurbishment factories at home, giving rise to a growing domestic industry of used electronic products, which, according to a 2013 study by the US. International Trade Commission, generated domestic sales of $19.2 billion compared to exports worth $1.45 billion in 2011.[65]

Need to establish a 3 R Economy in North America

What will it take to establish a flourishing homegrown 3R economy, which includes a domestic market for recycled materials? Broadly speaking, we need three conditions: high tech recycling and processing capabilities; controls on waste quality; and a local market for recyclable materials.

According to Mike Biddle, plastics recycling pioneer and founder of MBA Polymers, we will only be able to create the right market conditions for domestic recycling if we can innovate and invest in **high tech recycling and processing** plants. The EPA agrees, saying that education and stronger public and private partnerships are required to advance a domestic industry based on reduction, reuse and recycling.

Secondly, there need to be tighter **controls on waste quality**, including a common set of criteria for major scrap. To this end, the Bureau of

International Recycling (BIR) has recently published ISO-based guidelines on environmentally-sound waste management to help educate players in the global recycling market.[66]

One irony is that whilst China is gradually becoming more rigorous with respect to reducing contamination, we in North America are increasingly adopting co-mingling practices, whereby different types of recyclable materials are collected together. This tends to produce higher levels of material contamination than when recyclables are separated at source, as they are in countries such as Germany.

Co-mingling requires less effort by the public and tends to cost less for haulers because it avoids the need for separate trucks. It relies on highly automated sorting, which is fast but imperfect — a process that has been compared to trying to unscramble a scrambled egg. This results in much of the material having to be discarded or contaminating manufacturing processes.

Until we can reduce the higher levels of contamination which result from co-mingling waste, paper mills will continue to struggle with unusable contaminated paper that is wet or dirty, and manufacturers of glass containers will go on having to contend with contamination from window glass, Pyrex, metals, ceramics, gravel and stones as well mixed colors of glass, which do not work for some applications.

Waste diversion rates of major cities

San Francisco	100%
Seattle	83%
Los Angeles	81%
Toronto	78%
Minneapolis	72%
Sacramento	72%
Vancouver	69%
Ottawa	66%
Montreal	63%
Houston	59%
Calgary	58%
Orlando	58%
Philadelphia	57%
Chicago	55%
Boston	54%
New York City	53%
Denver	51%
Washington DC	44%
Dallas	41%
Charlotte	40%
Phoenix	40%
Atlanta	29%
Miami	28%
St Louis	26%
Pittsburgh	25%
Cleveland	22%
Detroit	0%

Figure 7 – Waste diversion rates of cities in North America

Fortunately, there is a growing online community that can help organizations ensure that as much of their clean waste materials are diverted from landfill as possible. If you have clean materials that you would like to recycle but don't know where to drop them off, check the following websites. *My eco-ville* at **http://www.myecoville.com/EcoPoint** allows you to search by material, location or organization in the USA. In Canada, see *3R Certified* at **http://3rcertified.ca/recyclers** for links to regional, national and international directories and exchange programs for materials recyclers.

A third condition for growing an economy that favors the 3Rs is to create **local markets for recyclable materials**. According to Bob Ensinger of the Institute of Scrap Recycling Industries, manufacturers need to be more proactive in creating sustainable designs, specifying recycled materials over virgin raw materials and investing in end uses for secondary raw materials.

What does all this have to do with waste management in offices?

The reality is that problems with the earth's dwindling resources and diminishing landfill sites, as well as pollution from hazardous materials are not going away. It is also clear that the forces of supply and demand for recyclables as well as different regulations across the globe and locally can have an impact on the way we manage our waste.

Even across North America, our waste management infrastructures, local regulations, landfill fees, and demand for materials vary. All need to be taken into consideration when planning our own waste diversion programs. For example, some municipalities have no infrastructure to store and sort recyclables. On the other hand, some remote areas that lack recycling infrastructure nonetheless have contracts with big hauling companies that have their own channels to transact different types of materials. Some jurisdictions ban the landfill disposal of cardboard. Some require commercial office facilities over a certain size to do waste audits and implement waste diversion work plans. In short, each region is different.[67]

An effective waste management program largely depends on local services, the support of senior management, and the premise that employees need to take responsibility for managing the waste they generate.

Waste management is largely dictated by contracts with our waste haulers and arrangements with the landlord

The link from our office waste to global markets generally begins with our waste haulers, most of whom have their own financial arrangements with brokers of recyclable materials, who in turn may deal with international brokers. This entire chain of transactions can shift depending on global forces of supply and demand.

The contract with our waste hauler largely dictates the types of materials that we recycle in our offices, the degree of source separation and how much we pay or are paid. Some haulers refuse to recycle certain materials because they do not have a market to sell them. Some haulers pay for high value materials such as aluminum cans or thick, clean, dry cardboard, depending on the quantities generated.

Some require co-mingling of recyclables. Others require source-separated recycling, which consists of keeping fiber components — paper and cardboard — separate from glass and plastic containers and cans. This may be more expensive to haul but results in lower levels of contamination and lower costs to process (sort) the collected recyclables. In offices, it is relatively straightforward to keep recyclables separated, and this can give an organization the maximum financial benefit from recycling due to the higher quality and value of the recovered material.

In leased facilities, where waste management may be the responsibility of the building owner or operator, recycling options for tenants may be limited by the availability of storage room and existing contracts. These issues can be discussed with the building owner or operator, and practical options can be implemented over time.

Best strategy: reduce
· · · · · · · · · · · · · · · · · ·

One of the basic principles of responsible waste management is to reduce the amount of materials needed or the amount of waste generated. This can save money that would have been spent purchasing excessive quantities, and the cost of disposing of materials at the end of their useful life.

To find the biggest savings, the first thing to do is to identify the key business operations — and the products and materials these use or generate in the largest quantities. Purchasing records can help to identify the best opportunities for waste prevention. In manufacturing operations, the savings from reducing materials and waste can be huge. Pepsi-Cola saved $44 million by switching from corrugated to reusable plastic shipping containers, conserving 196 million pounds of corrugated material. Dow Corning reconditioned steel drums, saving nearly $2.3 million and conserving 7.8 million pounds of steel, and an additional $530,000 by repairing and reusing 1.7 million pounds of wood pallets. And HASBRO reduced the thickness of corrugated shipping containers by 15%, which saved $400,000 and conserved more than 763,000 pounds of material.

In office operations, the savings are more modest than in manufacturing, and relate primarily to reducing paper. In the mid- to late-nineties, as offices transformed their operations to paperless, many companies saw huge savings, improved efficiencies and a reduced need for paper storage. For example, in 1994 and 1995, Bell South Telecommunications conserved 16 million sheets of printout paper and saved $3.5 million by implementing an electronic filing system. In 2000, Bank of America eliminated nearly 23 tons of paper used by subscribing to online magazines and newspapers, and changed to 15-pound rather than 20-pound paper ATM envelopes, which saved 228 tons of paper, and saved $500,000.

In 2000, Bank of America eliminated nearly 23 tons of paper used by subscribing to online magazines and newspapers, and changed to 15-pound rather than 20-pound paper ATM envelopes, which saved 228 tons of paper and $500,000.

That same year, the Ohio Bureau of Workers Compensation implemented a paperless medical claims imaging system, saving $483,000 in expenses, nearly 22 tons pounds of office paper and file folders and 2,500 pounds in toner cartridges.

Re-use
· · · · · · ·

Re-using certain items rather than disposing of them can save money that would be spent purchasing more items. It also reduces the cost of disposing of materials by extending their useful life.

In 2008, the US Postal Service, Great Lakes Area saved $52.5 million by reusing industrial equipment, electronics, and office furniture. Meanwhile, the Postal Service Western Area's conservation efforts saved the region $44 million by reusing and redistributing equipment and materials within the postal system, as well as diverting 35,000 tons of waste from the landfill.

There are many opportunities to re-use, including small actions that can really add up — for example, providing washable cups and dishes, and bulk drinking water, which avoids the need for throw-away containers.

For offices or individuals who want to participate in a grassroots global movement of people who are giving (and getting) stuff for free in their own towns, the Freecycle Network™ **www.freecycle.com** is a wonderful resource, made up of over 5,000 groups with almost 8 million members around the world. Each local group is moderated by local volunteers and membership is free.

Personal recycling and trash bins make employees more aware of how much trash they produce
· ·

Computer printout, white and colored ledger, newspaper, magazines, catalogues, marketing materials and telephone directories typically represent the majority of all waste generated in offices. For this reason, collection of recyclable waste paper should be provided at individual workstations, as well as near central photocopiers, printers and mail centers.

One approach to office waste is to provide each workstation with a paper recycling bin, as well as two small (1.5 liter) bins, one for landfill waste and one for recyclable waste. At the end of the day, the employees empty their own bins. This approach, compared to the traditional under-the-desk garbage cans, can result in significant savings due to the reduction in garbage, and reduced custodial costs when employees empty their own bins.

While this "empty-it-yourself" approach may seem extreme, it's actually very effective and is a great way to engage employees actively in the process of waste management. You are probably thinking that your employees would rebel at this concept. Our experience in buildings that we manage is that employees complain about it for a week or so — followed by a period of "quiet acceptance." After a month or so, the magic begins. Employees talk about it and, yes, even brag about it to visitors. It's an easy way to show others that they are participating in the sustainability effort and there is some honest pride in it. And because everyone in an office participates, it becomes an accepted part of the culture very quickly.

Central waste collection points
· ·

In addition to having bins at each workstation, central waste collection points should be located throughout the office in high traffic areas such as near elevators, coffee stations, photocopiers, lunchrooms or close to washroom facilities. These typically consist of a receptacle that has the appropriate number of compartments to meet separation requirements of the service provider — typically a receptacle for non-recyclable waste, a bin for recyclables: metal cans, glass bottles, rigid plastics and polystyrene, one for paper, and one for compost. This basic configuration can be expanded or reduced to meet the needs of the floor and can be complemented with external bins for batteries, or for office campaigns such as eye glasses for third world countries.

Bins should be checked frequently by cleaning staff to ensure they do not overflow and are wiped down periodically.

What about organic waste?

Organic waste in office buildings includes food waste and compostable paper waste such as paper towels. Most food waste comes from cafeterias and food courts; smaller amounts, consisting of apple cores, peelings, tea bags, coffee grounds and leftover food come from office lunchrooms, coffee stations, and individual workstations, where employees sometimes eat snacks and lunches. Paper towels generated in washroom facilities are also compostable. They occupy a large volume but do not have much weight. This also needs to be considered when determining storage requirements and costs.

There are certain important procedures to manage an organic waste stream, such as being clear as to what is and what is not acceptable by the organic processor. For example, much of the food waste from office buildings is coffee grounds that are not suitable for animal feed operations. Another necessary communication relates to the importance of not contaminating the waste with things like packaging. Ensure that there is adequate property management and staff support for handling organics — removing the waste from floor bins and cafeterias daily to reduce odors and pests (flies) and ensuring that organic collection occurs at least every second or third day, unless there is cold storage in the building.

Processing organic waste can take place on-site or off-site. On-site composting eliminates off-site collection costs and tipping fees, but there are additional internal costs for collection, storage, bulking, operating and maintenance and cleaning. It's important to review the technical and cost feasibility of composting. Because you are dealing with organic materials, there are issues surrounding safety and there may be local regulations about composting in your municipality. Before considering a composting option for your workplace, talk to local experts about the feasibility.

What to do with hazardous materials?

Offices may also generate small quantities of potentially hazardous wastes such as fluorescent lamps, batteries, and used paints and solvents from building maintenance operations. These should be safely stored and given to a licensed company to manage and dispose.

Some products such as printer cartridges and fluorescent lamps may be returned to the supplier or directly to recyclers, sometimes in the original shipping boxes as soon as enough of them have accumulated.

As for e-waste, unless you know for sure that your old computers and cell phones are going to one of the dozen or so existing clean recycling facilities, there is really no guarantee that they are not ending up in some e-waste village in Nigeria or Pakistan. Find out from your waste hauler.

Costing

The cost of waste disposal for offices varies greatly, and publicly available data is thin, but to give an idea of the order of magnitude, the Canadian federal government spends about $70/ton to dispose of its office waste. Other sources say the average cost is $100/ton. Some haulers charge by the pick-up, others by weight.

Multi-material recycling program costs are dependent on the cost to collect, separate and market the recyclable materials. Costs are typically priced as a fee that is based on the number of collection bins.

In most offices, paper is the only significant recycled material that has the potential to generate revenues. Depending on market conditions for mixed office paper and the volumes generated in a facility, office paper recycling services typically can either generate some revenue or be revenue neutral.

That said, depending on the type and quantity of waste, there can be resource recovery opportunities, savings and the possibility of revenues even for non-paper recyclables. For example, the University of Eastern Illinois collects and sells unwanted furniture that students leave behind in residences, and donates the proceeds to charity. In the past, Rutgers University has also re-sold 33 tons of unwanted furniture. Each year, the University of Eastern Illinois turns more than 10 tons of yard waste into mulch and compost, and the Medical University of South Carolina, transforms university cafeteria waste into fertilizer using vermiculture.

To give some idea of the revenue from recycling, in 2012, the California Refund Values (CRV) per pound of clean material at state certified recycling centers were $1.57 for aluminum cans; $1.00 for clear PET plastic bottles; $0.57 for HDPE plastic bottles (similar to the large water jugs); and $0.105 for glass bottles.

Unfortunately, in offices, the per ton costs for recycling materials such as glass and metal containers, rigid plastics or polystyrene on an individual material basis will always be higher than disposal costs due to their large volume to weight ratio. In fact, the ability to collect and recycle plastic PET beverage containers, HDPE plastic cleaning containers and polystyrene foam coffee cups, lids, plates and 'clamshell' trays is often limited in many regions.

Waste disposal charges typically include a collection or service fee, plus a tipping fee on a per ton or cubic yard basis. The costs for a recycling program should be assessed for the "basket of goods" when evaluating the per ton costs of diverting waste compared to the cost of disposing of it. To do such a comparison, also include equipment costs such as desk-side waste paper collection, mini-bins, central bins and carts, which may be part of the hauling service or be provided on a rental basis, as well as the office maintenance costs and any education or communications.

To minimize costs, the frequency of collection for recycling and garbage should not exceed the requirements in your facility and the contract should allow flexibility in service frequency. Waste and recycling contracts should include a provision to report the weight collected either on the invoices or in monthly reports, as well as the name, phone number and tipping rate structure for disposal facilities used.

Why do a waste audit?

Records of waste disposal and diversion for paper and other multi-material recycling should be kept as a running monthly summary. This ensures that the program stays on track, and helps to identify where improvements can be made. This data should be supplied by the waste hauler.

One way to monitor whether waste is being properly separated at source is to examine a sampling just to see whether employees are placing their waste in the proper bins.

Waste audits are more detailed. They serve to establish how much waste is being generated, exactly what type of waste, how much of it is recyclable, how much of the recyclable waste is going into the correct recycling bins. The quality of the data depends of course on the degree of sampling and the degree of sorting. Some audits use only a small sampling of bins, others are more rigorous — conducted over several days to get a good average, and detailing exactly what types of objects, such as paper cups, plastic film, aluminum trays, aerosol cans and so on, are finding their way into the dumpsters. This data is valuable because it can help to inform a more effective waste management strategy and make it possible to explore less wasteful options.

Audits vary widely in cost. Some waste haulers will do them for free; others charge a percentage of the savings found, and some certified waste

An independent audit can flag anomalies between the audit results and the amounts that are being reported and charged by the hauler.

auditors charge by the hour or on a contract basis. An audit could cost $1,000 or it could cost as much as $10,000. One advantage of doing an independent audit is that it can flag anomalies between the audit results and the amounts that are being reported and charged by the hauler. It may reveal for example, the need to do a calibration of the truck's weight, or indicate that the frequency of pick-ups could be reduced.

Communications

. . . .

As with any successful program, waste management can always be improved through ongoing communication and education to staff. Keeping employees informed, providing reminders and addressing problems (e.g. contamination) quickly can really improve performance. In addition, it's important to report successes to encourage continued participation in the program.

Modifications or changes to any diversion program (e.g. adding rigid plastics to the recycling program) should be communicated to staff through notices, emails and face-to-face contact.

Clarity of communications at collection points is critical. How many times have you seen someone standing in front of receptacles, trying to determine where to dispose of materials; after a few minutes, they give up and throw everything into one container. They want to do the right thing, but the instructions are not clear.

We suggest starting with a simple in-house audit of the materials typically thrown away in an office. Then, determine which of those items should be thrown into particular bins and clearly show which bins are for which items. Inevitably, there are going to be items that do not fit into any of the categories. Offer an "Anything Else" option. That's better than having those items end up, randomly, in one of the recycling bins.

Conclusion

The world of waste management is highly interconnected and global, and is driven largely by commercial forces of supply and demand as well as environmental considerations. Whilst most office management programs may appear similar, what actually happens to the waste once it leaves the building is often dependent on the local regulations and local infrastructure to store, sort and market the recyclables, as well as contracts that the waste hauler has. The best, most cost-effective and environmentally-responsible strategy for offices, therefore, is to reduce the amount of garbage — including recyclables — which we produce in the first place.

CREATING
A PRODUCTIVE
WORKPLACE

PART 2

CHAPTER 10

Employee Engagement and Employee Satisfaction

I strongly believe that you can't win in the marketplace unless you win first in the workplace.

— Douglas Conant, Former President and CEO, Campbell Soup Co.

Imagine working for an organization in which a fourth of the employees are totally turned off by their jobs, fully half the workers do just enough to get by, and only the remaining 25% are enthusiastic. Sadly, that's the profile of many firms in the United States.[1]

Engaged workers are the lifeblood of an organization. They're the ones who work with passion, feel a profound connection to their company and who go the extra mile to deliver. Engaged workers win the accounts, maintain customer loyalty, drive innovation and move the organization forward.

If you embrace this concept, are interested in knowing what is actually happening in the workplaces of the nation, and want to see a wealth of data that points to the fundamental drivers of productivity, then the Gallup study called *State of the American Workplace — Employee Engagement Insights for US Business Leaders 2013*[2] is a "must read," rich with data, analysis and insights.

The Gallup study corroborates many other studies that show that the vast majority of U.S. workers (over 70%) are "not engaged" or — even worse, are *actively* disengaged at work.

These employees are generally unmotivated, not likely to set goals and are simply putting in their hours, but with little energy or passion. These are what Gallup calls the "not engaged." They are friendly and make the right noises, but in reality they are doing just enough to get by and not get into trouble, and they tend to spend considerable time on their own personal business.

As for actively disengaged employees, these workers are not only unhappy and unproductive at work, but they also have a tendency to spread their negativity to co-workers. Their behaviors include making sarcastic jokes, speaking poorly about the company and the leadership, and looking for ways to put the blame on others. Some studies such as *Gallup* put the rate of actively disengaged workers at 25%. Others say it's not that high — more in the order of 5% — but even just a few bad apples are enough to create a toxic distraction. Workers who are actively disengaged are generally unhappy because they hate their job or the workplace culture, or quite simply, because they find that their bosses make them miserable.

The fact that the vast majority of employees are not reaching their full potential has huge negative implications for the North American economy and the performance of individual companies. Conversely, it should come as no surprise that companies with engaged employees have higher stock prices. NY Times best seller author of *Employee Engagement*, Kevin Kruse, has compiled a list of almost 30 studies[3] that link employee engagement to better service, sales, quality, safety, retention, profit and shareholder returns. Here are just a few examples:

- Engaged employees at Molson Coors were five times less likely than non-engaged employees to have a safety incident, and seven times less likely to have a lost-time safety incident.[4]
- A study of 23,910 business units compared top quartile and bottom quartile engagement scores and found that those in the bottom quartile averaged 62% more accidents, and 31%-51% more employee turnover. The study also found that those in the top quartile averaged 12% higher profitability.[5]
- Engaged employees in the UK take an average of 2.69 sick days per year; the disengaged take 6.19.[6]
- A study of 89 companies compared top quartile and bottom quartile engagement scores and found that those in the top quartile had 2.6 times higher earnings per share (EPS) than those in the bottom quartiles.[7]
- A study of 64 organizations showed that organizations with highly engaged employees have twice the annual net income than organizations whose employees have low engagement.[8]
- A study of 39 organizations indicated that those with highly engaged employees achieve seven times the five-year total shareholder return (TSR) than organizations with less engaged employees.
- Companies listed on the 100 Best Companies to Work for in America have produced 2.3 to 3.8 % higher stock returns every year.[9]

This shows that there's a significant financial advantage in companies where employee engagement is high compared to companies where employees are not engaged.[10] Kevin Kruse explains the "engagement profit chain" thus: "**Engaged Employees** lead to…**higher service**, quality, and productivity, which leads to…**higher customer satisfaction**, which leads to…**increased sales** (repeat business and referrals), which leads to…**higher levels of profit**, which leads to…**higher shareholder returns** (i.e. stock price)."

Employee engagement is not the same as employee satisfaction

It's significant that all of the above studies talk about "employee **engagement**" — rather than "employee **satisfaction**." This is a really important distinction, which has relevance to the way we design workplaces and the outcomes that we can expect.

It's possible for an employee to be well satisfied at work, but not be engaged. For example, Frank has a 9-5 job fairly close to home. The job is not too challenging, the work conditions are okay and the pay is reasonable. Frank's satisfaction rating is pretty high — but it's just a job. Is Frank engaged? Not particularly.

Employee engagement, on the other hand, is much more than being content with work conditions and pay. As Charles Rogel, an employee engagement and leadership expert at DecisionWise points out, job **satisfaction** begins and ends with feelings of contentment. Engagement is different. It's where employees feel personal satisfaction in the quality of their work, and like to be stretched beyond their comfort zone. Satisfaction may be enough to retain employees, and the bulk of employees may be strong, steady and satisfied like Frank, without ever budging outside of their job description. However, in today's competitive arena, it's **engagement** that results in innovation and moves the productivity needle in a meaningful way.[II]

Frank's job satisfaction is based on a transactional exchange between him and his employer: Frank fulfills the tasks in his job description. His employer provides remuneration, the tools to do the job, a basic level of respect and some perks. While increasing the perks — as in "let's bring in a foosball table" may increase Frank's satisfaction for a while, it probably won't move the needle in terms of his engagement. As a manager once said, "Engaged employees stay for what they give; the disengaged stay solely for what they can get."

Read any article on how to improve engagement, and you'll find that improving employee engagement is primarily a leadership function that has very little to do with pay and perks. In a White Paper called *MAGIC — Five keys to employee engagement*, Charles Rogel of DecisionWise says

"When we first look to join a company, we may be enticed by some salary promises, the company brand or cool perks. Important? Of course. But these factors — we call them 'satisfaction elements' — don't mean we're engaged. Engagement goes beyond satisfaction."[12]

Engaged employees stay for what they give; the disengaged stay solely for what they can get.

Increasing engagement in an organization is not about bringing in a ping pong table. It's about training mediocre bosses to become good leaders and mentors, and developing a culture where employees can find personal fulfillment at work in following five areas:

- MEANING — that is, helping employees find an aspect of the work that has personal significance to them
- AUTONOMY, in other words, empowering employees by giving them responsibilities and allowing them to make key decisions
- GROWTH, which comes from recognizing the strengths and successes of employees, improving employee skills, challenging them to push their boundaries and providing regular feedback
- IMPACT, which is about showing employees how they contribute to the big picture
- CONNECTION with organization and colleagues, and collaboration versus a paternalistic, hierarchical mentality

Charles Rogel and his colleagues at DecisionWise have coined this as MAGIC™. It's a good formula that results in employee engagement and drives the type of commitment and actions that can propel the organization forward. Note, though, — and perhaps this goes without saying, — that no matter how good the employer is at instilling the elements of MAGIC, engagement will not happen unless an employee is suited to the job and is the kind of person who is *receptive* to MAGIC™ leadership. For some people, no matter what — "a job is a job is a job."

One extreme example that illustrates the difference between satisfaction and engagement is described by Decisionwise CEO, Tracy Maylett, in an article called *When Engagement Replaces Satisfaction*,[13] where he describes the harsh living conditions of volunteers — typically university students — in developing countries, who do work such as bringing water to a small mountain village, teaching mothers about nutrition, building latrines, or other welfare and educational projects. What makes these volunteers willing to forego their comfortable, US-based surroundings for locations where poverty is the norm is that they are willing to temporarily overlook the "satisfaction elements" because they have chosen to be engaged in what they do. There, they find meaning, autonomy, growth, impact, and connection.

Employee satisfaction is the price of admission to employee engagement

One reason that the workplace is important to productivity is that employee satisfaction — which includes having a healthy, comfortable work environment — is a **pre-requisite for employee engagement**.

So what about start-up companies, working 7 days a week out of a garage with no pay or benefits, yet pumping out incredible energy and enthusiasm to get their idea out? Or those students who volunteer overseas, often financing their own way, risking their safety, working long hours for no pay, and living in harsh conditions? Clearly, their basic workplace satisfaction needs are not being met, and yet are they not fully engaged?

Indeed they may be engaged, but perhaps **not for long**. Start-up companies have a limited gestation period, and volunteer work assignments are generally for the summer vacation or a few months at most. Beyond that "honeymoon period," even in engaging organizations, a certain dissatisfaction — perhaps even a niggling resentment can creep in, fueled by the sense that the covenant is not entirely fair: "Surely they should at *least* pay for our trip and expenses, give us *some* time off, decent beds and clean washrooms, etc." Resentment may grow so that eventually it subsumes the ideals, kills motivation and undermines engagement. As Rogel says, "Employee satisfaction is the price of entry to employee engagement."

The point is that employee satisfaction does not directly result in employee engagement. Also, employees' passion for the work can endure for a period of time without employee satisfaction — call it the "honeymoon period," but usually — at some point, sooner or later, the engagement will evaporate.

Many workplaces don't meet today's norms for workplace satisfaction

Bottom line: A safe, healthy and comfortable workplace environment — one that is at least as good as — or better than the norm, is a "must-have" in the employee satisfaction equation, which, in turn is a pre-requisite for enduring employee engagement.

Many workplace environments simply don't meet basic norms in terms of acoustic and visual comfort and privacy, personal workspace location and features, office layout, ease of interaction, office furnishing, thermal comfort, indoor air quality, building location and amenities. Studies show that this can have rather significant consequences for employee wellness, wellbeing, productivity, and retention.

William Fisk of Lawrence Berkeley National Laboratory, conducting a survey of 100 U.S. office buildings, found that 23% of office workers experienced frequent symptoms of Sick Building Syndrome (SBS) such as respiratory ailments, allergies and asthma, resulting in lost productivity estimated at 2% due to sick days, as well as medical costs.[14] Fisk found

An employee's passion for the work can endure for a period of time even in adverse working conditions — call it the "honeymoon period," but usually – at some point, sooner or later, resentment builds up and the engagement evaporates.

that improving the **indoor air quality** (IAQ) reduced SBS symptoms by 20-50%, including asthma by 8-25%; and other respiratory illnesses by 23-76%. And it improved office worker productivity by 0.5-5%[15] — the wide range reflecting the uncertainty. However, considering only U.S. office workers, the corresponding annual productivity gain, even taking the most conservative value, would be $20 billion, and could be as much as $160 billion in the upper range.

Fisk and Olli Seppanon, from the Helsinki University of Technology showed similar patterns relating to **thermal comfort**. They developed a conceptual model that showed a decrease in performance of 2% for each degree increase of space temperature between 77°F and 89.4°F, with optimal productivity performance occurring when the space temperature was 72°F.[16]

Cornell University Professor, Alan Hedge has found a direct correlation between **thermal discomfort, poor indoor air quality, and noise discomfort** and the number of keyboarding errors, including the finding that workers who felt chilly made more errors, which increased the hourly labor cost by 10%.[17]

And Shin-Ichi Tanabe from Waseda University in Japan found that productivity dropped by 2.1% percent when the indoor **temperature** was 1°F higher than Japan's legal summer standard setting of 83.4°F. The study found also that individual **air velocity control** was able to reduce the perception of mental fatigue by workers.[18]

Beyond the basic requirement to provide a healthy and comfortable environment, there is a trend whereby companies are offering other perks such as a free bus service to work, dry cleaning delivery, health and gym facilities, free food, and flexible vacation. These perks focus on improving health and work-life balance, and providing fun and social connection at work. They also serve to demonstrate that the employer cares about employee wellbeing.

However, these perks are not sufficient to turn a job into a "calling." That's why it's so important to realize that while happy and satisfied employees may keep the widget line running, this does not necessarily mean that they will have the drive and personal commitment to treat customers better, innovate, and continuously improve the, thereby making a meaningful impact to the bottom line. As Tracy Maylett, CEO of DecisionWise puts it:

> Did those new coffee machines really increase productivity, or just make employees happy until they realize they don't have the Smoothie Man come in every Friday, like the company down the road? Satisfaction is not engagement. **Satisfaction is the "price of admission." It lets us play the game, but it's not what results in the win. Let's don't confuse the two.**[19]

Conclusion
. . . .

A prominent tech company was famous in the industry for its extraordinary workplace perks — everything from catered food and massages to bowling alley and slides, which were designed to attract and retain the best talent and generate a high level of employee engagement. To the company's surprise, the attrition rate was fairly high. The human resources department therefore set up a private group to ask former employees why they had left the company.

Some of the complaints had to do with satisfaction: including some disappointment that there were fewer fringe benefits than what they had been anticipating! Many of the complaints, however, had to do with engagement and a management style that was too bureaucratic — with too little mentoring.

Most employees thought they were entering the "Promised Land" — a sort of Nirvana and a fount of technical resources. What they discovered was that climbing walls, beanbag chairs and catered meals are important, but that no amount of this stuff can make up for the lack of MAGIC™ which is essential for employee engagement.

CHAPTER 11

Employee Surveys

Employees will only complain or make suggestions three times on average without a response. After that they conclude that if they don't keep quiet they will be thought to be troublemakers or that management doesn't care.

— Peter Drucker, Business Guru, Author, Professor of Business

Many employers don't "get" the difference between satisfaction and engagement. They make some cosmetic changes to the workplace and wonder why productivity is not improving, not realizing that there may be fundamental problems related to work overload, leadership, lack of recognition and so on.

As a result, many managers have, regrettably, become skeptical about employee surveys. A survey of 700 managers showed that in companies who administered an employee satisfaction survey, 27% of managers never reviewed the results at all, and 52% reviewed the results but felt no need to take action![20]

More progressive companies don't see it that way. Whereas in the past, the greatest value of satisfaction surveys was to learn how **clients** viewed the organization, this is giving way to a new paradigm — that **employee** mindset largely determines whether a product or service will be successful — because they are the ones who are developing, creating, delivering, and supporting what customers experience every day.

Perhaps the most basic employee satisfaction tracking approach is the Niko-niko calendar, also known as smiley calendar or happiness index. "Niko-niko" is a Japanese word for smiling. The approach, which was pioneered at Toyota production facilities, can be just a regular calendar on the wall, where each team member tracks their mood after each working day with a happy :-), a straight :-| or frowning smiley :-(²¹

Using this low tech tool, managers get a daily look at how happy people are. In the example in figure 8, we see some gloomy faces, which could signal that there's a concern. However, it doesn't indicate what the problem is. Naturally, there could be several reasons.

Because there are so many different possible causes of employee unhappiness, it's important to examine both employee satisfaction AND employee engagement.

In large organizations with many different business units occupying several facilities, **some departments may be more engaging to work in than others** depending on the nature of the work, the various management styles, and team dynamics. And where the different business units occupy different facilities, **some workplace environments may differ**.

New techniques and tools are being developed that are far more sophisticated than the Niko-niko calendar, including biometric sensing systems that measure employee happiness and job satisfaction in real time. Until these become mainstream, employee surveys can still provide a good snapshot.

There are many ready-made employee **engagement** surveys that capture and analyze how workers feel about their jobs, supervisors, teams and the organization as a whole.

Figure 8 – Example of a Niko-niko team calendar

November							
	Sun 2	Mon 3	Tues 4	Wed 5	Thur 6	Fri 7	Sat 8
Luke		🙁	😐	😐	🙂	🙂	
Josh		🙂	🙂	🙂	😐	🙂	
Edwin		🙂	😠	🙂	🙂	😠	
Anna		🙂	🙂	😐	🙁	🙂	

As for employee **satisfaction**, we like the approach by Lawrence Berkeley to gauge satisfaction with the workplace environment because it is streamlined, compared to some surveys, which appear to go on and on... The Lawrence Berkeley approach begins with a relatively small number of questions of a fairly general nature that serve to flag areas of concern. It then zeroes in specific problem areas.

For example, a survey might ask just the two following general questions related to acoustic comfort:

On a scale of 1-7

- How satisfied are you with the noise level in your workspace?
- Overall, does the acoustic quality in your workspace enhance or interfere with your ability to get your work done?

If there seems to be a problem, the survey then dives into greater granularity. For example, if — and only if the responses are negative, then the next question would be:

You have said you are dissatisfied with the acoustics in your workspace. Which of the following contribute to this problem (check all that apply)

- People talking on the phone
- People talking in neighboring areas
- Office equipment noise
- Office lighting noise
- Telephones ringing
- Mechanical heating, cooling, and ventilation systems noise
- Excessive echoing of voices or other sounds
- Outdoor traffic
- Other outdoor noise
- Other _____

If employers do an engagement survey AND a workplace satisfaction survey for each business unit, it then becomes easier to pinpoint whether a productivity issue is due to low engagement (i.e. need to improve management issues) and/or low satisfaction (i.e. need to improve the office environment).

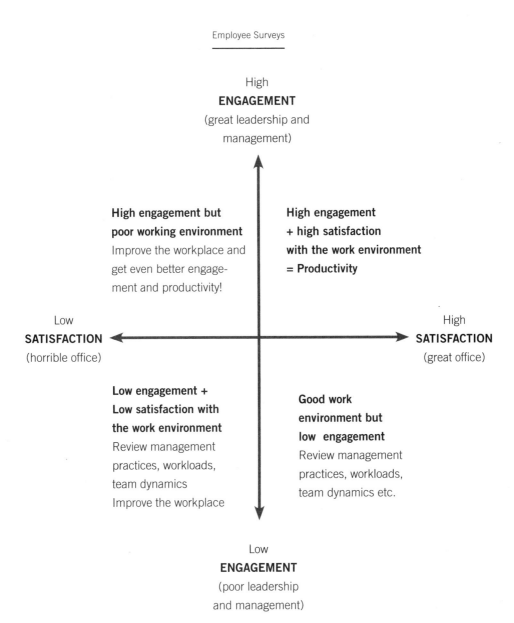

Figure 9 — Quadrant showing employee satisfaction and engagement

Poorly done surveys tend to do more harm than good by further disengaging and disappointing employees

Many companies place a Comments Box in the employee break room. Naturally, once they share their opinions with management, employees expect something to happen. If they never receive feedback or see a change based on their comments, it's unlikely that they will continue to make suggestions.

The same applies to employee surveys. Whenever someone says "Let's have the employees take a survey," it's really important to ask: "**Why** do we need a survey? How will we **use the information**?" and finally "Are we **prepared to invest the time and resources to take appropriate corrective action** based on the results?" Without such a commitment, a survey may actually further disengage and disgruntle employees.

Recently, the controversy about the validity of employee engagement surveys has been heating up, for example with articles in the popular press such as Maclean's magazine, *Employee engagement surveys: useless or very useless?*[22] The major criticism appears to be that there is no statistical basis to reduce such a complex concept as "engagement" into a single score, and that one cannot draw a direct correlation between an engagement score and performance.[23] Some critics also suggest that employee engagement surveys can have negative impact. For example, a 5% difference in engagement scores between two departments may not necessarily be significant, but can hurt morale in lower-scoring department as in "What are we doing wrong? We thought everything was okay, but now we are being told otherwise."

Advocates of employee engagement surveys argue that the psychology of attitudes and personalities — and how they link to behavior — has been undergoing rigorous academic research and scrutiny since the 1950s, and *can* be reliably measured over time.

Even critics generally concede that well-constructed engagement surveys, when used along with other sources of information, can elicit valuable feedback regarding organizational and individual objectives, the degree and quality of collaboration within and across teams in highly interdependent organizations, perceived support for innovation and risk taking, and the effectiveness of work structures.

Conclusion

Organizations of all sizes use employee surveys to gauge whether conditions are present that allow employees to do their best work. However, many managers are skeptical that surveys are of benefit because the information that they provide doesn't seem to lead to meaningful changes. To resolve this problem, it is important to differentiate between the terms "engagement" and "satisfaction" and to use surveys that have been scientifically designed. There are many such tools to choose from on the market.

For facility managers and human resources, employee satisfaction surveys can provide important data regarding the effect of the workplace environment on productivity.

CHAPTER 12

Productivity and the Workplace Environment

What high-performing companies should be striving to create:

A great place for great people to do great work

— Marilyn Carlson, Former CEO of Carlson Companies

We've talked a lot about employee satisfaction and engagement. It's time now to turn our attention to the P word. "Productivity" is a slippery word because it means so many different things to different people.

If the end goal, from a human resources perspective, is to engender engaged employees, and if — as the management gurus tell us — engagement is a leadership function rather than a question of hot chocolate machines and climbing walls, then what does this say about the role of the workplace in terms of improving productivity? And why is Google spending millions to turn its offices into fun parks for its employees?

There are several reasons that the workplace environment **does** matter. While the workplace environment doesn't contribute **directly** to employee engagement, it plays a significant role in ensuring employee satisfaction and avoiding dissatisfaction, which are pre-requisites for engagement. It also helps to attract top talent, meet the changing needs of the workplace, forge corporate a brand, and reflect the culture of the organization.

A poor office environment causes dissatisfaction

Has it ever occurred to you how we tend **not** to notice when things are okay, but we **do** notice when things **aren't** okay. For example, we take electricity for granted — until there's a power failure, and then we suddenly really miss it. We often overlook our spouse's or teenager's fine qualities and instead, zero in on their faults. It's human nature to take the good things for granted and notice the flaws.

The same happens in the workplace. Employees don't notice when things are good, but they **do** notice when things are not quite right. For example, employees may never give a thought about the fact that they have a safe working environment but do react strongly if something there is **not** safe. No one comments if the temperature, air quality and acoustics at work are fine. However, they do complain if the workplace is hot, stuffy and noisy. It probably doesn't occur to employees to notice that their office is really quite nice, but they do resent it if the other offices in the building are nicer. These dissatisfactions, if they remain unresolved, can mushroom into vexation, which can turn into active disengagement.

As we indicated in the previous chapter, employee dissatisfaction resulting from an unacceptable workplace environment can fester and begin to undermine employee engagement. It's important to note that workplace dissatisfaction can be even more acute for people who are in jobs that are inherently boring, where there was not that much engagement to begin with. These employees typically occupy low status positions, generally do repetitive tasks, are often undervalued, have minimal autonomy, and given the nature of their work, generally lack interesting challenges and opportunities. Providing a good working environment is essential to attract and retain these employees — certainly as important than for those who have interesting jobs.

If, in addition to not enjoying their jobs, these employees are feeling under the weather at work due to an unhealthy and uncomfortable work environment, they will certainly be less productive. With so many studies that correlate a poor work environment to reduced work output, it should be self-evident that taking corrective action where office conditions are not satisfactory should lead to **increased output efficiency** — quite simply, the value of work output in a given amount of time.

The question is, "how do we measure the value of work output?"

Improving satisfaction and decreasing dissatisfaction can result in greater work output

From the very earliest time-and-motion studies, examples abound that show that "time" is still the most generic and universal variable to measure productivity — or loss of productivity. For example, a survey of 3,200 employees by salary.com found that 21 percent of employees waste one hour per day, surfing sites that are unrelated to their work.[24] As Russ Warner, CEO of ContentWatch, the maker of Net Nanny noted, "This lost **time** represents money, and every hour wasted has a direct negative impact on the bottom line." Another illustration of how time is the most common metric for studying productivity is a study by Captivate Network, which estimated that the 2014 FIFA World Cup cost approximately $1.68 billion in lost productivity in the U.S. based on the typical viewing **time** at work, and an average salary of employed adults.[25]

Although time — whether measured in minutes, hours, days, weeks or months — seems to be a universal variable, there are many ways to measure the output in a given unit of time. These include number of calls or reports, employee turnover, tasks completed, errors, sick days, customer complaints, the time it takes to make decisions and so on. Note that these variables do not capture outputs such as creativity, team dynamics, innovative ideas and employee loyalty, which result from well-suited employees who experience meaning, autonomy, growth, impact and connection.

Naturally, each company has its own way of gauging efficiency. For example, some call centers have a Key Performance Indicator (KPI) known as "one call resolution." This is the ability of a customer service representative to be able to solve a client problem in just one phone call. One call center found that it takes an operator at least six months on the job to have acquired the knowledge, skills and experience to consistently deliver "one-call resolution." The problem with call centers though, is that the job is inherently stressful, dissatisfaction runs high, and there tends to be a high employee turnover. Improving the average productivity in a call center therefore depends largely on reducing dissatisfaction. This can be achieved by improving uncomfortable workstations, providing daylight, creating a relaxation room, or even supplying employee concierge services to assist those who can't leave their work phone to make a dental appointment, research summer camps or order a birthday cake for their kids.

From the very earliest time-and-motion studies, examples abound that show that "time" is still the most generic and universal variable to measure productivity – or loss of productivity.

A desirable workplace attracts top talent

In an earlier example, employees are initially happy about getting a new coffee machine for the office — that is, until they hear that the company down the road offers its employees Friday smoothies! In a market where companies are competing for top talent, this illustrates the importance of providing an enticing workplace. There is a reason why some companies often take their potential hires on a tour of their stunning premises before even sitting down for the interview. As one director confided, "By the time we've done the rounds of our drop-dead gorgeous office, the candidate has pretty much already decided that they want to work for us."

As one director confided "By the time we've done the rounds of our drop-dead gorgeous office, the candidate has pretty much already decided that they want to work for us."

The coffee machine versus the Friday smoothies illustrates the reality that norms and expectations can change. What was just fine before no longer satisfies. Fifty years ago, offices consisted of managers' offices along the perimeter, corner offices for executives, and in the interior, a bullpen consisting of dozens or even hundreds of clerks in a rigid arrangement of desks, usually in rows. Typically, these were noisy, poorly-lit and uncomfortable places to work. This eventually gave way to dull cubicle farms that gave more privacy and noise control, but which were devoid of daylight. Now, employees expect more.

Workplace reflects the changing nature of work

There is no doubt that we are experiencing a huge change in the way people work, which is impacting how we design the workplace. Some of the trends include the following:

- There is an exponential increase in the number of workers who are hired as free-lancers, independent contractors or temporary workers. One in three Americans (roughly 42 million) is currently a freelancer. By 2020, freelancers are expected to make up 50% of the full-time workforce.[26]
- By 2015, millennials will overtake the majority representation of the workforce, and by 2030 this hyper-connected, tech savvy generation will make up 75% of the workforce. Millennials are used to flexibility and being able to instantly connect with people regardless of their location.[27]
- Telecommuting is now so commonplace that almost all of *Fortune's Best Companies to Work For* allow employees to telecommute or work from

home at least 20% of the time. Offices need to provide good hoteling accommodation.

- When employees come to the office, they spend less of their time at their desk, and more of their time connecting and collaborating, which can entail a significant chunk of time moving around (which is healthier than sitting for hours on end). However, time spent locating one another and searching for an empty meeting room can represent many minutes of unproductive time. This has implications on how space should be allocated as a function of the various activities that take place. It also indicates the need for applications that help people to find one another and book space based on the status of a room — whether it's free, currently in use, or shortly to be used for a meeting.

Considered together, these trends have enormous implications in terms of the design of the workplace and space density — the allocation of space per employee. The result is an evolution from traditional individual offices where everyone comes to work every day (250-300 sf/person); to open plan offices with fully assigned workstations (200-250 sf/person); to a hybrid mix of unassigned and assigned workstations and support space for a more mobile workforce (100-150 sf/person); to fully unassigned workstations and support space (50-100 sf/person).

Workplace provides Connection
· ·

Beyond the functionality requirements and the health and comfort aspects such as thermal comfort, indoor air, acoustics, lighting and certain workplace amenities, which are "must-haves" for employee satisfaction, one area where the physical workplace can support employee engagement is by providing an environment that promotes **Connection**.

Connection means having a sense of belonging to something greater than the individual. For example, employees can feel connected to their manager, their team or their organization's brand. Branding is one way of connecting people emotionally to a company. For example, Disney employees are called "Cast Members;" Google employees are called "Googlers."

Fostering a sense of connection in the workplace is primarily a leadership role. However, the physical work environment can be a significant enabler by providing a look and feel that makes employees feel welcome, and a home base where mobile employees feel a sense of belonging. The workplace also reinforces connection through well-designed open office areas, areas for team meetings, and places for informal social networking.

Where the workplace reinforces the company **brand**, this can also strengthen the sense of connection that employees experience towards the company. Branding has expanded from consumer goods and services to include buildings. Branding a building is a way of connecting with the hearts and minds of occupants by reminding them that "Our brand helps to fulfill your expectations as an employee." Of course, as with all branding, this can be partly illusionary. For example, there is no ultimate proof that a green-certified building actually performs better than a well-run Class A building. Yet green certification has become such a basic requirement that virtually every Class A building now needs to be green-branded in order to be competitive.

Recently, a new area of building branding has emerged: "building wellness." WELL™ certification indicates that a building is super healthy in terms of providing occupants with the purest of air, water, light spectra and even organic snacks.[28] It could be debated whether wellness branding, in and of itself can drive more employee job engagement in terms of meaning, autonomy, growth and impact. However, it certainly can increase employee satisfaction and strengthen the sense of connection to the employer in terms of the health values that wellness branding represents. No doubt, this type of branding can also reinforce the Pygmalion effect whereby occupants figure that they must be healthier because they've been told that they are in a healthy building. And that's got to be good for morale.

Branding goes beyond the base building. Organizations also need to brand their office facilities. Millennials (i.e. reaching adulthood around 2000) have grown up in a world of marketing and brands. From the clothing they wear to their smart phones, branding is in their DNA. As a result, many organizations are weaving their brand into the look and feel of their offices.

Ivana Taylor, a small business consultant advises companies to "brandify" their office space with objects, images and colors that communicate the energy they want to project. For instance, orange, red or yellow give a sense of high energy. Green is associated with nature, growth and freshness. To communicate stability, trust or loyalty, use blues. And if power, ambition, wealth and luxury are the goals, then use some purple. White is the color of perfection, purity and cleanliness — a terrific foundation for just about any space. And to communicate power or mystery, use a lot of black.[29]

Although branding has perhaps never before been so important, brand **loyalty** is on the decline, so organizations have to work hard to keep their market position. Studies show that people tend to switch brands a lot faster than they used to.[30] The famous 80/20 rule (20% of customers account for 80% of the turnover has turned into the 60/40 rule and is slowly evolving towards a 50/50 rule.) One of the reasons for this is that companies can't always keep up with rising expectations as people keep comparing them to the 'best-in-class.'

For work environments, this means that designers need to be constantly thinking of ways to keep the brand fresh. And as with all branding, it's also about ensuring that the office is viewed by employees as continuing to contribute to their lives in a positive and relevant way. Some organizations have blended lifestyle and work to the extreme by providing perks including free haircuts, fitness equipment and laundry services.

Quantifying the link between physical changes to the workplace and improved the feelings of Connection is currently difficult other than by doing employee engagement surveys, but this is about to change, predicts Don Peck, in an Atlantic article called *They're Watching You at Work*.[31]

Peck describes what happens when big data meets human resources and recounts research by Sandy Pentland, Director of the Human Dynamics Laboratory at MIT, which measures human connections in the workplace. In a study carried out in 21 different organizations, 2,500 employees wore personal electronic "badges" that generated about 100 data points a minute, about their interactions as they went about their day. The data showed correlations between different areas of the workplace and the amount of interpersonal connections. Sensors recorded who was conversing with whom, the length of conversations, where the conversations took place, as well as biometric data such as the tone of voice and gestures of the people involved; how much those people talked, listened, and interrupted; the degree to which they demonstrated empathy and extroversion; and more. Pentland also wanted to see whether this data could serve to predict successful teams, as well as creative and productive individuals. About a third of team performance, he discovered, can usually be predicted by the number of face-to-face exchanges among team members. Interestingly, the study found that there is a certain level of interaction which characterized creative and productive individuals, and that **too much** interaction is as much of a problem as too little.

ABI Research forecasts that by 2018, more than 13 million employees will be wearing activity-tracking devices such as fitness bands, as part of their wellness programs — although commentators have warned that the trend may be affected by legal tests for privacy invasion and discrimination practices.[32]

There is a certain level of interaction which characterizes creative and productive individuals. Too much interaction can be as much of a problem as too little.

Workplace reinforces the internal culture of the organization
. . . .

Just as people have unique personalities, each organization also has its own distinctive internal culture, based on its values, expectations and psychological climate. These are the result of written and unwritten rules that have developed over time. They determine the ways in which the organization does business and deals with employees, customers and the wider community.

Naturally, an organization's culture has profound implications on productivity and performance, quality and customer care. The culture of an organization is also what determines how power and information flow through the hierarchy and the amount of freedom to express personal opinions, make decisions and develop new ideas. The company's culture affects every facet of its operations — from day-to-day behaviors such as employee attendance and punctuality to concern for the environment and social responsibility, including the creation of new products, production methods, marketing and advertising practices — and lastly, the character of the workplace.

Researchers have often attempted to define the many facets of company culture. Following the work of John Campbell in 1974, which described 39 cultural characteristics of organizations, subsequent researchers including Robert Quinn and John Rohrbaugh (1983) have distilled these into two dominant dimensions.[33]

The first dimension relates to the degree of **flexibility** within an organization. On the flexibility spectrum, we find dynamism and organic processes at one end, such as would be found in a start-up company. At the other end of the spectrum are **stability**, order, control, predictability and the type of mechanistic processes that would be expected, for example, in a more regulated government or service industry.

The second dimension describes whether an organization's strategy for success in the market is to focus primarily on getting its **internal** workings right ("If we build it right, they will come"); or whether it is has an **external** focus, comparing itself to the competition and striving to be the best in the marketplace.

If the two cultural dimensions are arranged in a matrix, this yields four main categories of culture as shown in figure 10: Creative, Controlling, Competitive and Collaborative.

There is no "one size" fits all for office layouts even within the same organization. Acknowledging organizational culture is important for space planners since the characteristics of an organization have spatial implications. A large number of private offices or cubicles and formal meeting rooms may be suitable for an organization that needs to be controlling and hierarchical such as a large insurance firm, or where individual work is the primary activity; but may not suitable for one where teamwork and flexibility are needed such as an advertising business.

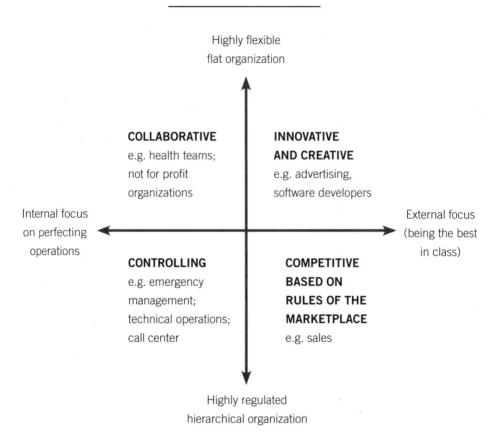

Figure 10 — R. Quinn and J. Rohrbaugh's quadrants describing organizational cultures

An organization that thrives thanks to a strong COLLABORATIVE culture requires sociable and friendly spaces that promote strong team-work and allow the necessary flexibility to come up with new approaches in order to achieve better internal efficiencies, processes, products and services. A CREATIVE culture needs spaces that enable individuals to get in touch with their own personal creativity and initiative, as well as spaces for teams to brainstorm and cross-pollinate ideas with a goal to produce the most cutting edge results in the industry. A COMPETITIVE culture needs a dynamic, entrepreneurial, corporate environment that reflects a hard-driving hierarchical leadership, standardized protocols and performance measures, and a focus on personal and team initiative to win market share and penetration. A CONTROLLING culture must provide an environment which reflects the hierarchical structure and allocation of spaces to achieve the most efficient processes and standardized results.

Conclusion
· · · · · · · · · ·

In a business environment characterized by disruptive technologies, many organizations are recognizing that their survival may depend in part on changing **management styles**, as well as changing the **work environment** to support rapid innovation. In fact, these two concepts are connected. The workplace helps define how an organization manages and motivates employees as well as how operations are conducted. The workplace can also be a source of satisfaction or dissatisfaction, which, in turn has an impact on productivity.

The next chapters address some of the key conditions that can make a difference in terms of employee satisfaction. There we examine various aspects of the workplace that can support or detract from productivity: space layout, acoustics, thermal comfort, indoor air quality, visual comfort, commuting, and amenities that support human connections and a work-life balance.

CHAPTER 13

Space Utilization

Nobody would consider building a manufacturing facility that they intended to use just one-third of the time. And yet that's what we routinely do with workspace. We realized that assigning resources based on utilization would significantly reduce Cisco real estate costs, and resolved to build a work environment based not on titles, but rather on the needs of individuals, by giving all employees a broad choice of workspaces and technology tools to do their jobs.

— Mark Golan, Cisco Vice-president for Workplace Resources

The way that space is utilized can have a huge impact in terms of making a workplace more environmentally sustainable AND more productive. The recent trend has been to reduce the amount of space per employee. This is achieved in two ways: by enabling employees to work off-site; and by designing offices with more thought than ever before to ensure that every square foot is being put to maximum use. This chapter illustrates some of the benefits of telecommuting and the impact that this is having on space utilization.

Space Utilization — a matter of environmental sustainability AND productivity

A well-thought-out allocation of space can have significant environmental benefits. Reducing the amount of space that needs to be heated, cooled and lighted can greatly reduce energy consumption and GHG emissions. Allowing employees to telework reduces the energy used for commuting to work every day, as well as GHG emissions and pollution, not to mention reducing pressure on the local transportation infrastructure.

There is also an impact on productivity as a new generation of employees largely expects the flexibility to work from anywhere — home, office, cottage or coffee shop. Improved laptops, personal digital assistants (PDAs), voice over internet protocol (VoIP) and communication platforms such as blogs, wikis, podcasts, instant messaging, social networks and web conferencing make this possible, with an unprecedented ability to collaborate among employees and with external stakeholders.

Not surprisingly, the IT cost of outfitting the "modern worker" with an arsenal of gadgetry and infrastructure is at an all-time high. Gartner Research estimates that the average IT spend per employee rose from $7,756 in 2000 to $9,419 in 2008 and over $13,000 in 2013.[34]

As they make large investments in new technologies, organizations are finding cost efficiencies elsewhere — the most obvious being physical facilities.

By using enabling technology, and carefully examining workforce patterns and the geographic dispersion of employees, a revamped workplace can optimize the occupant density and cost per seat, and ensure the best use of space in every corner of the office.

This in turn reduces rent, operating and maintenance costs. Deloitte Touche assumes an average seat cost of $12,000 in a traditional office compared to approximately $10,000 per full-time teleworking employee per year. The Gartner research notes that IBM slashed real estate costs by $50 million, McKesson saves $2 million a year and Sun Microsystems saves $68 million a year in real estate costs. Teleworking also avoids having to make special adjustments in the workplace for workers with disabilities.

To prepare for the workplace of tomorrow — align human resources, real estate and IT considerations

• •

Deloitte Touche in a white paper called *Why Change Now?* identifies three components that need to be considered holistically to prepare for the workplace of tomorrow. These are: workforce (HR), technology (IT) and workspace (Real Estate).

Working together, HR, Real Estate, and IT can lower costs by aligning workspace, technology and workforce patterns, using a 2-prong strategy: First, discontinue the practice of directly linking the amount of physical workspace to headcount. Next, redirect some of the real estate savings to technologies that will improve workforce performance and enhance employee satisfaction.

Rather than simply linking the amount of physical workspace to headcount, we should instead review the tasks that the employees do and their geographic location with a view to giving them greater flexibility and mobility. Based on this, we provide them with the tools they need both on-site and off, and design the layout such that every square foot of office space is being used.

This can generate considerable savings.

Deloitte Touche has found that in a traditional office, where the majority of employees work on location, approximately 14% of seats are unoccupied, which represents a significant cost. Using a hypothetical 4,400-employee facility and assuming an industry average per seat cost of $12,000 and a standard seat rate of 110 seats for every 100 employees, the facility would cost approximately $58 million to maintain each year. By eliminating 14% of the total space, the organization could realize cost savings of $8.1 million. By increasing the number of mobile workers, this would allow an even greater reduction in space and savings.[35]

Working together, HR, Real Estate, and IT can lower costs by aligning workspace, technology and workforce patterns.

There's no question that telework, using today's connectivity solutions, can save companies time and money in both direct and indirect ways.

"Work from home" attracts employees and reduces attrition
· ·

A plethora of studies also indicate that work from home ranks high in terms of attracting top talent. Global Workplace Analytics, a firm that Forbes describes as having possibly the most comprehensive data on emerging workplace issues, has reviewed 500 studies about telecommuting.[36] The data indicates that two thirds of people want to work from home. Over one third would choose telecommuting over a pay raise and say that the ability telecommute will be "somewhat to extremely important" in choosing their next job. In a poll of 1,500 technology professionals, over one third said that they would take a pay cut of 10% if they could work from home.

Gen Y'ers (i.e. born in the 1980s/1990s) are particularly attracted to flexible work arrangements, but others benefit as well. These include disabled workers, parents and senior caregivers out of the workforce, as well as retirees, many of whom would, if given the option, continue to work part-time from home, even with reduced pension and no health benefits.

Because telecommuting is considered a perk, it's not surprising that it helps to reduce attrition. 95% of employers say that telecommuting helps to reduce their turnover, which is significant when one considers that losing a valued employee can cost an employer $10,000 to $30,000. In a compensation survey of 1,400 CFOs conducted by Robert Half International, 46% said that telecommuting is second only to salary as the best way to attract top talent. In fact, many prospective hires would accept a lower wage for the perk of working from home.[37]

Reasons that working from home can be more productive
· ·

But can employees truly be as productive working from home? The answer, it seems, is yes. Global Workplace Analytics found that two-thirds of employers also report increased productivity among their telecommuters, due to **reduced absenteeism, a better quality of output**, and **worker efficiencies**.

The following are some findings in their review that relate to absenteeism: In traditional offices, over three quarters of employees who call in sick, really aren't, but do so because of family issues, personal needs, and stress. These unscheduled absences cost employers on average, $1,800/employee per year.[38]

Telecommuting can reduce this type of absenteeism by over 60% because flexible hours allow people to run errands or schedule appointments without losing a full day, and because teleworkers typically continue to work when they're sick (without infecting others) and return to work more quickly following surgery or medical issues.

As more organizations become global, teleworking is also catching on due to time zone differences. Employees in the U.S. may need to participate in a call in Asia Pacific at 2 a.m. These middle-of-the-night calls are becoming the norm and not the exception for worldwide companies.

According to the Global Workplace Analytics review, telecommuting productivity figures are impressive, not only in terms of reducing absenteeism but also improving quality of output. Best Buy, British Telecom, Dow Chemical, American Express and many others say that teleworkers are 35-40% more productive. Sun Microsystems says that employees spend 60% of the time they would normally spend commuting doing work for the company, and AT&T reports that workers work 5 more hours at home than their office workers. Alpine Access, a company that uses home-based workers to provide phone-based customer service for various companies including several Fortune 500 companies, says remote agents close 30% more sales than traditional agents, with 90% fewer customer complaints.[39]

Telecommuting has been found to reduce absenteeism as well as improve quality of work output.

Telecommuting also results in worker efficiency. For example, web-based meetings tend to be better planned and more apt to stay on message. Once telework technologies are in place, employees and contractors can work together without regard to logistics, which substantially increases collaboration options.

Remote work also forces people to be more independent and self-directed. And finally, teleworking lends itself well to goal-setting and performance measurement. Drucker, Six Sigma, and other management experts agree that goal-setting and performance measurement are key to successful management. For telework to work, it's even more important for employees to be measured by what they do, not where or how they do it.

Bring your own device (BYOD)

A growing trend is for companies to allow employees to use personal mobile devices if they wish. This is known as BYOD (Bring Your Own Device). A survey by *i-pass* of 1600 mobile workers in 2013 found that employees use fewer devices than previously, largely because they're using the same devices for both work and personal reasons. That said, they are accessing more data than ever.[40]

The *i-pass* survey found that mobile workers use about 1-2 GB per month, a number that is expected to grow with the proliferation of data hungry applications such as video streaming. In organizations that have a BYOD policy, this can represent significant savings for the employer especially when employees who use their own personal devices are paying their own data bills. *i-pass* also notes however, that this can also have a negative performance impact, where an employee is bumping against a data limit.

Also there are some cautionary issues that employers must consider, related to security, including what happens if an employee loses a smartphone that has unsecured data. A survey of 400 IT professionals by Decisive Analytics found that nearly half of enterprises that allow employee-owned devices to connect to a company's network have had a data breach. Most of these companies reacted by restricting data access rights (45%) or installing security software (43%).[41]

There is also a risk when an employee leaves the company that they could misappropriate, on their personal device, the phone number, company applications and data. Currently, only 20% of employees have signed a BYOD policy.[42] This can have serious consequences. For example, where an employee leaves the company and joins the competition taking their phone number with them, it follows that customers calling the number will then potentially be calling a competitor which can lead to loss of business for BYOD enterprises.

A survey of 400 IT professionals found that nearly half of enterprises that allow employee-owned devices to connect to a company's network have had a data breach.

Conclusion

Economist Brian Arthur, in his essay *The Second Economy*[43] argues that the internet and digitization are the biggest change since the Industrial Revolution. One of the results is that companies are downsizing their physical office locations as they increasingly adopt policies for sharing non-dedicated offices and implement technology to support their employees' ability to work anywhere and anytime. In order for a company to develop the most effective solutions, human resource departments, real estate executives and IT must work together.

CHAPTER 14

Open Offices and Productivity

Open offices have their advantages — and potential disadvantages. To create an *effective* open office, we must recognize the possible problems and make a conscious effort to eradicate them, so that the many benefits can be exploited.

— Dan Probst, Chairman of Energy and Sustainability Services, JLL

Yes, technology is changing the way we do business in offices, just as it is transforming the face of many industries. However, the impending death of the brick and mortar office is often overstated, for although technology has changed the way we work, there is still something different about interacting with people face-to-face.

Another interesting phenomenon is that in times of economic downturn or when companies are struggling, they often cut back significantly on allowing employees to telecommute. A good example of this is Yahoo's announcement in 2013, requiring employees to report to work.

Garrick Brown, director of research at Cassidy Turley says, "In times of struggle, the return to the brick and mortar office is often driven by management, who sometimes revert to old-world thinking about how to measure worker productivity, and become clock watchers instead of looking for results in terms of end product. But it can also be driven by worker paranoia. If your company is downsizing, suddenly you want to be highly visible in your workplace, regardless of whether you may actually be just as, if not more productive, working from your home office."44

No matter whether employees come to the office just once or twice a week, or every day, Stephen Siena, senior research analyst for JLL in Tampa believes that a major change in business culture is affecting the way offices are configured: the desire for more collaboration. This is impacting the way we allocate space and resulting in a shift to open office environments.

In this chapter, we review the pros and cons of the open office environment as it relates to new work styles and productivity. While there are various benefits, there is also overwhelming data indicating that there are many *poorly* designed open offices, and that employees often find it stressful and difficult to do their best work in this kind of environment. Some open offices may *look* great, but in fact, may be failing to meet some very basic requirements for a productive workplace. This may also partly explain why many people prefer to work from home.

Open offices are about transparency and collaboration
. . . .

The open office, as it was conceived in the 1900s, reflected the movement to increase efficiencies, making it possible to supervise large numbers of people doing boring jobs, such as workers in drafting and secretarial pools.

Today, open offices are designed with a different purpose in mind — to be beautiful and energizing, flexible, encourage collaboration, and make a statement about the corporate culture.

At the Bloomberg offices in Midtown Manhattan, layout and design are aimed at transparency and the dissolution of physical hierarchies. Even top-level employees work out in the open, or take their meetings in glass conference rooms, where any passerby can observe who has joined the meeting, how long it is lasting, and even get a sense of how things are going based on body language. This is all part of a culture that Bloomberg spokesperson describes as "institutional eavesdropping — the ability to sense what's going on in every part of the company through a sort of osmosis — by absorbing information peripherally while focusing elsewhere."[45]

The Bloomberg open office design is also intended to support a culture of collaboration. Editor Josh Tyrangiel notes, "In a deadline business, where every bit of missed communication can have an impact on the final product, open plan is pretty spectacular. It ensures that everyone is attuned to the broad mission, and … it encourages curiosity between people who work in different disciplines. So the art department and staff writers — who at most magazines are separated like lemurs and rhinos — end up mixing and lingering whenever they spot something of interest."

Compared to the traditional, rigid bullpen configuration — today's office is designed to be beautiful, energizing, and flexible; encourage collaboration, and make a statement about the corporate culture.

Open offices save money

While an open office environment can help to enrich and mold office culture and create opportunities for people to work and play closer to one another, another primary reason for their popularity is financial.

Today about 70% of offices have an open plan. Why is the open plan so hot these days? Karin Klein, a partner at *Beta*, a Bloomberg investment venture for technology start-ups, notes two reasons. The first is that the open office trend is largely an attempt to emulate the "cool" creative cachet of start-up enterprises, which thrive on teamwork and creativity. However, while this may have a visionary appeal, in many cases the real reason that startups have adopted the stripped down warehouse look is largely to save money. As Klein notes, "there's only so much room to fit card tables in the proverbial Silicon Valley garage."[46] An open office arrangement also allows flexibility to accommodate rapid growth or shrinking, which often typify start-up companies.

As Nikil Saval notes in his book *Cubed: A Secret History of the Workplace*, even the most utopian minded transition to an open office concept is chiefly motivated by the wish to save money by locating as many people in as small a space as possible.

The open office concept is also much better for accommodating a mobile workforce and managing the changes associated with high churn. And thanks to open furniture solutions and sophisticated technology infrastructure, it is less expensive to modify the layout in an open office compared to one that has hard wall interiors.

The increase in non-dedicated office space (sharing) and collaborative space, along with more on-site amenities and a growing acceptance of telecommuting, have reduced the need for space and resulted in more efficient utilization rates. As a result, the past decade has seen an increase in space efficiency from 50% to 80%, and a decrease in space per employee from 250 square feet to 150 square feet or less.[47]

But do open offices make workers more productive?

While the open office may be especially helpful in workplaces that require continual informal collaboration such as newsrooms, trading floors and political campaign offices, there is disconcerting evidence that open offices may not always make workers happier or more productive.

In a review of more than 100 studies, organizational psychologist Matthew Davis found that although they can foster a symbolic sense of mission and help employees feel that they are part of a laid-back, innovative organization, open offices can also result in reduced attention spans, less creative thinking and lower motivation — none of which is good for productivity.[48]

For example, in one study for a large oil company, psychologists measured employee satisfaction and productivity as they moved from a traditional office to an open one.[49] The study looked at employees' satisfaction with their surroundings, stress level, interpersonal relationships and job performance. Measurements were taken at three points in time: before the move, four weeks after the move, and, finally, six months afterward. The employees suffered according to every metric: the new space was disruptive, stressful, and cumbersome. Productivity fell. Another study of more than 2,400 employees, found also that employees in an open office took 62% more self-reported sick leave than those who had some privacy.[50]

Negative effects of an open office can be psychological, cognitive and physical

Many of the problems of open offices are caused by **noise**. A key finding of research on acoustics and productivity is that people in noisy environments tend to feel more helpless, less motivated and less creative than if they were in a quiet environment.[51]

Psychologist Nick Perham, who studies the effect of sound on how people think has found that office commotion reduces workers' ability to recall information, and even to do basic arithmetic.[52] Contrary to the belief that listening to music while working can be helpful, even this constitutes an acoustic distraction, which, Perham found, impairs our mental acuity.

Lost sense of control can reduce motivation. This effect takes many forms in the various studies. For example, subjects in a noisy environment attempt to solve fewer puzzles than they do when they work in a quiet environment. They also tend to make fewer ergonomic adjustments when sitting in a noisy open office than they would in a private space, (which increases the risk of physical strain).

When workers feel that they are not in control of their environment and their interactions, this can lead to feelings of helplessness, which

Open offices can foster a symbolic sense of mission and help employees feel that they are part of a laid-back, innovative organization, but they can also result in reduced attention spans, less creative thinking, and lower motivation — none of which is good for productivity.

are demotivating. This is the finding of three studies summarized in a paper called *Privacy at Work: Architectural Correlates of Job Satisfaction and Job Performance*,[53] which examines the relationship between architectural privacy, psychological privacy, job satisfaction and job performance. Results of all three studies showed a strong correlation between architectural privacy (physical barriers) and psychological privacy (a sense of privacy). For most employees — although to a lesser extent for clerical and mechanical employees — both forms of privacy were associated with workplace satisfaction, job satisfaction and job performance.

This is further supported by a 2005 study called *Effects of Control over Office Workspace on Perceptions of the Work environment and Work Outcomes*, which examined several different types of organizations ranging from an auto supplier to a telecom firm. Results were consistent — that the ability to control the environment had a significant effect on team cohesion and satisfaction. When workers couldn't change the way that things looked, adjust the lighting and temperature, or their personal interactions, spirits plummeted.

Privacy concerns can also be an issue. Some people find it stressful to write, edit and create with the constant feeling that someone is staring over their shoulder at their work-in-progress. And they may feel self-conscious about retreating to a more private area such as a meeting room, because they don't want to convey the impression that they are being anti-social or are trying to hide something.

Lack of privacy can also be a challenge when discussing certain business matters that require a high degree of confidentiality, for example human resources, finance, and legal. It can be quite difficult to conduct these important business calls when there is noise all around — or even worse, when everyone is being eerily silent!

There are also notable **health risks** from exposure to noise. Cornell University psychologists Gary Evans and Dana Johnson found that clerical workers who were exposed to open-office noise for three hours have increased levels of adrenaline, which over a prolonged period of time, can measurably increase risks of insulin resistance, heart disease, memory loss, immune system dysfunction and decreased bone mass density.[54]

Are open offices better suited to younger workers?

Many younger workers say that they prefer open offices. Indeed, there is often a perception that open offices are more suited to younger workers because they are better at multi-tasking than the older generation, and can therefore easily handle distractions. Because their minds are used to being attentive to many inputs at once — music, computer screen, a colleague's conversation, the ping of an instant message — it seems reasonable to assume that they could be more amenable to the idea of an open office that may have many distractions.

The preference for open offices by some young workers is supported by the findings from a 2012 study, which found that many generation Y employees (also known as Millennials), enjoy working in this type of environment.[55] Even though the subjects of the study agreed that open offices present noise and visual distractions, lack of privacy and an inability to control their environment, they generally felt that this was okay — a fair trade-off for the camaraderie and opportunity to socialize with coworkers, whom they often saw as friends.

But while the younger generation may be more amenable to working in an open office environment, given their predisposition to multi-tasking, are they more productive? Science says no. That's because the brains of multi-taskers — even those of millennials — can only be attentive to one or two tasks at the same time.

In fact, what we call multi-tasking is really task-switching. Even listening to certain music while writing is an exercise in task-switching. Psychologists tell us that there are many reasons that task-switching is not effective. Frequent switching from one task to the other takes significant brain power and prevents the mind from fully zoning into either activity. Jumping back and forth between tasks results in more errors. It also takes longer time to finish two projects than it would to finish each one separately.

Millennials have been described as having the attention span of a hyperactive squirrel. Growing up with constant social connection and accustomed to communicating using 140-character messages, the main distractions that millennials face are often the self-imposed distractions of constant use of social media and Internet.[56] Raised from an early age on several hours per day using digital devices, they expect the right to have some "me" time at work, and believe that as long as the job gets done, work and personal life can be blended.

Group/Time Wasted at Work (per day)	
Baby Boomers (1946-1964)	41 minutes
Gen X'ers (1965-1981)	1.6 hours
Millennials (1982-2000)	2 hours

Figure 11 —
Who wastes
the most time
at work?

Who works best in an open office environment?

So what type of people fare best in an open office where there are distractions? There are two cognitive traits that can largely determine how predisposed a person is to working in an environment that has a lot of distractions: cognitive inhibition and stimulus screening.

Cognitive inhibition is the ability of the mind to tune out stimuli that are irrelevant to the task at hand — in other words, the capacity of individual neurons to stop certain elements of thought. People with high cognitive inhibition are able to **block out distractions**.

Stimulus screening is the inverse of how emotionally "arousable" a person is. Arousable persons experience strong emotions easily, and once they become emotional, it takes them longer to get back to a normal, unemotional state. Arousable people have low stimulus screening. Persons with high stimulus screening are able to **reduce the stress of environmental stimuli** by prioritizing and focusing on important information.

Suppose the person next to me suddenly puts on his coat in middle of the morning, gathers up his stuff and leaves the office. If I have high cognitive inhibition, I will hardly notice. If I have high stimulus screening, then even if I *do* notice, I probably won't care.

However, if I have low cognitive inhibition, I will be quite distracted by the activity next to me. And if I also have low stimulus screening, this activity will arouse my curiosity. I will wonder "Why is he leaving right now? He looks a little upset. I wonder what he's upset about. Funny that he didn't mention that he was going somewhere. Would it be nosy of me to ask where he's going?"

A 2005 study found that people who are good at screening out distractions and do not get emotionally aroused by distractions — in other words, whose minds are able to zone out of their environment and be deeply involved in their task — have longer attention spans, which enables them to work effectively and productively in an open office, even an office that has many distractions.[57]

Subjects with low inhibitory ability reported lower job satisfaction when perceived privacy was low and task complexity was high. Subjects with high stimulus screening had higher performance and job satisfaction scores.

Heavy multi-taskers tend to be poor at blocking out distractions. Moreover, according to Stanford University cognitive neuroscientist Anthony Wagner, heavy multi-taskers are not only easily distracted by irrelevant environmental stimuli, but they are also worse at switching between unrelated tasks. So for example, if a habitual multi-tasker is interrupted by a colleague, it will take them longer to settle back into what they were doing.[58]

The conclusion: Although multi-taskers are more accepting of distractions in the workplace and embrace the open office culture, this arrangement may be undermining their performance more than they realize.

What about collaboration?

"The theory that when people are in proximity they'll jump in on each other's conversations to create new and unexpected ideas? That never happens. When we're mushed together, our primary goal is to *not* talk to each other. It's professional courtesy. This tension, of talking versus silence, is a real problem for me in an open space.

Supposedly, by all of us being squeezed together, we're to form a beating heart of collaboration. And yet, because we're sitting together, we're doing everything we can to create the sense that we're apart. It's incontrovertible proof, right here, almost every minute of my working day, that the open-office movement has the opposite of its intended effect.

Outside this office, I'm a talkative guy. A total extrovert. In past lives, when I've had offices, colleagues would pop in for a question, and we'd end up chatting for 30 minutes. Real ideas actually came out of those meetings. So did new relationships.

But here, over two and a half years, I've barely gotten to know my colleagues — and it's because every time I open my mouth, I feel bad knowing that I'm definitely distracting someone.

— Jason Feifer, Senior editor of Fast Company http://www.fastcompany.com

As this open-office worker notes, lack of control over personal interactions and the fear of disturbing others can lead to co-workers feeling distant, dissatisfied, and resentful instead of feeling closer.

Conclusion

The office environment is a major contributor to how happy employees are at work. Dissatisfaction with the work environment directly links to a lack of job satisfaction and lower productivity. Summing up the advantages and disadvantages of open offices, we get something like this:

On the positive side:

- Open offices convey a sense of community.
- They support transparency, and help employees to sense what's going on in every part of the company.
- Having collaboration areas promotes the sharing of ideas.
- Common areas result in more impromptu interactions.
- When managers sit with employees, this abolishes physical hierarchies.
- Open offices are more flexible and therefore better suited for a mobile workforce and a high churn rate.
- They reduce the cost of change compared to hard wall interiors, thanks to open furniture solutions and sophisticated technology infrastructure.

Possible negative effects of an open office include the following:

- Noise and lack of privacy are the key sources of dissatisfaction in work environments.
- Overhearing irrelevant conversations is detrimental to any task that requires cognitive processing. Tasks requiring complex verbal processes are especially likely to be disrupted.
- The inability to have confidential conversations in open-plan offices is cited as a major source of job dissatisfaction.
- Uncontrollable noise doesn't just lower productivity, it also decreases overall motivation.
- Perceived lack of visual privacy in open-plan offices is a major contributor to job dissatisfaction.
- Open-plan offices can, in some cases actually *discourage* collaboration, due to lack of privacy.
- Excessive, uncontrolled social interaction leads to overstimulation and loss of focus.
- Loss of control over the workplace can produce feelings of helplessness, which in turn reduces motivation and creativity in some individuals.

In the next chapter we explore ways to emphasize the benefits and mitigate the harmful effects of an open office environment.

CHAPTER 15

Designing a Productive Open Office

Companies should take advantage of the research and give thought to furniture design and how it fits the needs of employees and their work habits. But don't let utility override personality: Remember, your employees spend more time at work than almost anywhere else, so it should also be a comfortable and inspiring environment, with wall colors and art that support your company's image and culture.

— Lois Goodell, Principal and the director of interior design at CBT Architects

Advances in technology, the growing acceptance of telecommuting as well as an increased focus on collaboration have had an impact on the way offices allocate space, giving rise to the open office concept. Benefits of an open office include increased space use efficiency, more flexibility and less cost to make changes.

On the other hand, open office arrangements can have a negative impact on productivity due to lack of privacy, visual and acoustic distractions and uncontrolled social interactions, which can cause lack of focus. Loss of individual control of one's immediate environment can also decrease motivation and creativity in some individuals.

Fortunately, there are many design solutions that can help to counteract these negative effects in an open office environment and support productivity. That is the subject of this chapter.

Create office neighborhoods

By now it should be clear that simply creating an environment where everyone can see and hear everyone else will not necessarily lead to more collaboration.

For example, a uniform arrangement such as "benching," which consists of lots of rows of tables in a vast open space, fails to recognize different work styles and the fact that some tasks require collaboration, while others require individual deep thinking or confidentiality.

Most of the problems of open offices that were raised in the previous chapter can easily be solved by careful space allocation and the use of appropriate furniture. The answer is to have different types of spaces — some for heads-down focused tasks and privacy, some for connection between two or three people, and others for collaborative work. Each activity has its own space requirement and furniture solution.

For example, cubicles have changed but not disappeared entirely. Small, acoustically designed work booths that provide seating and a small desk surface, offer a place to retreat for a private phone conversation or concentrated work.

Other acoustical, "sound cone" types of products include high alcove, acoustically designed sofas, similar to tall padded restaurant booths. Not only do people outside not hear what's going on inside, the sofas are also high enough that there's no visual distraction. These spaces have power strip plugs to charge equipment.

Many people seek refuge in conference rooms to find some peace and quiet, but this does not work well because conference rooms are for conferences, not for individual work.

Many offices set aside a "Quiet Zone," where no conversation and no cell phones are allowed.

Many people seek refuge in conference rooms to find some peace and quiet, but this does not work well in the open environment because conference rooms are for conferences, not for individual work. Individuals who use conference rooms are blocking out groups of people who want to use the same space. The most efficient answer is to provide space for both conferences, as well as quiet individual workspaces.

As the individual workstation has contracted, so too has the concept of the conference room mutated. Former offices have been transformed into small conference rooms for just four or five people, and even smaller two- or three-person "cubbies," many of which wouldn't be identified as conference rooms at all.

Keep different types of work areas in close proximity to one another

The different types of work areas should be acoustically isolated but in close proximity so that people can transfer from one work mode to another very easily.

If someone needs to go all the way to another floor to find an available private space, they probably won't bother. Instead, they are more likely to remain in the open office and suffer. Similarly, if a small group needs to meet on the fly but has to walk a long distance to find the nearest conference room, they are more likely to have their impromptu meeting on the spot, which can be distracting to people who are trying to concentrate.

Short sightlines help to avoid visual distractions

Visual distractions should also be addressed so that people aren't continually seeing things happening 200 feet away in the office. By designing appropriate sightlines, this helps to create different zones and neighborhoods, which can also satisfy the need for employees to have their own "neighborhood" with their own team. One way to do this is with a curved layout, which has also been linked with positive emotions, and greater creativity and productivity.[59]

Consider curves

On the topic of curvilinear arrangements and furniture, it appears that people prefer them over straight edges and sharp angles. In one study of over 100 people, curvilinear furniture provoked significantly higher pleasure ratings, and comments such as "I like the rounded shapes. They make the furniture look comfortable and inviting", and "The rounded furniture seems to give off that calming feel."

Restore a feeling of control

Efforts should be made as much as possible to allow employees to have some control over their immediate workspace. Some companies offer employees a choice of seating — from traditional, ergonomic chairs to non-traditional balls or kneeling chairs.

According to Google spokesperson, Jordan Newman, Google allows hundreds of its software engineers to design their own desks or work stations out of what resemble oversize Tinker Toys. Newman notes, "Some have standing desks, others have treadmills so they can walk while working. Employees can express themselves by scribbling on walls. The result looks a little chaotic, like some kind of high-tech adult refugee camp, but that's how the engineers like it."[60]

Even a simple pin-board to post pictures and messages can help employees feel that the space is "theirs" with consequent benefits to productivity.[61]

Don't forget ergonomics
· · · · · · · · · · · · · · · · · · · ·

An ergonomic chair is not ergonomic unless it is adjusted to the individual. This needs to be emphasized even more in an environment of non-designated workstations.

Repetitive strain injuries to the wrist, elbow or shoulder are among the most common and costly occupational health problems of office workers. Many problems could be avoided by correctly adjusting furniture. Messaging and training on how to adjust a workstation are essential.

What does Feng shui say about open offices?
· ·

The principles of Feng shui to arrange rooms in ways that are pleasing and health-giving has popular appeal. Based as it is on the ancient Chinese concept of "Chi" or life-force, Feng shui's scientific credentials may be lacking; nevertheless, many leading companies and business leaders are reportedly using Feng shui as a business tool to increase their potential and protect their assets.[62]

Feng shui aficionados include the chairman of Microsoft, Bill Gates and Virgin boss Richard Branson. Coca Cola used Feng shui at its headquarters in Atlanta and reported an increase in productivity as did Hong Kong Disneyland. The Body Shop founder, Anita Roddick says that her headquarters and shops around the world have been designed using the principles of Feng shui. When McDonalds' replaced their garish yellow and red plastic with leather seats, earth tones, plants and trickling water, they were reportedly following Feng shui principles.

Banks that reportedly use Feng shui include Bank of America, Royal Bank of Canada, Citibank, HSBC, Texas First National, Mutual of New York, Guaranty Trust Bank of England, Chase Manhattan and Standard Charter Bank of London.

Donald Trump has been famously quoted as saying: "You don't have to understand Feng shui for it to work. I just know it brings me money."

Many hospitals now also follow principle of Feng shui by using wide corridors, plants and paintings to create soothing energy, in contrast to the traditional classic long, straight, narrow hallways, which make energy accelerate and cause stress.

Donald Trump has been famously quoted as saying: "You don't have to understand Feng shui for it to work. I just know it brings me money." Indeed, some principles of Feng shui are not easy to explain. However, others make perfect sense even to people who have not mastered all the nuances.

For example:

- Create a spacious, well-lit entryway opening to a friendly and welcoming foyer or reception area. A clear brand — for example the company logo provides a strong statement of reception when positioned above the eye line. That's because when we look upwards, we are inspired, as opposed to looking downwards. Many companies put their logos on floor mats. That's wrong! The last thing you want is to have people grinding dirt into your logo.

- Daylighting or lighting which mimics natural daylight is important. Reddish or yellowish traditional lighting is not good for our energy levels.

- Curvilinear shapes are preferable, a principle that is supported by research showing that these forms trigger more activity in brain regions associated with reward and aesthetic appreciation.[63] The research also indicates that sitting in circles provokes a collective mindset, whereas sitting in straight lines triggers feelings of individuality — something worth thinking about if team cohesion is the goal.

- As a general rule, these are the 3 Feng shui guidelines to follow when deciding on the best positioning of workstations: a view of the door (the so called commanding position); a solid wall behind (for protection and stability); and space and a good view from the working area (good Chi). Facing a wall is considered bad Feng shui because there is nowhere for the energy to flow.

- Different colors as represented by five Feng shui elements, have different psychological effects.[64] **Fire** colors (red, purple, strong pink) are high energy. **Earth** colors (earthy and sandy colors) bring stability and balance and health. **Metal** colors (white, gray) bring the qualities of calm, crisp clarity precision, efficiency and eliminate distractions. **Water** colors (blue, green) bring refreshing energy of calm, ease, purity and freshness, and abundance. Exposure to both blue and green has been shown to enhance performance on tasks that require generating new ideas. **Wood** colors (brown, green) bring the energy of vibrant health, vitality and growth. The wood element is also an expression of abundance, thus it is reportedly used as a Feng shui cure for wealth and prosperity.
- Other Feng shui must-haves for the office are air-purifying plants and high energy items such as bright, inspiring art with vibrant colors.

Conclusion
· · · · · · · · · ·

Designing an effective open office is far more subtle and complex than just opening up the floor plate and sitting everyone at tables in the open. What is needed is a variety of thoughtfully conceived work spaces, tailored to the needs of a company's employees, which also takes into consideration the activities and who needs to be near whom. This requires forethought and workflow mapping.

CHAPTER 16

Acoustic Comfort

Some days I need to put on my headphones to isolate myself from the "tic tic tic tic tic" noise of everyone typing. But music in my headphones is too intense and just adds other sounds and it prevents me from concentrating.

— Fast Office Staff,

The 10 Worst Things about Working in an Open — We asked you what you hate about your open-office layout. And oh boy, did you tell us! http://www.fastcompany.com

About a year ago, Bob was talking with a colleague, or at least he was *trying* to talk with a colleague in a Kansas City convention hotel lobby. But this hotel lobby, supposedly designed for informal business face-to-face chats and phone conversations, was being literally BLASTED with music. He looked around and saw one man on this cell phone with his finger plunged into his non-phone ear. He saw a woman crouching in a corner, also on the phone, struggling mightily to somehow manufacture a quiet space where she could hear. The contortions were painful to watch.

After a few minutes of shouting at each other, Bob and his colleague stepped outside into the parking lot, just so they could actually converse. Lo and behold, the area was filled with other groups of people standing around, deep in conversation. They had all been forced out of the lobby by one of the biggest detractors to workplace productivity — noise.

If we think of all the places where we want to do business: airplanes, airports, lobbies, coffee shops — bad acoustics dominate, with loud speakers and sound-reflecting surfaces that turn these spaces into virtual echo chambers. Granted, these places are not designed to allow quiet. But even offices are often noisy — filled with beeping office equipment, cell phones that ring intermittently, conversations and comings and goings.

When Bob isn't travelling, he sits at one of the virtual "drop-in" work stations near a kitchen area. He wears earphones — standard equipment issued to employees in the office. Without them, the refrigerator and ice machine would drown out his phone calls.

In this chapter, we discuss the most common complaint in open offices: **noise**; its effect on people; and some of the sound solutions that can be very effective.

Soundscape — a necessary part of the human experience

Every minute of our lives, we are moving through changing soundscapes of traffic, wind, conversations, domestic hubbub, babies crying, music piped into public spaces, air blowing through ductwork, dishes clattering, the sound of footsteps, vehicles and so on.

Even when we are not aware of the sounds, they are affecting us physically, psychologically, cognitively and behaviorally. Many of our reactions are primal. For example, birdsong makes us feel safe because it signals the absence of predators. The sound of trickling water is soothing because

The sound of trickling water is soothing because water supports life. The warning sound of wind and thunder before a storm makes us sit up and take notice. Soundscapes make up an important part of our human experience.

water supports life. The warning sound of wind and thunder before a storm makes us sit up and take notice. Soundscapes make up an important part of our human experience. They also help us to orient ourselves physically in space. This is one challenge that Deafblind people or astronauts in soundless space must learn to overcome.

Have you ever wondered what it would be like to be in a completely soundless environment? One place where no sound can be heard at all is the anechoic chamber at Orfield Laboratories in South Minneapolis.[65] The lab, which is 99.99% sound absorbent and holds the Guinness World Record for the "world's quietest place," is used to test the sounds that products make, for example, the sound of artificial heart valves, the sound of the display of a cellphone or the sound of a switch on a car dashboard. It's also the lab that motorbike maker Harley-Davidson used to make their bikes quieter, while still sounding like Harley-Davidsons.

Stay there too long though and you may start hallucinating. In fact, the company's founder and president, Steven Orfield sometimes challenges people to sit in the chamber in the dark. One reporter stayed in there for a record 45 minutes. "When it's quiet, ears will adapt," says Orfield. "The quieter the room, the more things you hear. You'll hear your heart beating; sometimes you can hear your lungs or your stomach gurgling loudly. In the anechoic chamber, *you* become the sound. This can be so disorientating that people have to sit down." Mr. Orfield admits that he can last a very respectable 30 minutes in his chamber, despite having an off-putting mechanical heart valve that suddenly becomes very loud indeed once he's inside.

When does sound become a problem?
. . . .

We need to hear sound. Noise though, is defined as *unwanted* sound. In other words, sound that we would prefer did not exist because it produces a negative **physical, psychological** and **cognitive** effect. In an office environment, noise includes comings and goings, noisy copy machines, ringing phones, air conditioning and conversations of office workers. A study called *Noise in Multiple Workstation Open Plan Computer Rooms: Measures and Annoyance* found that the for the majority of office workers, the most annoying sounds are: conversations; whirring and beeping from office equipment; the conversation and kaffuffle of people arriving/departing; and sounds from ventilation and air conditioning.[66]

Unfortunately, we cannot eliminate noise completely from the workplace. There are going to be conversations going on around us. In fact, we want people to talk. Equipment makes noise. It's unavoidable. But how much is too much?

Some Common Sounds	
Noise Source	**Decibels (dBA)**
Whispering	34
Conversation	60
Vacuum cleaner	69
Heavy traffic	90
Jet aircraft (overhead)	115
Human pain threshold	120

Table 2

There are several different ways to characterize sound, the key measures being: intensity (loud or quiet); frequency (high pitch or low pitch); and duration (how long the sound lasts). **Intensity** is the most common way to describe sound because it is the easiest to measure using decibels; but **frequency** is also very important. The Occupational Safety and Health Administration and the Environmental Protection Agency address **both** intensity and frequency by describing sound in terms of "Decibels on the A scale of a sound meter," where **higher frequencies are weighted more heavily**.

The American Society of Heating and Air Conditioning Engineers recommends that open office plans should fall in the 49-58 dBA to avoid interfering with verbal communication and complex mental tasks.[67]

Other research indicates that performance is negatively affected when noise reaches a decibel range of about 50 dBA,[68] which equates somewhere between a moderate rainfall and a normal conversation. The *Swedish Work Environment Authority* recommends even lower background sound levels in the workplace, in the range of 35 to 40 dBA.[69] In other words, it doesn't take very much noise to start detracting from work performance!

So, does noise affect productivity? You bet it does! After surveying 65,000 people over the past decade in North America, Europe, Africa and Australia, researchers at the University of California, Berkeley, report that more than half of office workers are dissatisfied with the level of speech privacy, making it the leading complaint in offices everywhere.[70] Study after study shows that workers in a noisy environment have a harder time **concentrating**, make more **errors** and score lower on tasks that require **memory** or reading **comprehension**.

Another troublesome finding is that prolonged exposure reduces office workers' **motivation** to persist at a difficult task.

More than half of office workers are dissatisfied with the level of speech privacy, making it the leading complaint in offices everywhere.

Is noise really a problem in the workplace?

Before we took measurements in Bob's open office, our initial impression was that overall, it was actually pretty quiet. Wrong. Decibel readings ranged from a low of 55 dBA in areas where people were working on computers to a high of 95 dBA near the kitchen area, where Bob sits. While there was a huge range across different parts of the office, the average was 72 dBA, which equates to something like the sound level of a vacuum cleaner.

How is this affecting Bob and his colleagues who happen to also be sitting in the noisy areas? Noisy offices can increase feelings of being in a negative mood. There are also negative health effects. Certain levels of noise reduce concentration, which results in stress, which, in turn causes the measurable release of adrenaline and noradrenaline.[71] **Noradrenaline** constricts almost all blood vessels, while **adrenaline**, sometimes called the emergency "fight or flight" hormone, causes constriction of tiny blood vessels, but dilates the blood vessels in the skeletal muscles and the liver.

Both hormones increase the rate and force of contraction of the heart, thus increasing the output of blood from the heart and increasing blood pressure. The hormones also have important metabolic actions. Adrenaline stimulates the breakdown of glycogen to glucose in the liver, which raises of the level of blood sugar. And both hormones increase the level of circulating free fatty acids. It's no wonder that prolonged exposure to stress can cause insulin resistance, heart disease, memory loss, immune system dysfunction and decreased bone mass density.

Office workers exposed even to relatively low levels of office noise (55 dBA) compared to workers in a quieter environment have higher levels of adrenaline — an indication that workers in these conditions experience clinically-measurable levels of stress.

Cornell researchers Evans and Johnson found increased levels of adrenaline in office workers exposed even to relatively low levels of office noise (55 dBA) compared to workers in a quieter environment — an indication that workers in these conditions were experiencing clinically-measurable levels of stress.[72]

How important is quiet?

Gloria Mark was working as a professor at the University of California in Irvine when she decided to look at interruptions and how they affect productivity. Her study, which addressed the issues of multi-tasking and interruptions, found that when a worker is interrupted from a task, it takes on average a little less than 25 minutes to re-engage and fully focus on that task.[73]

Of course interruptions can take many forms — people, e-mails, texts, etc. But the most detrimental are those uncontrollable random interruptions that the individual worker has the least control over.

Block noise at the SOURCE, along its PATH or at the RECEIVER
· ·

Noise-cutting solutions can be implemented at any of three points within the soundscape: at the source; along the noise path; or at the receiver. **Reducing noise at the source** or stopping the noise before it starts can be achieved with practices such as providing quiet areas, where phones must be turned off, no conversations are allowed, and any noise-producing activities moved to another location.

Another effective solution is to acoustically separate the work areas for the different types of tasks: collaboration, connection, concentration and confidentiality. This can be done by dividing the office into "noisy zones" for the kitchen, the collaboration areas, the copiers and whatever else generates noise — and "quiet zones" for individual workstations. This is discussed in *Chapter 15 — Designing a Productive Open Office.*

Controlling noise along its path can be done with features such as sound-absorbing ceiling systems, furniture and partitions made of soft materials, cushioned carpeting, rubber mats or anti-vibration machine mountings for office equipment. Another solution is sound masking, which ensures that noise from conversations does not travel more than 10 to 15 feet away. However, perhaps the most common way of **controlling noise at the receiver** nowadays is with the use of personal headphones, either to cover up noise with music, or with noise-cancelling capabilities.

Sound masking is the *addition* of noise

. . . .

Sound masking differs from active noise control because it is the *addition* of sound to cover up noise. A good analogy to explain sound masking is to imagine a flashing light source in a dark room. If all the ceiling lights are then turned on, the flashing light will no longer be noticeable because it has been masked. For this to work though, the masking light needs to be similar to the flashing light in terms of color and brightness. If the masking light is a different color or is too dim, then the flashing light will still appear.

Sound masking is similar. In offices, sound masking is designed to mask human voices. The human voice can be characterized as a bunch of frequencies (think of them as notes on the scale) all playing at the same time. Figure 13 shows the spectrum, or balance of loudness for the different frequencies of the human voice. As you can see, the profile of a human voice is typically a sort of haystack shape.

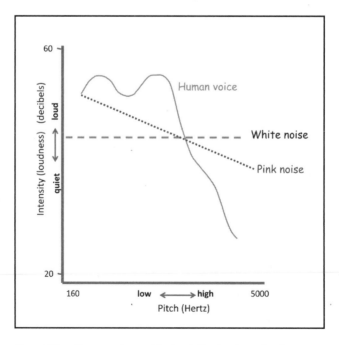

Figure 12 — Frequencies and their relative loudness for the human voice, white noise and pink noise

178

White noise contains the same amount of energy at all frequencies, and because of the sensitivities of human hearing, sounds very hissy and annoying. Pink noise has a balance that sounds less hissy, but it is still quite annoying and nowhere near suitable for effective sound masking. Both white and pink noise are really only useful as scientific calibration signals.

True sound masking provides enough energy at the right frequencies to effectively mask speech while including enough other energy to be comfortable and even soothing to the listener. The effect of masking is that speech privacy is maintained, and annoying sound distractions are reduced.[74]

Sound masking systems are often installed in ceiling plenums, in an open ceiling and even under raised floors. Studies report productivity gains of 8 to 38% through the use of such systems. When software giant, Autodesk installed sound masking in its open-plan building in Waltham, they ran the system for three months before telling the employees — and then, one day, turned it off in order to gauge its impact. "We were surprised at how many complaints we got," said Charles Rechtsteiner, Autodesk's Facilities Manager. "People weren't sure what was different, but they knew something was wrong. They were being distracted by conversations 60 feet away. When the system's on, speech becomes unintelligible at a distance of about 20 feet."[75]

Controlling sound at the receiver with headphones
. . . .

One industry that is doing well as a result of the open office trend is headphone manufacturers — with significant growth for high end products. The trend toward open office design with minimal partitions has made headphones more popular. They are the new "walls" in open office environments.[76]

However, many studies say that listening to music while working does not always help with concentration. For example, research shows that listening to music with **lyrics** is linked to lower scores on tests of concentration for reading or writing tasks. That's because the brain must work harder to force itself not to process strong verbal stimuli such as catchy lyrics, which compete with the work. Workers listening to **music that they either love or hate** also score lower for concentration, compared with workers who don't have strong feelings about the music, or who work without music. That's because people naturally pay more attention to music they strongly like or dislike. This pre-occupation hurts our ability to focus. Bottom line: The more brain power work is needed screen out unwanted input, the less remains for tasks. And the longer one tries to concentrate amid competing distractions, the worse the performance is likely to be. Attention takes mental effort, and we can get mentally tired.

That said, individuals respond differently to music and their reaction depends very much on what they are used to. Many people say that they *need* some background noise to help them concentrate. For them, a familiar piece of music without lyrics is an effective sound-blocker that helps them to focus — so effectively, in fact, that if you tap them on the shoulder, they may practically jump out of their skin!

"I often have music playing softly in the background while I'm writing scripts or working on director notes. Instrumentals work best as I can get distracted by songs with lyrics. Music relaxes my mind on one level, leaving me room to think creatively."

— Joanne Ingrassia, Video producer/director

"Having music in the background really interferes when I'm writing a report or a proposal, but the steady, logical beat of techno definitely helps when I'm writing code."

— Jean Marc Skopek, Senior programmer

"I like to have melodious classical music in the background when I'm writing. Something like Bach's harpsichord and violin sonatas or anything Mozart works for me."

— Dennison Berwick, Author and travelogue writer

How Loud Is That Music?
· · · · · · · · · · · · · · · · · · · ·

Thanks to the digital revolution, never has music been so accessible. And never have we seen so many people with headphones — not just millennials; and not only for listening to music, but also for talking on the phone.

Although listening to music with headphones can help to drown out unwanted noise, this can have another, less desirable long-term effect — permanent hearing loss. According to the Stony Brook School of Medicine, most portable music devices produce 95 to 108 dB of sound in the middle of their volume range, and 115 dB toward the top end of the spectrum. At 95 dB, hearing damage can occur after four hours of listening to music. However, at 108 dB, damage could start occurring between 30 minutes to an hour. And at 115 dB, damage could occur after only 15 minutes.[77]

It might be a good idea, therefore, for employers to occasionally remind their employees to limit their headphone use in the office.

Noise reducing headphones could be the better way
· ·

For those of us who don't *need* background sounds to concentrate, noise-reducing headphones can be a better (and safer) way to help concentration than listening to music.

Noise-canceling headphones were first developed by Bose Corp. more than 20 years ago for use by airline pilots. Today there are models that can help cancel the higher-frequency sounds of speech and other ordinary activity.

"Headphones can screen out as much as three-fourths of office noise," says Steven Orfield, president of Orfield Laboratories Inc., the firm that operates the anechoic chamber we mentioned earlier. "But when you take them off for a couple of minutes, everything is going to sound way too loud for you while your ears adjust. You may find yourself speaking louder to others."

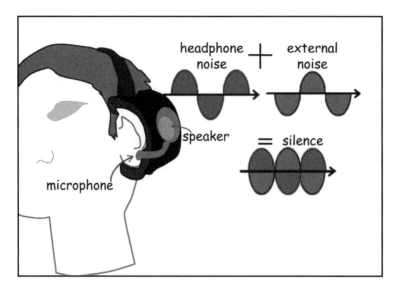

Figure 13 — Noise-canceling headphones

The way noise cancelling headphones work is well described in *How Stuff Works.*[78] Noise-canceling headphones come in either **active** or **passive types**. Passive noise reduction occurs as a result of the materials of the headphones themselves muffling some sound waves, especially those at higher frequencies. **Active** noise-canceling headphones add an additional level of noise reduction by actively **erasing** lower-frequency sound waves. How do noise-canceling headphones do this? By creating their own sound waves that mimic the incoming noise in every respect except one: the headphone's sound waves are 180 degrees out of phase with the intruding waves.

Conclusion
. . . .

Working in noisy soundscapes is not just a problem at the office. Think about where today's workplace exists. By 2015, over one third of the workforce in the U.S. will be considered "mobile," meaning they are not tied to a specific desk or work station.[79] They will conduct business in multiple public areas like coffee shops, airports, airplanes, hotel lobbies and even outdoor areas, where there are constant interruptions by announcements, advertising messages, music and noise.

Do some coffee shops play music just loud enough so that people don't linger too long? "Please come and drink our coffee and even stay a bit, but don't park here to work for any length of time." A good way to shoo people out is to make it so noisy that it's hard to talk or even think. On top of it all, you have coffee grinders whirring, cappuccino machines hissing and on-going clanging and clattering of behind-the-counter activities. It adds up to a cacophony that is pretty effective in making people, who want to work, gulp down their coffee and head elsewhere. Maybe that's their hope.

Obviously, we have little control over these public spaces, so it becomes more of a personal battle with each of us figuring out how to filter out the noise. Perhaps one day, the people running airports will consider incorporating places where announcements are not blaring every few minutes. A review of recent press coverage indicates that hotel, restaurant and coffee shop owners are beginning to hear (no pun intended) the growing cries for quieter environments.[80]

As businesses focus more on the impact of the workplace on employee productivity inside or outside the formal office, we think noise control will be a growing concern. And the good news is that it's relatively easy to improve.

CHAPTER 17

Visual Comfort

Design is defined by light and shade, and appropriate lighting is

enormously important.

— Albert Hadley, The Story of America's Preeminent Interior Designer

Revolutionary lighting technologies are resulting in significant gains in energy efficiency. But the biggest potential benefit from improving lighting in the workplace may be the effect it can have on productivity.

Many offices still contain outdated lighting that was configured primarily to support paper-based tasks. Also, many of these systems were installed before the effects of daylight on health, wellbeing and productivity were well understood.

Now that almost everyone is staring at monitors for hours at a time, the excessive lighting levels, flicker, glare and lack of daylight associated with old lighting can be a major cause of eyestrain, headaches, and general dissatisfaction, all of which can greatly reduce productivity.

Offices that are considering a lighting retrofit for energy-saving purposes would therefore do well to also examine the question from a productivity angle — the topic of this chapter.

Lighting affects productivity
· ·

Loss of productivity from poor lighting is famously illustrated in a Cornell University study, which was conducted to explain data from the American Society of Interior Designers, showing that 68% of employees are dissatisfied with their office lighting, as well as data from another study in Silicon Valley, indicating that 79% of VDT users wanted better lighting.[81] The Cornell study, which was conducted at a Xerox facility, aimed to quantify the relative merits of the various office lighting methods, including parabolic down-lighting and indirect lighting. Researchers asked workers to report the amount of time they lost from the types of symptoms often associated with poor lighting. More workers who had parabolic lighting reported lost time, and a high percentage (20%) reported a loss over 15 minutes a day due to eye focusing problems, compared to only 2% of the group that had indirect lighting. The study, although it is not recent, is still widely quoted because it provides a notional estimate of the financial loss from reduced productivity, which was estimated at 15 minutes per day or over an hour a week per employee — the equivalent of a full week of lost time per affected employee per year.[82]

Conversely, productivity **gains** from correcting poor lighting conditions are also being measured. For example, when a San Diego federal building changed T12 bulbs with magnetic ballasts, (which produce a flicker associated with eye strain) to T8s with electronic ballasts, they found that employee productivity improved by 3% in the office areas, and by 15% in courthouse, correctional, and post office spaces. These benefits were conservatively valued at almost $1.3 million a year, in addition to reduced energy costs of more than $275,000.[83]

With the exciting advances in lighting technology and recent findings on the effects of lighting and daylighting on workers' health and wellbeing, there has never been a better time to re-visit the lighting design of an office and its effect on productivity.

Daylighting and views — we crave them even if we don't exactly know why

Human beings are naturally drawn to windows and natural light. There seems to be something almost magical about daylight; the more we can get, the better we feel. Even if the average person can't scientifically explain why, we just know that daylight affects our moods and energy levels; when days get shorter, many of us get the "winter blahs."

Scientists believe that human evolution in a natural — rather than a built environment — is responsible for our gravitation towards daylight and our sensitivity to it. Light is associated with those seasons that produce new life, which perhaps helps to explain our archetypical perceptions of summer and winter as captured in literature and even in dictionary definitions:

Summer: a period of fruition, fulfillment, happiness, or beauty

Winter: a period of time characterized by coldness, misery, barrenness, or death

The reason that we are drawn to **views** can also be traced back to our early origins, when survival depended on our ability to view — from a secure vantage, and without being seen — any dangers approaching from afar. From this position of relative security, our ancestors could relax, feel at peace, reflect on life and make plans. Even in this day and age, we still get the same feeling from looking at a great view.

What is the physiological effect of daylight?

Until fairly recently, it was believed that the main benefits of daylight were primarily **psychological**, in terms of raising comfort and reducing stress. Scientists tell us that exposure to daylight is linked to the release of serotonin, known as the "happy hormone" — which may explain why most people enjoy being out in the sunshine. It may also be why bring-

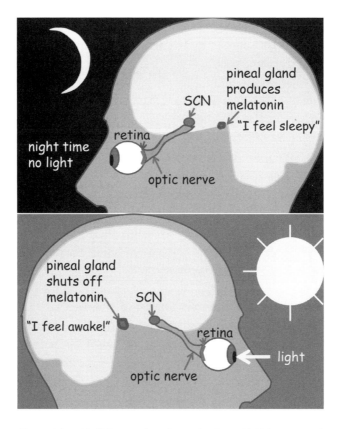

Figure 14 — No light = melatonin production.   M Light = no melatonin

ing more daylight into a store through skylights seems to result in greater "shopper energy" and about 6% more in sales figures — a finding which has been widely reported in retail trade journals.[84]

Seasonal Affective Disorder (SAD), a condition that affects as many as half a million Americans, and which causes severe depression, irritability and fatigue in the winter, was properly identified and defined as a **physiological** trait only as recently as the 1980s. With so many people suffering in their everyday life, job performance and personal relationships, not surprisingly, early studies focused primarily on finding treatment options. It was only in the early 2000s that scientists started to really study the causes of SAD in order to determine *why* the change of seasons from bright summer to dark winter days can have such a debilitating impact on some people.

This is what they found.

Our bodies work according to a biological "clock" consisting of a group of nerve cells smaller than a grain of rice, called the suprachiasmatic nucleus, or SCN, which is located in the hypothalamus, an area of the brain just above the optic nerve. The SCN regulates the 24-hour rhythm that determines *when* many of our bodily functions occur, including appetite. One of the most important roles of the SCN is to establish **sleep-wake patterns**.

This is how. The amount and type of light which enters our eyes causes a signal to be sent via our optic nerves to the SCN, which is exquisitely sensitive to cycles of light and darkness.

As daylight dims and night falls, the SCN instructs the pineal gland to produce melatonin, a hormone which makes us sleepy.

In the day time, when light hits the retina in our eyes, messaging goes through the optic nerve informing the SCN. The SCN then instructs the pineal gland to STOP producing melatonin. In the absence of melatonin, we feel awake.

In response to the sun's 24 hour cycle, a similar pattern becomes embedded in the SCN. As the seasons change progressively, so too does SCN clock progressively re-set itself. A couple of hours before our habitual bedtime, it signals to the pineal gland that it is time to start releasing melatonin. As dawn approaches, close to the time that we are used to getting up, the SCN signals that it is time to shut off the melatonin so that we can rise 'n shine. This explains why many people wake up at exactly the same time every morning without the help of an alarm.

This schedule needs to be reset however, when there is a gradual or abrupt major change in the day-night cycle. For example, when we jet across the globe and suddenly day and night are reversed, it can take a day or two for the circadian clock to readjust itself so that melatonin is produced at night once again, rather than at 3:00 in the afternoon. People with SAD experience an inability to shift and re-set the circadian clock when days get shorter as winter sets in.

By the way, you may be wondering how the SCN of blind people can determine when to instruct the pineal gland to release melatonin. Many blind people, even though they may lack the main photoreceptors known as rods and cones, still retain other photo-receptors in the retina called pRGCs, which are also effective at informing the SCN of light conditions. However, *totally* blind people, who cannot perceive the light-dark cycle at all, do tend to suffer from significant circadian abnormalities, which are manifested as insomnia and daytime sleepiness.

Daylight spectrum
· · · · · · · · · · · · · · ·

Daylight is composed of many color wavelengths that shift in their relative intensities throughout the day. As the spectrum shifts, the different color compositions that enter the eye modify the hormonal response in humans.

For example, at dawn (6-9 AM), daylight consists largely of blue light, in the spectrum range that effectively *suppresses* melatonin, thereby causing us to feel awake. In the late afternoon and towards evening, daylight contains more red, orange and yellow — that part of the spectrum that does not suppress melatonin production.

It's interesting to think that for thousands of years of our evolution, humans spent evenings in the reddish, golden glow of firelight. Taking a lesson from our ancestors, the best way to protect our production of melatonin as evening progresses, would be to shift to low wattage bulbs with yellow, orange, or red light.

By now it should be clear to you why even pinpoints of light at night — particularly blue lights from alarm clocks and other electronic gadgets prevent us from getting a good night's sleep. It isn't necessary to be staring directly at a TV or computer screen; even the tiniest amount of blue light penetrating through closed eyelids, suffices to prevent the pineal gland from releasing melatonin, which will affect the quality of our sleep — a good reason to invest in an eye mask for sleeping.

Many teenagers and young adults tend to feel more awake at night.

They are also more sensitive to the effects of light than older people. Watching TV or a video game just before bedtime certainly isn't going to help them get a good night sleep.

For thousands of years of our evolution, humans spent evenings in the reddish, golden glow of firelight. Taking a lesson from our ancestors, the best way to protect our production of melatonin as evening progresses, would be to shift to low wattage bulbs with yellow, orange, or red light.

Mal-illumination — a problem of the modern age

Since the dawn of history and until relatively recently, humans have lived and worked outdoors in the light of day and ended their day around a softly glowing fire. This is in contrast to our modern lifestyle, made possible by electric lighting, which has effectively reduced us to contemporary cave-dwellers, sadly lacking exposure to the varying intensities and color-spectrum of daylight that our brains need in order to receive the cues that nature intended.

Today, most people suffer from *mal-illumination*, brought about because we often get up in the dark, lack daylight during the day, and experience too much artificial light at night.

How does this modern, round-the-clock lifestyle affect our metabolism? Disruption to our circadian rhythm by late-night artificial light or being roused from sleep by an alarm that is beeping in the dark — can have a profoundly disturbing effect on our bodies and brains.

For example, our circadian clock controls not only our daily cycle of sleep, but also our level of alertness and ability to organize information in such a way that we can remember it later. If our internal clock isn't functioning properly, it causes the release of too much gamma-amino-butyric acid (GABA), a neurotransmitter, which inhibits our brain in a way that can lead to **short term memory problems** and difficulty retaining new information.[85]

Lack of sleep also affects the release of hormones that regulate satiety and hunger. For example, when we are sleep-deprived, our body decreases production of leptin, the hormone that tells our brain that there is no need for more food, while also increasing levels of ghrelin, a hormone that triggers hunger. This can lead to **weight gain**. Both too little and too much sleep can also increase the risk of **type 2 diabetes**. A 15-year study of more than 1,000 men found that those getting less than six or more than eight hours of sleep a night had a significantly increased diabetes risk. A similar pattern was also observed in the relationship between sleep and **coronary heart disease**.[86]

Sleep problems have even been related to an elevated risk of **cancer**. Melatonin is an antioxidant that helps to suppress harmful free radicals in the body and slows the production of estrogen, which can activate cancer. When our circadian rhythm is disrupted, our body may produce less melatonin and therefore may have less ability to fight cancer.[87]

How important is daylight to productivity?
· ·

Naturally, we all have to earn a living, and therefore most of us can't spend our lives out of doors in the daylight in order to stay healthy and free of disease. So what about the millions of us who spend a good part of their lives in an office environment?

Researchers at the Interdepartmental Neuroscience program at Northwestern University in Evanston, Illinois, who studied the impact of working in a windowless environment, concluded that there is a strong relationship between workplace daylight exposure and office workers' sleep and quality of life. An abstract of the research can be found in an online supplement of the journal SLEEP.[88]

A well-known 2003 study by the California Energy Commission (CEC) linked daylight exposure to increased levels of concentration and improvements in short-term memory tasks.[89] In an earlier study, the CEC had also reported that students exposed to more daylight performed 7% to 18% better on standardized tests.[90]

Federated Logistics introduced daylighting into their Los Angeles warehouse primarily to reduce energy but found that natural light also reduced errors in product identification for repairs, warehousing and shipping.[91]

The Institute of Information Science at the University of Nebraska found that poor workplace lighting leads to lower productivity, as measured by sick days, lower employee satisfaction levels and increased turnover rates.[92]

The research is endless, all showing the positive effects of daylight on mental performance and worker health.

Daylighting — What does this mean for office design?

By now, it should be clear that the answer is to provide as much daylight as possible in an office. How much is enough? To get a sense of magnitudes, a sunny day at high noon is equivalent to 100,000 lux of brightness, while indoor lighting only provides around 300 to 500 lux.

Illuminance (lux)	Example
120,000	Brightest sunlight
110,000	Bright sunlight
20,000	Shade illuminated by entire clear blue sky, midday
1,000 – 2,000	Typical overcast day, midday
<200	Extreme of darkest storm clouds, midday
400	Sunrise or sunset on a clear day (ambient illumination).
40	Fully overcast, sunset/sunrise
<1 lux	Extreme of darkest storm clouds, sunset/rise

Table 3

To give us an idea of how much daylight we need, Oxford University neuroscientist Russell Foster notes that the average person needs exposure to 1,000 lux of daylight to enjoy the *maximum* benefits of daylight. "When you are exposed to 1,000 lux, you are getting enough light for full alertness." says Foster.[93] As a point of comparison, light therapy for people who suffer from seasonal affective disorder (SAD) consists of somewhere in the order of 10,000 lux of daylight for 30 minutes in the morning or 2,500 lux for two hours per day. A 2009 study, *Indoor Exposure to Natural Bright Light Prevents Afternoon Sleepiness* showed that just a half hour of exposure to bright daylight (>1,000 lux) by sitting adjacent to windows, reduced normal post-lunchtime drowsiness and increased alertness in healthy subjects almost as effectively as a short nap.[94] Having a day-lit dining area can help people get their dose of daylight. Being located in a pleasant, walkable neighborhood is also conducive to getting people out of their desks and outdoors in fresh air and daylight on their lunch break.

Some workplaces have integrated lighting circadian lighting controls that adjust the color and intensity of light over the course of the day, corresponding to the changing spectrum of daylight. Gradually brightening lights in the morning acts as a dawn simulator to a high-intensity light, which helps to awaken occupants, increase morning alertness and achieve optimal daytime energy. This, along with ultraviolet light to allow the body to generate Vitamin D, is one of the requirements for a building to attain WELL™ certification. Naturally, the benefits of providing circadian lighting controls will not be as great if occupants have bad sleeping habits at home — staying up until the wee hours of the morning, and falling asleep with the TV on and gadgets blinking in the night.

Short of providing this level of lighting sophistication in the workplace, the bottom line is, quite simply, to provide as much daylight as possible to as many workers as possible. A good place to start is by looking at workplace layout. It will determine to a large extent what is possible in terms of daylighting in the desk areas.

Obviously, not everyone can have a window seat. Plus, there are significant considerations that have to do with glare on monitors. One way to compensate for lack of daylight at the desk is by locating common areas — such as meeting rooms, lounges, coffee nooks and exercise rooms — in parts of the office that get daylight.

In a traditional office, with private offices up against the window-line, opportunities for daylight to reach throughout the floor-plate are limited. But there are options. Using full or partial windows for interior walls allows daylight to permeate private offices and reach interior spaces. If privacy is an issue, frosted glass or high windows can still let some daylight through.

Spreading the light in an open office landscape is easier, although even in an open floor-plate, daylight from windows can be virtually lost 20-25 feet away from the window.[95] One way to get the light deep into the space is to reduce the height of cubicle partitions. Light shelves that look like airplane wings can be placed in front of windows and angled to maximize light reflectivity and direct daylight farther into work spaces. Depending on the building, solar tubes may be used to funnel daylight into the workplace. These can be conduits with highly reflective interior surfaces that essentially "pump" daylight through roofs and walls to reach workers who would otherwise not have any access. More sophisticated versions use fiber optic cables to transmit the daylight to interior spaces. Finally, LED technology has advanced to the point that artificial lighting more closely mimics daylight. New LED translucent panels use particles to diffuse light to mimic the atmosphere, creating a close-to-real daylight.[96]

Beyond layout and structural changes, there are simple ways to spread light throughout the workplace using light colors on walls, ceilings, desktops and cubicle walls to help the daylight reflect into the space.

Drapes or blinds are generally needed to block out glare and unwanted solar heat gain during the day. However, there are types that let some light through and can be easily adjusted to different lighting conditions throughout the day. For example, some vertical-slatted blinds are perforated with small holes to let daylight in, which stops glare and stills fill the space with daylight

Sensor-driven lighting systems can change lighting levels, depending on the amount of daylight available at any moment. Several technologies are starting to make these solutions economically-feasible including wireless controls, which are far less costly to install that wired systems. A centralized system can be connected to lights to deliver the correct light levels. There are now also economical sensors that can be connected to one or several light fixtures for pinpoint adjustments.

Views
• • • • • •

Views are important because when people look at nature, it helps restock their mental energy. Sally Augustin, an applied environmental psychologist and author of *Place Advantage, Applied Psychology for Interior Architecture*, has spent years studying people's experience in homes, workplaces and hospitals. She explains it this way:

> "Think of energy in your brain as one big pot of stuff churning around like lava. When doing knowledge work, you deplete your mental resources, whether it's your job or playing chess. When mental stocks come down, we become irritable, cognitive performance and social performance decline, and we don't get along well with others. But when we look at something that interests us — something that doesn't require a lot of attention to monitor, we build back up our mental energy. Our mood and performance improve. This happens when looking at nature, but also anything that produces a natural, soft fascination. My brain is almost exactly the same as some relative I had several thousand years ago. Our brains change so slowly that things that made us comfortable in the environment in which we evolved are comforting to us now. Watching the countryside allows us to look at our world softly, easily, and consider what might happen to us next."

The ideal view to restore mental balance should be pleasing to the eye, while also subconsciously allowing us to observe any approaching threats. Augustin says to imagine a home perched on a hill overlooking a rolling English countryside. The green landscape is pleasing to the eye and, subconsciously, we can see danger approaching. From this vantage we feel more secure, which allows our mind to relax, drift and replenish.

"You don't want to be deep in a jungle setting," she says. "That's because danger lurks in the jungle, and you can't see very far ahead. I like that phrase, 'It's a jungle out there,' because what it means is life is stressful, like a jungle."

Most offices don't offer a view of green nature. "The good news is that they don't have to," says Houzz Editorial Staff Mitchell Parker in an article called *Why We Want a House with a Great View*.[97] Mitchell describes **biophylic** ways to trick our minds into receiving restorative benefits from nature by "re-creating that ancestral environment in which we can relax and contemplate nature without feeling threatened." His tips include incorporating natural building materials, water, fire, art and even fish.

A **green view** is wonderful, but according to Sally Augustin's research, there are restorative benefits even while looking at cityscapes. The only catch is there needs to be a body of **water** visible — a lake, pond, ocean, or even a water fountain in a courtyard. Somewhat realistic **landscape art** — rather than abstract — can have restorative benefits too. **Plants** add a psychological boost, as long as they do not constitute a jungle-like setting, which makes our ancestral brain uneasy at the possibility of unseen, lurking wild animals. "In a 10 foot by 10 foot room, three or four plants are great," Augustin says. "You get the green effect, but you're still able to survey your environment. If you have 50 plants in the same room, you've basically re-created a jungle."

What about glare?

. . . .

Daylight and views are wonderful, but anyone who has tried to work on a computer outside on sunny day knows that glare can be a problem.

In fact, while natural light is beneficial for all the reasons we have mentioned, the awful truth is that bright sunlight constitutes poor visual ergonomics for computer work.

Glare results when there is a high level of contrast between the intensity of light in the foreground and background, for example, if a bright window is positioned behind a computer screen. In glary conditions, the eyes have to constantly adapt to the difference in contrast between dark and light areas, resulting in eye fatigue, headaches and reduced visibility.

Direct glare occurs when there is a bright light source directly in the user's field of view, for example, when a worker is facing a window or where electric lights shine directly onto the screen. Indirect glare is caused by reflections when light from windows or overhead lighting is reflected off reflective surfaces. Masking occurs when light levels are too high.

The best way to avoid glare is to locate the workstations so that computer monitors are set up at right angles to windows and to long runs of overhead fixtures. This will eliminate bright light from directly striking the eye and reduce screen glare. If glare or masking from windows continues to be a problem, draw the blinds.

Direct glare from overhead lights can also be controlled by fixtures that are suspended from the ceiling with the lamps oriented "up," creating indirect light that is reflected off of the ceiling. This lighting is ideal for computer work.[98]

The best way to avoid glare is to locate the workstations so that computer monitors are set up at right angles to windows and to long runs of overhead fixtures.

Intensity of lighting

As with glare, there is also a contradiction between our need for sunshine and what constitutes optimal lighting for computer work.

In Chapter 6, we discussed lighting levels with a view to energy efficiency. What are the optimum lighting levels for productivity?

Good lighting should enable people to easily view their work without straining their eyes. The type of work being performed will determine the intensity of light required. Reading and writing paper documents requires much more intense lighting than computer work. While lights need to be sufficiently bright for paper tasks, they should not be so bright as to cause reflection, glare and masking on a computer screen.

Office lighting that is either too bright or not bright enough increases the risk of workers developing eye health problems. Computer users should be working in rooms in which the brightness is between 200-500 lux. In spaces where there are no other sources of bright light, lighting at around 300 lux is most appropriate. The Illuminating Engineering Society of North America (IESNA) puts out a handbook that recommends lighting levels for different types of spaces and tasks.

Task Lighting

Until recently, it was assumed that more lighting was always better. Now we know that this is not the case, particularly for computer-based work. However, the lower lighting levels that are becoming the norm can be a problem for paper-based tasks.

Task lighting is an effective way to ensure that illumination is being provided where it is most needed, and more economically than most energy efficient ceiling lights, for the simple reason that the task lighting is located closer to what is being lit. Another huge advantage of task lighting is that workers have control over their lighting as needed for the tasks that they are doing.[99]

Flickering lights

Light flicker occurs when the voltage supplied to a light source fluctuates. When flicker is severe, the light appears to flutter and be unsteady. The severity of the flicker depends on several factors, including, but not limited to the kind of light, the age of the light tube and whether the ballast is working properly.

Lamps operating on AC electric systems (alternating current) produce light flickering at a frequency of 120 Hz (cycles per second), twice the power line frequency of 60 Hz. What this means, simply put, is that the power is turning on and off 120 times a second (actually the voltage varies from +120 volts to -120 volts, 60 cycles per second and is at zero volts twice in one cycle).

The flicker is not visible in incandescent lights, and most people do not notice it in fluorescent lights either. That's because when a light is flickering at a frequency greater than 50 Hz, it is no longer possible to distinguish between the individual flickers, and the flashes appear to fuse into a steady, continuous source of light. The faster the flickering, the more steady the light appears.

That said, even though we don't notice it, the sensory system in some individuals can somehow detect the flicker. As a result, ever since fluorescent lighting was introduced in workplaces, there have been complaints about headaches, eye strain and general eye discomfort, which have been associated with fluorescent light flicker.

The type of ballast, which controls the electrical supply to fluorescent lights, affects the frequency of the flicker. There are two kinds of ballasts in fluorescent lights: magnetic, and the higher frequency electronic ballasts. Magnetic ballasts change the voltage supplied to the fluorescent lamps but do not alter the power line frequency of 60 Hz. Electronic ballasts take the 60 Hz supplied power and convert it to a much higher frequency (20,000–60,000 Hz). The resulting flicker frequency is so high that the human eye cannot detect any fluctuation in the light intensity — rendering it essentially flicker-free. An added benefit is that electronic ballasts produce less hum than that emitted by other kinds of ballasts. In a study called *Fluorescent Lighting, Headaches and Eye-strain*, the use of high frequency electronic ballasts in fluorescent lights resulted in more than a 50% drop in complaints of eye strain and headaches — and even fewer complaints of headaches among workers exposed to lights with electronic ballasts as well as more natural light.[100]

So if you have noticed light flicker in your office, here's what to do: Make sure that bulbs are replaced on a scheduled basis. Old bulbs tend to flicker more and they are not as bright. Check that all parts of the light fixture, especially the ballast, are functioning properly. And finally, consider upgrading to fluorescent lighting that uses electronic ballasts.[101]

Conclusion

Today's exciting lighting technologies can be combined with design principles to create a lighting approach that takes full advantage of daylight and artificial lighting. The result is a more productive environment that cuts energy costs. In other words, a workplace that is greener and more productive.

CHAPTER 18

Thermal Comfort and Indoor Air Quality

Thermal comfort as defined by ANSI/ASHRAE Standard 55 is the condition of mind that expresses satisfaction with the thermal environment and is assessed by subjective evaluation. Maintaining this standard of thermal comfort for occupants of buildings or other enclosures is one of the important goals of heating, ventilation, and air conditioning design engineers.

— Wikipedia

One of the few places that sustainability and productivity have at times conflicted is in the area of temperature control and ventilation.

It's a simple fact — Increasing the amount of heating, air conditioning and ventilation increases energy use (and costs). The easiest, no-cost way to reduce energy consumption in the workplace is by temperature set-back at night and on weekends, changing temperature set points to higher levels in the summer and lower set points in the winter, and by reducing ventilation rates.

Unfortunately, skimping on energy for heating and cooling and ventilation can potentially create a productivity problem — or worse. When people are uncomfortable, either too warm or too cold, or feeling sleepy from lack of oxygen, their productivity declines; when they are breathing polluted air for 8 hours a day, five days a week, they can actually get sick.

In this chapter, we show how it is possible to achieve a balance between energy management, and health and productivity as a function of indoor air quality and temperature. Because heating, cooling and ventilation are largely controlled by the landlord, this is one area where there can be a win-win — energy savings for the landlord and/or tenants and comfortable occupants.

Here's how a typical ventilation system works

An understanding of HVAC can help us to see where energy savings can be made and where health and productivity may be affected.

- The cycle begins with fresh air drawn in through dedicated openings in the wall or roof.
- Some air that has already circulated through the building may be added to the fresh air. This can save energy during the heating season if the re-circulated air is warmer than incoming fresh air. Conversely, it can help save on air conditioning in the cooling season if the re-circulated air is cooler than the incoming fresh air.
- Prior to being pushed through the building, the air is first cleaned. This is done primarily by filtering, although there are other measures that may be used in specialized applications such as hospitals or clean rooms to clean the air. These include filtration of molecular-sized particles, and technologies to capture volatile organic compounds (VOCs) and even kill bacteria.
- Next the air is "conditioned" — either by heating or cooling it. Temperature settings determine the degree of heating and cooling.
- The clean, conditioned air is then pumped throughout the building. The amount of air that is pumped is controlled centrally or by zone. Some

buildings have carbon dioxide sensors throughout the building that tell the ventilation system that it needs to pump more or less fresh air, depending on how much CO_2 has built up.

- Having gone through the building, the air becomes quite contaminated with carbon dioxide from the occupant's breathing, as well as a cocktail of particles and VOCs from manufactured wood products, furnishings and carpeting, electronic equipment, cleaning materials, and other products. It's not surprising that indoor air contains much higher concentrations of some pollutants than outdoor air.

- The contaminated air from the occupied spaces is then sucked away through separate grilles and ductwork and is exhausted to the outside. Some of the used air may be recirculated. Prior to exiting the building, the "used" air may pass through a heat exchanger to extract or absorb heat to pre-condition the fresh air coming into the building. In the winter, heat is extracted from air that is about to exit in order to warm up the fresh incoming air. In the summer, it's the opposite: the cooled exiting air is used to suck out some of the heat in the in-coming fresh air.

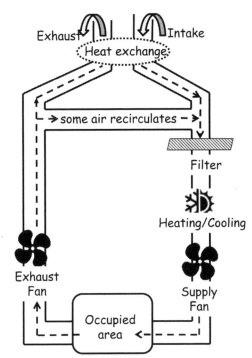

Figure 15 — Ventilation

From the diagram, we can see that energy is needed for pumping the air, and heating and cooling it. Energy is also needed to force air through filters — the finer the filters, the more energy is needed to push the air through.

We can reduce the energy by **reducing the amount of fresh air** that has to be pumped, and heated/cooled; and by **adjusting temperature settings** — lowering them in the wintertime, and increasing them during the hot season. However, these energy saving measures must be fine-tuned, or else they can cause occupant discomfort — or worse, illness, when the air is too contaminated.

Sick Building Syndrome and Building Related Illnesses

The World Health Organization estimates that 30% of the buildings in the United States experience indoor air quality problems. There are two classes of health problems that can result from contaminated air in buildings. The first are symptoms which go away when the occupant leaves the building, such eye, nose, and throat irritation, headaches, dry cough, dry or itchy skin, dizziness, nausea, difficulty in concentrating, or fatigue. These symptoms are associated with "**sick building syndrome**." They can make people really miserable, and have an impact on productivity. Even more serious though are "**building related illnesses**," which do not disappear when the occupant leaves the building. These include sinusitis, bronchitis, asthma, humidifier fever, dermatitis, Legionnaire's Disease, and Pontiac Fever.

Reducing fresh air ventilation
without compromising air quality

In some situations, air contaminants generated **outdoors** may be brought into the building. Indoor air quality is greatly impacted by the air quality outside of the buildings — for example a building in heart of Los Angeles compared one located on a high plateau such as Alberquerque in New Mexico. Another consideration is the location of the air intakes, which should be as far as possible from known sources of pollution such as parking lots, the air exhausts from the building, drift from cooling towers, stagnant water or areas that have bird droppings. Screens and filters help to bar the entry of external particles into the air stream entering the building.

Some sources of pollution occur **within** the building, from activities such as cooking, and off-gas emissions from building materials, furnishings, office equipment and cleaning products.

To control air pollution that is generated from inside a building, it must be ventilated with adequate amounts of outdoor air. However, we can reduce the amount of fresh air that is needed by controlling pollutant sources. In fact, controlling pollutants at their source is the most effective way to combat indoor air problems.

Controlling pollutants

One way to clean the air inside a building is to continuously ventilate it with fresh air. That uses a lot of energy. Another way is to scrub the air using one or more of several technologies.

The most common is **filtration**. Filtration traps airborne particles by size. The effectiveness of a filter is given using a **Minimum Efficiency Reporting Value**, or **MERV** rating. The higher the MERV rating is, the more effective the filter. ASHRAE recommends MERV 8 for commercial buildings. LEED requires MERV 13. Some specialized areas may install filters as high as MERV 14. The following table shows the range of MERV ratings.

MERV	Min. Particle Size	Typical Controlled Contaminant	Typical Application
1-4	> 10.0 µm	Pollen, Dust mites, Cockroach debris, Sanding dust, Spray paint dust, Textile fibers, Carpet fibers	Residential window AC units
5-8	3.0-10.0 µm	Mold, Spores, Dust mite debris, Cat and dog dander, Hair spray, Fabric protector, Dusting aids, Pudding mix	Better Residential, General Commercial, Industrial workspaces
9-12	1.0-3.0 µm	Legionella, Humidifier dust, Lead dust, Milled flour, Auto emission particulates, Nebulizer droplets	Superior Residential, Better Commercial, Hospital Laboratories
13-16	0.3-1.0 µm	Bacteria, Droplet nuclei (sneeze), Cooking oil, Most smoke and insecticide dust, Most face powder, Most paint pigments	Hospital & General surgery
17-20	< 0.3 µm	Virus, Carbon dust, Sea salt, Smoke	Electronics & Pharmaceutical manufacturing cleanroom

Table 4 — MERV ratings for filters

Filters rated at MERV 14 or greater can remove airborne particles of between 0.3 to 1.0 micrometers with a capture rate of at least 75% for particles.

Most buildings can achieve adequate filtration using filters with a high MERV rating. For specialized areas such as clean rooms there are more rigorous technologies. For example, **HEPA filters** can remove more than 99.97% of particles 0.3-micrometer or larger. HEPA filters are not often found in offices because they are more costly than conventional filters, need more energy to overcome the filter resistance and may need frequent changing. To increase the life of HEPA filters, it is best to first pass the air through a conventional filter (pre-filter) to remove coarser impurities, so that the HEPA filter doesn't quickly become clogged, thereby requiring less frequent replacing.

Although the capture rate of a MERV filter is lower than that of a HEPA filter, a high-grade MERV filter can be just as effective as a HEPA machine. That's because a central air system with a conventional filter can move a significantly greater volume of air in the same period of time than a HEPA machine. The main problem with many filters though, is that they lack an airtight seal, so air can pass around them. This problem is worse for the higher-efficiency MERV filters because they are denser and increase air resistance.

Activated carbon is another technology that is usually reserved for specialized areas. Activated carbon is a porous material that can change volatile contaminants from a gaseous phase to a solid phase and adsorb them. The VOCs accumulate (adsorb) on the surface forming a thin film, often only one molecule thick. However, activated carbon does not remove larger particles. For this reason, activated carbon is normally used in conjunction with other filter technology, especially with HEPA.

Ultraviolet germicidal irradiation (UVGI) can be used to sterilize air that passes UV lamps via forced air. The system can be a freestanding unit with a fan to force air past the UV, or it can be integrated into an existing forced air system. The UV lamps should be placed next to a good filtration system to remove the dead micro-organisms.

Provide local exhaust for specialized activities

Some specialized activities need their own local exhaust and should be kept under negative pressure. For example, fumes from **garages** should be exhausted directly before they have a chance to enter the building. Fumes and odors from activities such as **cooking** or **labs** should also be exhausted by providing fume hoods. **Chemicals** and **cleaning products** should be kept in separately ventilated storage.

VOCs — avoid them or remove them

Some **building materials and finishes** inside the building emit unhealthy volatile organic compounds (VOCs). What are VOCs? Simply put, VOCs are chemicals containing carbon that that are emitted as gases from some solids or liquids. A sliced onion, human sweat, or fresh cookies emit VOCs but these are not harmful to human health, compared to the VOCs from, say, a new vinyl shower curtain, a burning cigarette or oven cleaner. There are electronic devices that can detect VOC ppm concentrations.

Benzene, methylene chloride, hexane, toluene, trichloroethane, styrene, heptane, and perchloroethylene are VOCs that are known to make people sick. Products containing these chemicals, which should be avoided altogether include some carpets, paints, adhesives and sealants, and manufactured wood products containing certain glues, finishes, and waxes. Enormous progress has been made to reduce the amount of VOCs in these products, with certificates such as *Green Seal*, and the Carpet and Rug Institute's (CRI) *Green Label Plus* certification program for carpets and under-carpet adhesives.

In addition to several materials used in construction and interior design, many **cleaning products** also contain VOCs in ingredients such as quaternary ammonium compounds, phthalates or butyl. Any strong artificial fragrances or reactions that produce foam fizz, bubble are indications that VOCs are likely being released, which are not good to breathe.

So how do we remove VOCs from the air in buildings? The best solution of course is to completely **avoid** products that contain VOCs. However, we don't live in a perfect world, and most buildings contain products that emit VOCs. These are usually **removed** through ventilation, which as we know, is an energy-intensive approach.

The good news is that relatively inexpensive chemical ways are being developed to remove VOCs and ozone.[102] For example, Berkeley Lab Technologies is working on a manganese oxide (MnOx) compound, which, when applied to a regular filter in the existing HVAC, catalyzes (i.e. facilitates) the oxidation of several VOCs to carbon dioxide and water. The MnOx catalyst on the regular filter, can be used in conjunction with activated carbon fiber (ACF) filters to remove additional VOCs from gas streams. So the way it works is that the regular filter removes particles, the catalyst removes aldehydes and other specific VOCs, and the activated carbon filter adsorbs remaining VOCs and ozone. This can remove formaldehyde and acetaldehyde in indoor air by 80%, using just a fraction (15-20%) of the energy that would otherwise be needed to remove the VOCs through ventilation.

Mold

· · · · ·

One nasty contaminant found in many buildings is mold, which can trigger allergic reactions, asthma attacks or other lung ailments. Molds grow in areas that have become damp, for example from leaking pipes, condensation, excessive humidity in the air, or rain entering into the building fabric. The damp and mold may be apparent or not — for example, when it occurs in the building foundation or in wet insulation behind a ceiling or wall.

Mold can be mitigated by ensuring that your landlord and facility manager regularly inspect the building and HVAC for evidence of dampness; take prompt steps to identify and correct any sources of dampness; and dry out affected areas. Where mold is found it should be cleaned, wearing protective gear. Carpets or drywall that shows signs of mold should be carefully removed.

Avoid spreading pollutants from renovation projects
· ·

Renovations generate dust, fumes and odors not to mention high concentrations of VOCs found in some products such as particle board, and some paints and carpets. Where the rest of the building is being occupied during renovations, it is important to seal off the ventilation supply and return ducts in the construction area. Also seal doors and other openings between the construction area and occupied areas with an air-tight barrier, sealed on both sides. Activities which may generate excessive dust, noise or odors should be scheduled for when the building is not being occupied. Keep the construction area as clean as possible, with frequent vacuuming and rather than dry sweeping. Finally, allow sufficient time for drying and off-gassing of paints, carpets and other furnishings before occupying the space.

Green clean
· · · · · · · · · · ·

Most reputable cleaning companies offer "green cleaning." In addition to selecting low VOC cleaners, their equipment and procedures result in deep cleaning, which benefits the air that occupants breathe. For example, vacuum cleaners with HEPA filtration remove dirt and allergens as small as .3 microns. Hot water extraction equipment makes it possible to deep-clean carpets and remove enough moisture such that carpets can dry in less than 24 hours, thereby avoiding mold. Automated scrubbing machines with variable-speed pumps reduce the amount of cleaning fluids needed, as do microfiber cloths and mops. These have polyester/nylon fibers that retain a positive charge, which attracts dust (which is negatively charged). The micro-fibers, which are approximately 1/16 the thickness of a human hair, have split edges that can penetrate the microscopic surface pores of most flooring materials, trapping microbes, dust, and debris more effectively than traditional products.

How much ventilation is enough?

There are two general criteria for acceptable air, as defined by ASHRAE. First, the air contains no known contaminants at harmful concentrations. Secondly, 80% of occupants do not express dissatisfaction.

The achieve this ASHRAE recommends either a minimum ventilation rate for a specific type of space OR indoor air quality procedures to control known contaminants to some specified acceptable levels.

In North America, the rule of thumb for ventilation rate is 10 L/sec per person of clean air. One way to determine whether there is enough ventilation is to do carbon dioxide measurements. Carbon dioxide, which is breathed out by occupants is a proxy measurement that indicates how stale the air is. Outdoor air contains 400 ppm of CO_2. Indoor CO_2 should not exceed 1,000 ppm at any of the workstations. A simple desk carbon dioxide monitor, the size of an alarm clock can be had for under $200.

During the night or weekend, when the building is empty, it's common practice to cut back on ventilation as an energy-saving measure. This can result in a build-up of VOC contaminants, which should be flushed just before occupants arrive in the morning, using enhanced ventilation. Depending on how long the ventilation has been reduced (longer on weekends than night weeks), the building may require 2 air changes or more. This could take an hour or more of enhanced ventilation, before reducing the ventilation back down to regular occupancy cycle.

Carbon dioxide, which is breathed out by occupants is a proxy measurement that indicates how stale the air is.

Is underfloor ventilation better?

Underfloor ventilation, which is less common in North America than Europe, has many advantages, provided it is carefully designed, installed and maintained. Most office buildings deliver air through metal duct-work to terminal units located in the ceiling, which supply the required amount of conditioned air to a room in response to thermostats. The air is then returned to the mechanical room through the space above the ceiling, called the return plenum.

This is not terribly efficient because some of the air inevitably is short cycled — going directly from supply to return, without actually circulating in the room. This shortcoming can be avoided with under-floor air distribution, in which the air enters the room from the floor and is removed via the ceiling.

In this arrangement, which is similar to the raised floor cooling systems found in some data centers, the conditioned air is supplied through a raised floor supply plenum, which is about 10-18 inches deep and can also house the power and data cabling. (note: the plenum in a data center can be up to 3 feet deep). The air enters the room from vents in the floor and leaves through a ceiling return plenum or through the sidewall of the core.

The reason that under-floor air distribution is more effective than conventional overhead cooling is because all the air must go through the space to the return in the ceiling or sidewall. Thus there is no chance of short cycling of the supply air. Underfloor distribution also uses less energy. Unlike ceiling diffusers that need pressure to move the air down to the occupants, underfloor distribution has no need to push air into the room to reach the occupied zone but instead uses natural convection. The warm, contaminated air forms a stratified region above the occupied zone, which is exhausted out the ceiling plenum along with the heat from lighting.

Under-floor air distribution also allows highly localized controls, with the possibility of installing adjustable vents at each work station. It also allows for higher ceilings due to the absence of supply air ductwork.

A raised floor is effective provided it is properly zoned, either by segmenting the plenum under the floor or controlling the vents in the floor tiles. Gaps between raised floor tiles, which allow air to leak can result in complaints about cold feet-typically from those who wear open toed shoes. An infrared camera makes it possible to locate leaks and seal the gaps. Also it's important to manage discharge temperatures, air flow rates, and air flow direction to make sure that people will be comfortable around the head as well as at ankle level.

It should be noted that underfloor systems are best installed in new buildings and that they do require thoughtful design, careful implementation by the construction team, and commissioning to assure success. Improper application or poor installation of an underfloor plenum can result in significant comfort complaints as well as concerns about excess humidity, which have implications for mold. While robotic cleaning systems exist to clean the underfloor plenum, what is most important is to ensure that there has been a thorough cleaning for dust and debris during construction and before occupancy. While a cleaning robot would theoretically be good, this is not always practical where there is a lot of cabling.

Temperature

Have you noticed how hard it is to concentrate if you are too hot or too cold? All you can think of is how uncomfortable you are. It's not surprising that being too hot or too cold can seriously affect employee accuracy, efficiency, and output.

Occupant surveys offer a means to systematically measure this performance, and also to provide diagnostic information for building designers and operators. A University of California study reviewed over 34,000 survey responses to air quality and thermal comfort questions in 215 buildings in US, Canada, and Finland.[103] Results showed that 80% or more of occupants were dissatisfied with their thermal comfort in 89% of the buildings surveyed. This would indicate that most buildings appear to be falling far short.

Naturally, everyone has a different internal thermostat, so the ideal working temperature varies by person. The best we can hope to accomplish is a temperature range that is reasonable for most workers.

Research from the Lawrence Berkeley Laboratory indicates that the optimal temperature range for maximum productivity is between 68 and 74 degree (Fahrenheit), so a reasonable target would be 70-72 degrees.[104] It may be possible to temper this a bit in winter months, when workers could adjust to slightly cooler temperatures with an added layer of clothing, like a sweater.

Unfortunately, this range still will not work for everyone and so people often make their own temperature control adjustments, using fans or space heaters, counter-acting much of the energy efficiency gains from changing the set-points in the first place. We also have the issue of thermostat adjustments by people in the workplace. If area thermostats are accessible, it is inevitable that some people will turn them up and within a short period, someone else will turn them down. Or vice versa. All these personal strategies for controlling temperature really underscore its importance. People will go to great lengths to find their ideal, personal temperature.

To avoid these thermostat wars, we strongly recommend that thermostats not be accessible for adjustment by any employees. It simply does not work as an effective strategy for making people comfortable and more productive.

Fortunately, applications are being developed which individual occupants can use to report on their cellphones whether they are too hot, too cold or feeling just right. These signals are sent to the BAS, which sets a temperature that will provide optimum satisfaction for the population. Thus buildings can "negotiate" energy saving measures with their occupants, factoring in the perceptions of all. An assistant professor at the University of Southern California, Becerik-Gerber and colleagues in social psychology and computer science have developed such a smart phone application. To make up for increased heating or cooling, the application also asks those users demanding more energy-intensive conditions if they'd be willing to compromise a bit, and it tells them what the resulting energy savings would be. "If people understand the consequences, they're more tolerant," says Becerik-Gerber. The optimized settings are then put in place and monitored automatically.

Coordinating the preferences of hundreds of occupants is especially acute in today's popular open-plan offices where people with very different preferences often share space. But Becerik-Gerber's simulations indicate that her algorithms can satisfy some 70 percent of occupants—while reducing overall energy consumption by more than 30 percent.[105]

Optimizing thermal comfort and energy savings
· ·

As with ventilation, temperature has energy implications. And as with ventilation, it **is** possible to reduce the energy needed without negatively affecting thermal comfort. Some of these measures are controlled by the landlord, and a few can be managed in the leased space. Ensuring that windows are properly sealed, adding window film to reduce solar heat gain, installing blinds to keep out the summer heat and retain heat in winter, and implementing temperature setback are discussed in *Chapter 7— Energy for Heating, Cooling and Ventilation.*

Temperature and ventilation provisions in a green lease
· ·

Landlord and tenant should agree on reasonable temperatures and ventilation to ensure occupant comfort at the same time as considering energy. For example, the lease could state that the occupied temperature of the building should not be less than x° in the summer or greater than x° in the winter; and that unoccupied temperature of the building should not be less than x° in the summer or greater than xo in the winter." Suggested temperatures that contribute to efficient building operation are:

- Summer occupied: 72°F at 60% relative humidity
- Winter occupied: 70°F
- Summer unoccupied: 82°F
- Winter unoccupied: 60°F

Similarly, there could be a clause that ventilation should meet the most recent ASHRAE or any supported standard for indoor air quality, for example Standard 62.1 — 2007 *Ventilation for Acceptable Indoor Air Quality.* Alternatively, the clause could require compliance through demand-controlled ventilation, which provides fresh air only when it is needed—based on occupancy, CO_2 levels or other factors. Over-ventilation is widely considered one of the reasons that some green-certified buildings have not performed as well as expected with respect to energy use.

There should also be a lease provision that the landlord should perform Existing Building **Commissioning** (EB-Cx) or that there should be a program of ongoing "continual" or "continuous" commissioning. Existing building commissioning ensures that the building is running as efficiently as possible while meeting current tenant needs. "Continual commissioning" refers to the process of collecting data and analyzing it manually at certain intervals—typically monthly. "Continuous commissioning" refers to uninterrupted monitoring of system performance data via a building automation system (BAS) and/or stand-alone data-loggers, which are programmed to continuously evaluate the data collected and generate an output message if the measured parameters fall outside of their programmed ranges.

Ideally, Existing Building Commissioning should cover the whole building — tenant premises and base building together — so that tenant systems may be calibrated to function properly with Base Building systems. However, it may be necessary to delineate the "Base Building," as distinct from the "Tenant Premises." For example: the base building could be defined as the structure and shell of the building, the common, public, service and utility portions of the building and each building system up to the point at which it connects to any facility controlled by any tenant. In that case, the lease could contain a requirement that the tenant has a reciprocal obligation to commission its space or conduct a basic energy and operational audit of lighting, plug loads, data centers and supplemental HVAC at regular intervals.

The lease should also indicate that within a stated timeframe, recommendations of the Existing Building Commissioning Study or Energy Management Plans should be implemented that do not exceed an agreed dollar value cumulatively and do not violate the terms of any other existing lease obligations.

Conclusion

· · · · · · · · · ·

Whatever temperature or ventilation strategy a workplace follows, working with the landlord and making employees part of the effort will make it even more effective. Involve employees in the discussion of what you are trying to achieve in terms or their comfort and energy control. Communicate the range of temperature/ ventilation rates you are trying to achieve and ask for cooperation to minimize the use of space heaters or fans, which both negate the energy savings and alter the temperature levels for surrounding employees.

CHAPTER 19

Health,
Work-Life Balance
& Productivity

Happiness is not a matter of intensity but of balance, order,

rhythm and harmony.

—Thomas Merton

Thanks (or no thanks) to the proliferation of communications technologies, employees are increasingly tethered to their work, around the clock. Many people even sleep with their cell phones practically on the pillow. Not surprisingly, the boundary between work life and personal time is becoming blurred.

Yet as more employees bring their work home, the opposite is also happening. Organizations are integrating many aspects of "home" into the workplace. Haven't we all marveled at the lengths some companies will go to provide creature comforts and a feeling of family and community in the workplace, with their cafes, catered meals and snacks, bean bags, napping rooms, climbing walls and ping pong tables, gyms, shuttle services and haircuts! (And as a side note, is it not ironic that the companies that create the gadgets that enable us to work **away from the office** are among those that are offering the most attractive, exciting, playful and homey environments to entice their employees to spend as many of their working hours **at the office**!) Is all of this "pampering" being done out of kindness of heart, or does it have something to do with achieving a higher level of productivity?

In previous chapters we talked about basic health and comfort requirements in the workplace, failing which, employees will be physically miserable or even ill — and consequently, less productive. These include being neither too hot nor too cold, having good quality air, daylight, a view to the outdoors and comfortable lighting, and an environment that's free of acoustic distractions.

In this chapter, we take another look at these, and also address an additional dimension of employee wellbeing that characterizes "the workplace of the future." It is the recognition that employees have **"non-work" needs**, which, if they are not met, can affect their ability to be focused and engaged — resulting in less than optimal productivity. Meeting these non-work needs is often thought of simply as achieving "work/life balance," but what does this mean, exactly?

In today's world, work/life balance is largely a question of time management — in other words, being able to fit everything into just 24 hours: not just work, but also commuting, eating, sleep, exercise, errands, family obligations, community and social involvement — and if possible, some down time. The workplace of the future also recognizes that **poor health** due to a hectic pace and sedentary life style, combined with **stress**, whether it is work-related or due to there not being sufficient hours in the day, are major factors that reduce productivity. Where employees suffer from lack of work/life balance, poor health or stress, their work output will be affected.

Where employees suffer from lack of work/life balance, poor health or stress, their work output will be affected.

Workplace of the future addresses
non-work needs, health and stress management
· ·

Whether employees work in a futuristic office or a traditional one, studies show that most people are working longer hours than ever before — and are feeling more stressed. And while work appears to be dominating people's lives more than ever, some things have not changed: First, there are still only 24 hours in the day. And secondly, no matter how committed an employee is, everyone needs to "recharge", and everyone has preoccupations and a busy life outside of work, which often includes family responsibilities.

These challenges can be addressed by choosing a good office location as well as thoughtful workplace design and HR policies related to the work environment. This not only enhances productivity but differentiates an organization, thereby enhancing its ability to attract and retain employees.

"Wellness" — the new buzzword
· ·

First we had "Sustainability" in the workplace. Next came "Productivity." Now we have a new buzzword: "Wellness." Having employees physically feel "well" within the formal workplace is the foundation of the wellness concept. In fact, there is now a "wellness" certification, much like a LEED certification, which is awarded by the Well Building Institute, a subsidiary of Delos Inc. Many of the WELL™ criteria go beyond the standard best practices found in most green and healthy offices. An executive summary of the criteria can be found at **http://nowinteractive.net/delos-downloads/WBS-Executive%20Summary-Apr2014.pdf**.[106]

Clean Air
· · · · · · · · ·

Research indicates that the air we breathe in the workplace affects our well-being and our ability to function effectively.[107] Sick Building Syndrome

(SBS) occurs when air quality severely impacts the health and well-being of people in a building. Short of something as severe as SBS are concerns about odors, particulate matter and CO_2 in the air. The answers include sufficient air circulation, demand ventilation that is based on CO_2 monitoring, and particulate filters as well as controlling pollution at source by minimizing of chemicals in the air from furniture, carpeting, cleaning products or other activities, like copy machines as well any construction and renovation activities. Some newer buildings offer underfloor ventilation, which helps to ensure a good air circulation.

Taking this to the next level, the WELL™ criteria ensure that occupants are breathing absolutely pure air by requiring a high level of filtration, carbon filters to adsorb VOCs, HEPA filtration to remove microbes, and ultraviolet sanitation to sterilize the air. There is also continual air quality measurement and feedback to the user. Some WELL™-certified buildings provide aromatherapy.

Thermal Comfort
. . . .

When people are too hot or too cold, this can become a personal distraction that erodes productivity and which can escalate as a focal point for complaints. Facility Managers may sometimes find that people complain even when the temperatures are within generally acceptable norms. However, these concerns, if they are not addressed, can give the impression that the employer is unresponsive to employee concerns. Whether they are justified or not, unless these complaints are properly dealt with, they can spread and fester into a real HR problem.

One way to address thermal comfort issues is to make sure that thermostats are calibrated and check that employees are not blocking vents with furniture, papers, boxes and books. Some newer buildings have underfloor ventilation which offers a higher degree of personal control. It is also important to communicate to employees what the temperature set points are. Employees should be encouraged to leave a sweater at work.

Also people are often cold when they do not move around enough. Encouraging some form of physical activity by providing an exercise room and a fitness program or yoga class with an instructor, results in employees who are healthier, more mentally alert — and warmer.

Advances in technology are making it possible to sharing information about air temperature and air quality through display screens in the workplace. These read-out screens can display many other types of information including energy consumption, to make employees participants in the process of making the space greener and more productive.

Acoustic control

As discussed in Chapter 16 on acoustic comfort, an employee-centric workplace recognizes the need to provide acoustic accommodation for different types of activities: collaboration, concentration and connection. This can be achieved with "quiet zones" or "worker pods" for focused activities that require concentration, as well as acoustically separated areas with sound-absorbing materials, where small groups or large can engage in collaborative work, have meetings, or connect with their colleagues without causing noise distractions around them. Some employees in open offices like to wear sound cancelling ear phones. Another alternative is sound masking.

Food and beverage

The old concept of a single cafeteria or vending room in a corner of the workplace has been displaced with inviting lounge areas, featuring bulk drinking water, multiple snack and drink options and fancy coffee/cappuccino makers for any employee that needs a caffeine fix. Organizations are also finding that they can use the food and beverage areas to reinforce healthy eating habits. Some even provide healthy snacks. For example, Google doesn't just want employees to be happy. When Google discovered that its free food practices were leading to weight gain, it made changes to encourage smaller and healthier food choices. Plate sizes were reduced and healthier eating alternatives were made more accessible than less healthy options.

Beyond addressing the basic needs of hunger and thirst, cafes and dining areas are natural congregation points, promoting informal collaboration and social interactions.

The WELL™ criteria take this to a higher level, by requiring the further treatment of drinking water to remove any potential impurities such as sediments, heavy metals, residual chlorine, prescription medications and other organic contaminants. There are also criteria for placing edible herb plants throughout the office (organic of course) as well as readily accessible fresh phytomedicinals, and designing a kitchen with ergonomically designed kitchen/pantry spaces that encourage optimal nutrition intake with herbariums and anti-microbial surface protection.

Cleanliness
· · · · · · · · · · ·

Certain design features and a rigorous cleaning protocol can impact productivity by reducing the chances that employees will get ill due to something in the workplace. Some questions to consider … Are surfaces in food areas/restrooms easy to clean? Are washrooms designed for easy maintenance, with wall-hung toilets, ceiling-hung partitions, non-porous (e.g. ceramic) floors, walls and backsplashes? Are these areas cleaned and disinfected frequently — at least during the night cleaning program? Do washrooms have "touch-free" features to minimize touching, including a maze entrance (no doors). Are there signs encouraging proper hand washing? Are there hand-sanitizers throughout the workplace? Is there a program to disinfect FTOs (frequently touched objects)? Are employees encouraged to disinfect desktop electronics? Do cleaning procedures use cleaners with low VOCs and microfiber cleaning implements? Are first aid supplies readily-accessible? Are there spill clean-up kits?

Workplace design and practices to control the spread of infectious diseases in the workplace not only help stem illnesses, but their very presence sends a message to employees that the organization cares about their well-being.

Visual comfort
· · · · · · · · · · · ·

Chapter 17 discussed lighting strategies that include abundant daylighting, proper lighting levels (not too high), views and visual resting spots, and avoiding glare and fluorescent light flicker. Recently, another aspect of lighting in the workplace that is getting increasing attention is circadian lighting rhythms. It almost sounds a little mystical, but research indicates that our inner clocks are driven to some extent by lighting intensity and color during the day. Our physiological response to these external cues determines to some degree, our level of alertness, fatigue, digestion and the production of certain hormones.

The WELL™ criteria address circadian rhythms by requiring lighting levels in the workplace to change during the day to mimic the natural environment, including dawn; gradually increasing lighting intensity during the day, and providing blackout blinds for night time. There is also a requirement providing ultraviolet light to allow the body to generate Vitamin D.

There is great interest by the science community, as well as an increase in sophisticated technologies to isolate and measure health-related variables and their effect on workplace productivity. This data may reveal how progressive features such as circadian lighting, advanced air purification and phyto-medicinals in the workplace affect productivity, and any measurable advantage there may be compared to a mainstream, well-designed, healthy, productive and attractive workplace.

Exercise
· · · · · · · ·

Giving employees a place to stretch or exercise during the day is becoming common in the modern workplace. Why? Because it introduces a number of important productivity-enhancing opportunities. First, exercise helps employees maintain their health. Even a small regime every day can have an impact. Second, it breaks monotony by providing a completely different activity than regular work. Third, it is a good way to address fatigue by getting people active. Finally, providing a workout area, even if it is just a room with exercise mats, tells employees that the employer wants them to be well.

Some employers take this farther with locker rooms, exercise equipment, subsidized gym memberships and fitness programs.

One company portrays healthy living in graphically interesting ways, for example, attractive infographics depicting calories burned on the way up the stairs, and compared to the number of calories in an apple or a bag of chips. Placement is crucial — on the stairwell walls, in the break room or inside a quiet room. These dynamic messages convey a culture of education and consistently reinforce the concept of health.

WELL™ criteria also include the requirement to provide attractive stairs in a building to encourage walking instead of using an elevator, access to hydrotherapy facilities and spas for people recovering from injuries or with muscle and joint pain, and specific fitness programs with feedback for each individual.

Rest
· · · · ·

OK, this is controversial and may even seem counter-intuitive. People in the workplace can actually benefit from a rest area or, heaven forbid, a place to take a short nap? Research indicates that at certain times of the day, such as after lunch, people are fatigued. Rather than try to fight through it at sub-optimal performance levels, a 10-15 minutes of rest or sleep would enhance productivity well beyond that small time investment.

Commuting
· · · · · · · · · ·

While organizations do not traditionally view employee commuting as a component of the workplace, they should. In fact, one of the most important satisfaction aspects of workplace cited by employees is their commute.

The initial selection of an office or workplace location should be carefully analyzed in terms of commuting convenience for the existing or projected workforce. Is it close to public transportation? Can people walk easily or ride bicycles?

While organizations cannot move buildings to new locations for better commuting, there are measures that can be taken to better accommodate employees who must report for work at the office. Are there facilities to park bicycles, and showering facilities? Does the building offer a shuttle to nearby transportation points? Staggered hours to avoid rush periods? Transportation discounts?

Some organizations have found that a robust, well-supported carpooling program can have a significant impact on the culture of the organization, speaking to green values as well as employee pocket-books. For employees, saving money is not the only perk. *Travel Smart*, an organization in Vancouver that offers tips and tools on alternative forms of commuting, points out that carpooling also makes for a less stressful commute, noting on its website, "For example, if your car needs to go to the shop, you can always ask on your carpooling buddy to drive that week. It's also a great way to get to know somebody (and their taste in music) outside of the work environment. And when it's not your turn to drive, you can use that extra time in the morning to eat breakfast, prepare for your 9 a.m. meeting, or get some shut eye. Perhaps the greatest benefit to carpooling is driving in the high occupancy vehicle (HOV) lane during rush hour traffic. And if it makes you feel safer, most drivers have a tendency to drive with more caution when there is a passenger in their vehicle."

Car-pooling can also be an effective mechanism to generate informal cohesive networks, and bridge silos by offering an opportunity for social contact among employees who may work in completely different parts of the organization. When employees spend an hour a day together driving to and from work, informal conversations can spawn relationships and give rise to some interesting cross pollination of ideas. Employers can incentivize car-pooling by providing a data-base for employees to make car-pooling arrangements as well as perks such as preferential parking.

Local Amenities

. . . .

Nearby amenities such as such as banks, ATMs, cleaners, groceries, a drug store, restaurants, day care facilities and so on, can enhance the work-life balance of employees by making it more convenient to run errands.

How does this contribute to productivity? First of all, by allowing people to fit necessary personal activities into their workday with less scheduling difficulties, thereby avoiding having to take time off work to be able to deal with personal errands; and secondly, because a big part of the productivity equation is to free the mind from these kinds of preoccupations.

More organizations are realizing the importance of local amenities when choosing a new location for their office. *Walk Score*® is an easy, web-based tool to assess any neighborhood in the world in terms of how "walkable" it is.[108] Just enter an address, and it will generate a "walk score" using a 100-point scale, which is calculated based on the walking distance to various categories of amenities. *Walk Score*® rates an address as per the following categories:

Walkscore		
90-100	Walker's Paradise	Daily errands do not require a car
70-89	Very Walkable	Most errands can be accompllised on foot
50-69	Somewhat Walkable	Some errands can be accomplished on foot
25-49	Car Dependent	Most errands require a car
0-24	Car Dependent	Almost all errands require a car

Table 5

The *Walk Score*® website also allows locations to be scored, specifically, for either transit or biking convenience.

Obviously, an existing workplace has little control over the amenities in the neighborhood. However, some organizations review the amenities that are available locally, and then augment them as needed with on-site amenities such as vending machines, ATMS, or company-sponsored on-site services — for example, enabling employees to pick up convenience items, drop off their dry cleaning or dirty laundry and pick it up when it is clean without leaving the workplace. Some workplaces even offer employee concierge services.

All of this indicates a trend whereby organizations understand that making the lives of workers better also makes it easier for them to concentrate, be more productive — and feel appreciated.

Take a cue from call centers

Call centers have become laboratories for measuring workplace productivity. While they don't reflect the complicated dimensions involved in the infinite workplace roles, they offer some basic, measurable standards such as number of calls, customer satisfaction levels, and so forth. Because call center operations require speed, concentration, and accuracy, this makes it easy to apply and study specific workplace variables, apply rigorous controls and produce measurable results that are scientifically and statistically valid. For this reason, call centers are often a focal point for research into the ideas we are discussing. With attrition rates as high as 75% and training costs for new employees in the order of $6,000, it is no wonder that organizations with call centers are working diligently to keep workers healthy, comfortable, happy — and productive.

In an article called *How to Build a Better Call Center*,[109] Jeff Beer discusses how some companies are doing it. Zappos, the on-line shoe retailer, uses perks such as free lunches and a nap room to create a worker-friendly environment for its call center employees. "When Mullen, the company's advertising agency, went looking for ideas back in 2010, it found the answer in Zappos's call center," says Beer. The *Happy People Making People Happy* campaign featured audio from actual customer calls." Director of Customer Loyalty, Rob Siefker says, "It's a very fun environment. I don't think you hear that word associated with [call] centers very often."

In another case study, Rogers Communications worked with Scienta Health to analyze the workplace practices and habits of its call center operators. The results showed that many suffered from headaches, obesity and other preventable problems. "Because of the unrelenting pressure to process more calls, employees were cutting down on water consumption (and hence, bathroom breaks), and stress and lack of time were leading to unhealthy food choices," notes Beer. As a result, the company launched an initiative with Scienta that offered advice, healthy food and online health-monitoring tools like pedometers, as well as team health challenges to help encourage a change. After a year, senior vice-president Paul Nielsen noted that this had a huge effect on employee health, job satisfaction and performance. "Our sales performance has gone up incredibly, and while that's due to a number of factors, this certainly was a major contributor," he says. The program is now being considered for all of Rogers' 6,000 customer-service employees."

With attrition rates as high as 75% and training costs for new employees in the order of $6,000, it is no wonder that organizations with call centers are working diligently to keep workers healthy, comfortable, happy — and productive.

Finding fun and community at work

The need for people to feel connected runs deep. Yet our busy lives often make it difficult to find the time to make connections in our own home-based communities. Many organizations try to bring community into the workplace. Salary and dental benefits are great, but employees also need a workplace that they look forward to each morning.

Consider Google's workplace philosophy to "create the happiest, most productive workplace in the world." According to Google spokesperson, Jordan Newman, Google uses workplace design to support this concept and continuously communicate the company's commitment to employees. Just take a peek at the company's website, and you will see that Google fills the workplace with fun visual experiences, coffee areas, food bars and congregations zones. Even pets are allowed. And in addition to exercise equipment, there are massage rooms as well as free yoga and Pilates classes, and "nap pods" that employees can use at any time. On its headquarters campus, Google makes 1,000 bikes available for employee use.[110] Google uses the workplace to foster employee loyalty, which increases retention and saves millions in hiring and training costs.

The following are some examples of other companies that have shifted the paradigm towards better treatment of their human capital.[111] These companies are thriving, which indicates that their way of operating not only works, but works well.

- *Valve Software*, creator of a gaming platform, has made Thursdays "company lunch days," where a caterer brings in food and everyone gets together and chats in the enormous lunch room. The company also offers "free massage Fridays," and once a year, an all-expenses paid vacation for all employees, which starts with a chartered airplane and ends at an exotic location with a beach and a swimming pool. Even when employees feel the need to hide out in the bathroom, songs by Scorpion, Poison, and Queen are known to blast through the bathroom speakers and get employees pumped to return to work. Who would not be motivated after singing "We Are the Champions" while washing their hands!?!
- Event production company, *Red Frog Events* has a bar with kegs and a flat screen that plays sports. After five years of working for the company, employees (plus one guest) can choose to travel to Africa, Asia, Europe or South America for an all-inclusive four-week sabbatical trip. Fridays are themed "Whiskey Fridays!"
- *Dropbox* offers employees needing a work break, use of a full music studio and equipment, game rooms with Starcraft, Dance Dance Revolution, ping pong, and more. Each and every day at work, employees get free breakfast, free lunch, and free dinner and tons of free snacks and drinks.
- *Zappos* holds Weight Watchers meetings on site and has a reimbursement program. There is also an on-site fitness center that is open 24/7.

Whether these measures are appropriate for all organizations may be debated. However, while all of this may just sound like good fun or excess, the truth is that many companies, such as those in above example, are devoting the same level of intellectual firepower that they use in their business operations to implement practices that optimize and drive human performance in the workplace.

Conclusion — how much is enough?

How much is enough, and at what point do these employee wellness features and workplace amenities constitute over-coddling of employees? Consider this. For most organizations, people are the most expensive aspect of their operations. Companies spend incredible amounts of money to maintain equipment and upgrade systems, but often fail to invest in the most important and costly resource, their people. As more organizations realize this and focus on the wellness of their employees, those that don't will find themselves at competitive disadvantage, experiencing difficulty in attracting the best workers in the marketplace, and risking loss of productivity as a result of employee dissatisfaction.

Think about some of the examples of high productivity offices and then look around your workplace. What does it say about your organization? Be honest. Does it show that you value employees and want them to be healthy and happy? Or, is it simply designed to give people a place to do their jobs — without much thought about how those jobs are accomplished or who those people are?

CHAPTER 20

Is Your Portfolio Green & Productive?

The heart of science is measurement.

— Erik Brynjolfsson, Professor MIT Sloan School of Management

While telecommuting continues to grow in North America, *The State of Telework in the U.S.* reports US Census statistics that indicate that we are still a long way from completely virtual organizations that have no need for office space.[112] Of the total employed workforce of approximately 146 million in the USA, 50 million employees hold jobs that could be done through telework, but less than 3 million — or only approximately 2.3% of the workforce actually consider home their primary place of work. More than 75% of these employees earn $65,000 per year, putting them in the upper 80th percentile relative to all employees. Based on current trends, the number of telecommuters is expected to reach almost 5 million by 2016, a 69% increase from the current level, but still a relatively small proportion of the workforce. *The State of Telework in the U.S* reports that the biggest barrier to teleworking is management fear and mistrust.[113]

When she was criticized for reversing the popular work-from-home policy, Yahoo CEO Marissa Mayer defended her decision, saying that it was not an issue of trust. Mayer acknowledged that "people are more *productive* when they're alone," and then stressed "but they're more *collaborative* and *innovative* when they're together. Some of the best ideas come from pulling two different ideas together."

In spite of some of the disadvantages of working at the office, office life will always maintain some attraction for both employers and employees, for there is a limit to how long or how effectively people can work at home alone. This would suggest that there will always be brick and mortar offices — but they will likely consist of a hybrid of office-plus-remote-worker support.

The take-away is that because of changing occupancy requirements, corporate real estate executives will be major facilitators in terms of: 1) determining how much space is needed and location(s); as well as 2) providing a green workplace that supports employee health, comfort and wellbeing — which in turn, contribute to employee satisfaction, leading to improved productivity. Our focus in this book has been on the latter. In this chapter, we look at a way to gauge which green + productive improvements would provide the greatest value.

"People are more productive when they're alone, but they're more collaborative and innovative when they're together. Some of the best ideas come from pulling two different ideas together."

— *Melissa Mayer, CEO Yahoo*

Measuring productivity from a real estate perspective

Addressing peaks and valleys in the workflow and the varying headcounts at different times of the year will require on-demand, flexible space rather than a fixed space that risks being underutilized during non-peak times. This presents a challenge of significant complexity for facility managers, IT and HR, who must manage resources. [114] As "the workplace" now refers to workplaces both within and outside a company's portfolio of leased or owned properties, this is creating a demand for accurate and consistent information on workplace usage. John Hampton, Senior Vice President, Corporate Solutions at JLL believes that placing better, deeper, more accessible and more relevant data at the heart of corporate real estate decision-making will be the key to addressing the challenges of underutilized corporate real estate space.[115]

With growing pressure to improve productivity of leased assets, corporate real estate executives will need to track data about all processes and operations to be certain of making the best determinations based on the most accurate information. They will do this using big data and analytics for up-to-the-minute information on the workforce and workflow; space usage patterns; whether employees are present, absent, have just stepped out to grab lunch, are on paid leave or non-work related absence; the type of space and resources they need; facility maintenance; security, visitors; and even biometrics. This focus on worker enablement is what will drive real estate productivity.

Using integrated workplace management systems (IWMS), facility managers will also be expected to know at any moment in time: what spaces they are leasing, at what cost and under what terms; the number

There will always be brick and mortar offices, but they will consist of a hybrid of office-plus-remote worker support. This will present a challenge of significant complexity for facility managers, IT and HR, who must manage resources.

of rooms and percentage of space that is being used by each department and user group; whether space is being used for focused work, collaborative work, learning or social networking; and costs — per square foot and person, including costs for operations such as energy, water, waste management, cleaning and security.[116]

Measuring the effect of workplace improvements on employee productivity

As big data and analytics help to drive both people and real estate productivity, there will also be a need to consider health, comfort and wellbeing, which are critical for employee satisfaction. In a 2012 productivity study of 32,000 employees, almost half of them admitted to performing "below par" and not being as fully engaged as they could be.[117] The study found that employee engagement is affected by two things: 1) corporate culture, leadership and the relationship between employees and managers; and 2) a *physical work environment* that needs to be energizing and promote physical, emotional and social well-being.

As we have been discussing throughout this book, a vast array of scientific field studies show that correcting workplace health and comfort deficiencies can dramatically improve employee satisfaction — a pre-requisite for lasting employee engagement, and a "must-have" to avoid *loss* of productivity. Some studies claim productivity gains of 20% and more from making such improvements.

The question — particularly if you are a skeptic — is how can these contributions to workplace productivity be measured in a meaningful way in *your* office, and how are current deficiencies detracting from work output? Unlike energy reductions that translate directly to dollars saved, productive employee output from improved health, comfort and wellbeing is harder to quantify. Many of the productivity studies that we have mentioned in this book have been conducted in laboratory-like conditions, with narrowly defined variables and rigorous scientific controls — which are not practical to replicate in a real work environment. Also each study has its own definition of productivity. All of this makes it highly unlikely that one could exactly replicate the results of these academic studies in a real-office setting. Besides, if one were to add up all the claims of increased productivity from correcting deficiencies in lighting, acoustics, thermal comfort, air quality, social cohesiveness and so on — the sum total would be absurd.

Until now, a corporate real estate executive has had to rely on observation or feedback of employees who are too hot or cold, sleepy from lack of oxygen, distracted and irritated by the noise around them, headachy from glare, exhausted from a tiresome commute, feeling isolated in the workplace and depressed by their drab surroundings. Even cynics will generally acknowledge that these employees are assuredly less productive than if they were in a healthy, comfortable, dynamic and engaging environment, and that very likely *some* gains in productivity can be expected from addressing the deficiencies. The real issue is how much productivity improvement can an organization *realistically* expect from modifying the workplace environment — and can these changes also be green? JLL has developed a realistic, measured approach to gauge the potential gain, in financial terms — from improved energy efficiency and from taking corrective action where there may be a loss of employee productivity due to adverse conditions in the workplace.

Many of the productivity studies that we have mentioned in this book have been conducted in laboratory-like conditions, with narrowly defined variables and rigorous scientific controls — which are not practical to replicate in a real work environment.

"Green" and "Productive" are not synonymous

As we discussed earlier, greening an office does not necessarily lead to increased productivity. For example, reducing the space that is heated, cooled and lighted can produce energy savings, but it can adversely affect productivity if employees are packed like sardines without attention to noise, visual comfort, privacy and amenities. Reducing HVAC levels to save money can hamper work output if employees are too hot or too cold. The aim of a green + productive workplace is to achieve a balance: an office that is not only sustainable and energy efficient, but also provides a comfortable physical environment where employees can do their best work, better support business goals and are more inclined to stay with the organization and — be productive.

The challenge of measuring office productivity

Measuring productivity is challenging. Employee productivity has traditionally been defined as unit of *input* (payroll and other expenses) per unit of *output*. In a manufacturing facility or a call center, it is easy to measure outputs such as the number of widgets produced or calls answered.

However, it is more difficult to determine output for business units that are part of a complex system of interlinked processes. For example, IT, public relations, R&D, customer service, human relations and accounting are all elements of a collective process, each contributing different types of outputs. From a real estate perspective, it is almost impossible to assign input-to-output values to individual office facilities and to compare these values from one office to another in a meaningful way.

Using cost as a proxy

Understandably, organizations are reluctant to invest in changes in the workplace without having some indication of what the financial benefit might be. Where the input-to-output ratio of an office is difficult to measure, cost can serve as a proxy for calculating potential energy or productivity benefits. For example, it makes sense to focus on achieving greater productivity in a business unit that has high energy costs, or high labor costs, such as an operation with thousands of employees, or a corporate office with employees who have large salaries and are expensive to replace.

There is a "3-30-300" rule of thumb that organizations typically spend approximately $3/ft^2 for utilities, $30/ft^2 for rent and $300/ft^2 for payroll. While these figures are just archetypes, they are useful to provide orders of magnitude between the three areas of expenditure. According to 3-30-300 model, the greatest financial savings of greening a workplace may not be in terms of energy or rent but productivity. A 2% energy efficiency improvement would result in savings of $.06/ft^2 but a 2% productivity gain is worth $6/ft^2.

The best strategy, therefore, is to identify measures that improve employee productivity and will *also* result in space efficiency, resource conservation or energy efficiency.

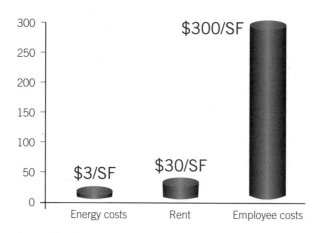

Figure 16 — Relative costs of occupancy

Base-lining "green + productive"

To find out how much energy savings and productivity gains an organization can *realistically* expect, JLL has developed *Green + Productive*

Workplace™ (G+P), an online application that baselines the current state of a portfolio, and identifies the potential energy and productivity gains that could be possible. The assessment addresses:

- *Energy, water, waste and use of resources* including lighting, heating and cooling, plug loads and server rooms, green purchasing, use of paper, recycling programs, commuting, green tenant programs
- *Space use efficiency and layout* that reflect workflows and offer an optimum environment for individual tasks, employee interaction, team building, operations and customer service
- *Productivity features* including acoustic and visual comfort, thermal and indoor air quality, amenities and measures that help impact employees' health, comfort and work-life balance

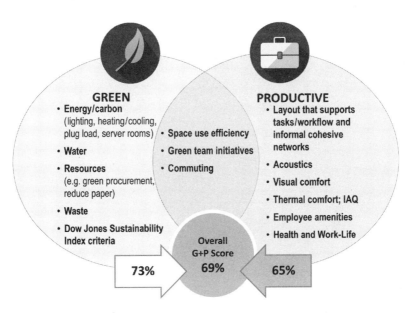

Figure 17— Overall Score; Green score; and Productivity score

From the assessment data, the *G+P*™ application provides "green" and "productive" indices for each facility in a portfolio and for the portfolio as a whole. The reports begin at a high level and become increasingly granular.

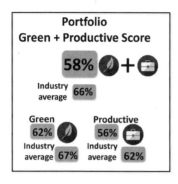

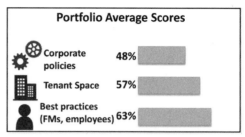

Figure 18 — Portfolio (average) scores

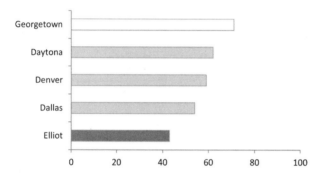

Figure19 — Overall percentage scores for individual facilities

	Overall score	Green	Productive	Space	Best practices (FM/ employees)
Georgetown	○ 71	○ 73	● 60	● 68	○ 73
Daytona	● 62	○ 70	● 62	○ 71	● 52
Denver	● 59	● 55	● 65	● 56	● 63
Elliot	● 43	● 62	● 38	● 61	● 39
Dallas	● 54	● 49	● 62	● 46	● 59

Figure 20 — Percentage scores for individual facilities (green; productive; space; best practices)

	Energy	Water	Waste	Commuting	Occupancy	Workplace	Governance
Georgetown	62	0	83	79	35	39	79
Daytona	65	63	78	75	68	65	63
Denver	59	39	45	66	75	86	66
Elliot	43	68	68	47	60	57	47
Dallas	49	65	40	90	42	40	62

Figure 21 — Percentage scores for individual facilities (energy; water; waste; etc.)

Providing an industry comparison

These scores serve as indices that give high level indications of performance. As with any rating, the power of an index as a management tool is its ability to capture the information contained in a large number of variables in one number. As such, the scores are a good way to compare the performance of different entities — in this case, office facilities or portfolios, or to compare performance of the same entity over time.

But just as an index is a good way to condense a great deal of information into one number, it is equally important to be able to drill down and examine the data.

$G+P^{TM}$ can be used to compare the performance of offices in a portfolio, and over time — generally every 12 months. Scores can also be compared to all of the facilities in the database.

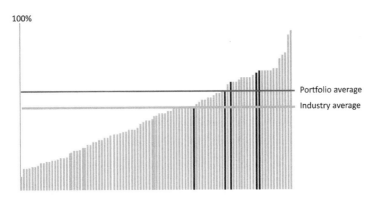

Figure 22 — Comparing Overall G+P scores

Determining potential operational savings and productivity gains

The $G+P^{TM}$ report also provides estimates of potential energy savings and productivity gains that could be achieved relative to the baseline. The calculations are based on the archetypical 3-30-300 input ratios: $3/ft² per year for energy, $30/ft² per year for rent, and $300/ft² per year for payroll. The estimates are not intended to be exact, but simply to flag energy conservation opportunities, and address areas which could be causing the organization to lose out significantly in terms of productivity due to conditions in the workplace that need to be corrected. The estimates are deliberately conservative; by erring on the side of caution, these potential energy savings and productivity gains are not only realistic but could very well be surpassed.

The following two examples illustrate productivity-oriented improvements, based on the assessment of a theoretical "Office X," a 25,000 ft² facility with 100 employees. In this scenario, the assessment has identified two areas of weakness: acoustic comfort and space layout — and provides a rationale for improving the situation, based on the findings of the $G+P^{TM}$ assessment.

Acoustic Comfort

Challenge: Due to an entirely open office layout, there is noise distraction from conversations, including speaker phones used at workstations. The open-office has no sound masking, and there are no designated quiet areas for tasks that require a high level of concentration. A recent employee survey also showed a high rate of dissatisfaction with the acoustic conditions in the space. The resulting distractions cause stress and irritation, negatively affecting employees' ability to concentrate.

Solution: Some measures that would improve the situation are to: i) designate a "Quiet Zone" in the office where no talking or cell phones are permitted — a place where employees engaged in "heads-down" tasks are able to concentrate; ii) partition some small meeting spaces where speaker phones can be used without disturbing others; and iii) install sound masking.

Anticipated productivity gain: The following are examples from independent studies of the impact of appropriate "speech privacy" and related acoustical conditions on office workers: [118]

- Ability to focus on tasks: 48% improvement
- Elimination of distractions (especially overheard conversations): 51% improvement
- Reduction of stress (measured physical symptoms of stress): 27% improvement
- Error rates/accuracy (performance of standard "information work" tasks): 10% improvement

However, let us assume an ultra-conservative estimate of only 1% improvement in productivity and work quality due to fewer distractions, the ability to concentrate fully on tasks, and having a place for making conference calls without disturbing others. This 1% improvement is equivalent to about 25 minutes per week per person in enhanced work performance or quality of work, not to mention increased worker satisfaction. Or put another way, taking this corrective action represents a **reduction in the loss of productivity** — that is to say, it would restore productivity which is currently being forfeited due to poor acoustics.

Financial impact: Assuming $300/ft^2 for payroll, Office X spends around $7.5 million per year on salaries. A conservative productivity gain of just 1% would generate an improved quality of work/productivity equivalent to $75,000.

Payback: While each office is unique, sound masking costs are estimated at around $1-$2 per square foot. Partitioning five small meeting rooms might cost in the order of about $20,000, although this would depend on materials. Designating a "quiet zone" in the office carries no cost. A conservative payback estimate would be 1-2 years.

Improved space layout

Challenge: Office X also lacks sufficient space for team meetings of various sizes. There is too much space for individual work requirements, and insufficient space for collaborative tasks. Despite the open office concept, the layout does not foster social cohesion. Because of acoustic distractions, most people retreat into their own soundscape using headphones. Business units are isolated from each other on different floors, and circulation routes offer little opportunity for face-to-face encounters. There are no informal areas to promote informal interactions. A survey indicated that most employees have little opportunity to interact informally other than with their supervisor and immediate peers.

Solution: The situation could be improved by: i) installing more small meeting rooms for collaborative tasks. This could be done using moveable portable dividers for more flexibility; and ii) integrating circulation routes and lounge and café areas for informal interactions among immediate peers and others in the organization.

The strategy for improving layout could be integrated with complementary strategies for improving the acoustic environment.

Anticipated productivity gain: Studies indicate that significant productivity gains can be achieved when a space enables casual meeting, leading to friendly familiarity and trust — which in turn contributes to a climate of collaboration. MIT research shows that 40% of creative teams productivity is directly explained by the amount of communication they have with others to discover, gather, and internalize information. In other MIT studies, employees with the most cohesive face-to-face networks are 30% more productive.[119] Adding coffee machines, cafés and other informal areas can provide a place to "bump into" colleagues and accommodate social interaction. Assuming a conservative estimate of just 1% improvement in productivity/work quality, the gain would be, as in the case of acoustic comfort, the equivalent of about 25 minutes per week per person in quality of work, improved health and alertness from people getting out of their chairs and moving, and increased worker satisfaction. Another way to view it would be the equivalent of gaining another full-time employee — without assuming their salary and benefit package.

Financial impact: As in the previous example, assuming $300/ft^2 for payroll, Office X spends around $7.5 million per year on salaries. A productivity gain of just 1% would generate improved quality of work/productivity equivalent to $75,000.

Payback: While the cost of changing the layout depends on how much construction is involved, a conservative estimate for payback would be 2-4 years.

Relative orders of magnitude for energy savings and productivity gains

$G+P^{TM}$ calculates conservative **energy savings estimates** for energy management, heating & cooling, lighting, plug load and server rooms. It does the same for **productivity gains** (or if you prefer "reduced productivity losses") that would be achieved from taking corrective action with respect to space layout, health and comfort.

These relative orders of magnitude are summed up in a portfolio report, and are described in greater detail in each individual facility report.

Potential energy savings

	Energy Management	Heating and Cooling	Lighting	Plug load	Server room	TOTAL
Georgetown	$2,000	$800	$200	$2,000	$600	$5,600
Daytona	$5,000	$1,500	$4,100	$2,900	No savings	$13,500
Denver	No savings	No savings	$10,400	$13,400	$9,000	$32,800
Elliot	$6,200	$7,800	13,200	$14,200	No savings	$41,400
Dallas	$15,000	$7,500	$41,300	$33,800	$15,000	$112,600
					TOTAL	$205,900

Potential productivity gains ("reduced loss of productivity")

	Acoustic comfort	Visual comfort	Thermal comfort, IAQ	Layout, comfort health,	TOTAL
Georgetown	$200,600	No savings	$100,300	$150,400	$451,300
Daytona	$26,200	No savings	$52,500	$39,300	$118,000
Denver	No savings	No savings	No savings	$56,200	$56,200
Elliot	$159,900	$159,900	No savings	$239,900	$559,700
Dallas	$660,000	$ 200,100	$660,000	$294,900	$1,815,000
				TOTAL	$3,000,200

Figure23 — Estimated energy savings and productivity gains in the Portfolio report

A review of the potential energy savings and productivity gains serves to flag and prioritize areas which should be further investigated because they represent significant value, which is currently being forfeited due to energy inefficiencies or work environments that are not as healthy or comfortable as they should be. The tables tell a story at a glance. The individual facility reports give more granular information.

The case for being green *and* productive

The purpose of creating a green + productive workplace is to improve an organization's bottom line by:

- Making better use of space
- Reducing the use of resources including energy
- Providing a healthy, comfortable and efficient workplace where employees also feel a sense of connection with one another
- Demonstrating corporate social responsibility. A green + productive workplace is also an indicator to investors of good management practices.

Although there are accepted metrics for sustainability and energy efficiency, the science of measuring productivity outputs is still imperfect. JLL's *Green + Productive Workplace*™ tool does not presume to completely solve this complex problem. However, it does provide a practical approach to flag where corrective action would make workplaces more sustainable, energy efficient and more productive. By applying $G+P$™ metrics, an organization can compare different offices across its portfolio or against a larger aggregate database, or it can measure progress for a particular location over time.

The tool helps organizations establish how green and productive their office portfolios *currently* are compared to what they *could be*, flag necessary improvements and then estimate a credible order of magnitude of the possible financial benefits. By using conservative estimates and developing integrated strategies that address sustainability and employee health, comfort and wellbeing, the holistic approach provides a structure for informed and balanced decisions, and acts as a thoughtful approach for investments. As a result, you *can* make your workplace greener and more productive using a quantitative approach. Really.

End Notes

Introduction
. . . .

1   **Want productivity? Then go green. Simple**, Donna Kelly, the Fifth Estate, Dec. 2012, http://www.thefifthestate.com.au/archives/41855/

2   **Green Offices in Australia: a User Perception Survey**, Lynne Armitage, (Institute of Sustainable Development and Architecture, Bond University, Gold Coast, Australia), Ann Murugan, (Institute of Sustainable Development and Architecture, Bond University, Gold Coast, Australia), Hikari Kato, (Institute of Sustainable Development and Architecture, Bond University, Gold Coast, Australia)

   Performance & Perceptions of Green Buildings – A study based on the experiences of working, renting and owning Green Star certified buildings, 2010, Institute of Sustainable Development and Architecture, Bond University in association with Green Building Council of Australia

PART 1 — Greening the Workplace

CHAPTER 1 – Why Go Green?
. . . .

3   **Green Behaviour: Barriers, Facilitators and the Role of Attributions**, L. Butterworth & A. McDowall, Richard Plank, City University London, in a compilation of studies called "Going Green: The Psychology of Sustainability in the Workplace", edited by Dean Bartlett, London Metropolitan University and published by the British Psychological Society, 2012

4   **Fortune Magazine Names Business World's Green Giants**, GreenBiz, March 2007, http://www.greenbiz.com/news/2007/03/21/ fortune-magazine-names-business-worlds-green-giants

5   **How "RAD" GE and ARCA Reduce Refrigerator Landfill Waste and Greenhouse Gas Emissions in 12 States**, GE Appliances and Lighting Fact Sheet, http://www.arcaap.com/ PDFs/GE_ARCA_RAD_FACT_SHEET.pdf

6   **Science Meets Sustainability, Dupont Sustainability Report 2013**, http://www.slideshare.net/DuPont/dupont-sustainability-report-2013

7   **Walmart – The Responsibility to Lead, 2014 Global Responsibility Report**, http://corporate.walmart.com/global-responsibility/environment-sustainability/ global-responsibility-report

8 **Going Green Means Saving Green**, Scott H. Lawson MS, CIH President, Scott Lawson Companies, IEN, industrial Equipment News http://www.scottlawsoncompanies.com/wp-content/uploads/2011/05/www.ien.com_article_going-green-means_116185.pdf

9 **The 2013 UPS Corporate Sustainability Report**, http://sustainability.ups.com/resources/sustainability-reporting/

10 **Speaking Sustainably: Why Most CSR Reports Fail**, Jim Nail, http://speakingsustainability.com/2011/01/13/csr-reports-fail-leadership/

11 **Your M&S 'Plan A' Report 2014**, http://planareport.marksandspencer.com/downloads/M&S-PlanA-2014.pdf

12 **Corporate Social Responsibility and Consumers' Attributions and Brand Evaluations in a Product-harm Crisis**, J. Klein, & N. Dawar, Working paper 203-217, International Journal of Research in Marketing 2004, http://www.sciencedirect.com/science/article/pii/S0167811604000266

13 **CSR Provides "Reputation Insurance" when Products Fail**, Network for Business Sustainability April 2013, Patrick Callan http://nbs.net/knowledge/csr-provides-reputation-insurance-when-products-fail/

 Corporate Social Responsibility and Consumers' Attributions and Brand Evaluations in a Product-harm Crisis, Working paper 203- International Journal of Research in Marketing N. 2004.217 Klein, J. & Dawar

14 **Walmart 2012 Global Responsibility Report – Beyond 50 Years: Building a Sustainable Future**, http://corporate.walmart.com/microsites/global-responsibility-report-2013/pdf/Walmart_GRR.pdf

15 **World Watch Institute 2008 Innovations for a Sustainable Economy**, Chapter 3, L. Hunter Lovins, http://www.worldwatch.org/files/pdf/SOW08_chapter_3.pdf

16 **EPA Green Power Partnership**, http://www.epa.gov/greenpower/partners/partners/fedexpressoaklandhubfacility.htm

 Q&A With Mitch Jackson, FedEx Expert on Sustainability, http://access.van.fedex.com/qa-mitch-jackson-fedex-sustainability/

17 **Q&A With Mitch Jackson, FedEx Expert on Sustainability**, http://access.van.fedex.com/qa-mitch-jackson-fedex-sustainability/

18 **Green Dandelion, Sustainability at the University of Rochester–provided to you by Facilities and Services**, 2013, http://blogs.rochester.edu/thegreendandelion/

19 **CSR for HR**, Elaine Cohen, Green Leaf Publishing

20 **Green Recruiting Helps Bring in Top Talent**, Workforce Management, Aug. 2007, Charlotte Huff, http://www.workforce.com/articles/green-recruiting-helps-bring-in-top-talent

21 **Three Reasons Job Seekers Prefer Sustainable Companies**, Network for Business Sustainability, June 2013, David Jones, University of Vermont's School of Business Administration and Chelsea Willness, University of Saskatchewan's Edwards School of Business, http://nbs.net/knowledge/three-reasons-job-seekers-prefer-sustainable-companies/

22 **GE and mtvU Launch Search for Best Student Ideas to Green College Campuses; Winner of mtvU GE ecomagination Challenge to Receive Earth Day Concert and $25,000 Grant to Implement Idea**, GE Citizenship, http://www.gecitizenship.com/site-map/; http://www.genewscenter.com/Press-Releases/GE-and-mtvU-Launch-Search-for-Best-Student-Ideas-to-Green-College-Campuses-Winner-of-mtvU-GE-ecomag-580.aspx

23 **Harnessing the Power of Informal Employee Networks – formalizing a company's ad hoc peer groups can spur collaboration and unlock value**, Lowell L. Bryan, Eric Matson, and Leigh M. Weiss, http://www.mckinsey.com/insights/organization/harnessing_the_power_of_informal_employee_networks

CHAPTER 2 – Green Policies, Directives and Guidelines
. . . .

24 **How Small Green Team Can Transform Large Corporation**, Carbon 49 – A blog on sustainability for Canadian businesses, Nov 2013, Derek Wong, http://www.carbon49.com/2013/11/small-green-team-transform-large-corporation/

25 **Green Workplace Survey Brief**, Society for Human Resource Management (SHRM), Justina Victor, Evren Esen, Steve Williams, http://www.shrm.org/research/surveyfindings/articles/documents/shrm%20green%20workplace%20survey%20brief.pdf

26 **Sustainability 2.0: Beyond Green Teams**, Green Lodging News 9/24/2012 Francesca Quinn, http://www.greenlodgingnews.com/sustainability-20--beyond-green-teams

CHAPTER 3 – Green Teams
. . . .

27 **Green Teams That Work**, Green Steps http://www.greensteps.edu.au/news/green-teams-work

28 **Twelve Ways to Turn Green Intentions into Green Actions**, Carbon 49 – A blog on sustainability for Canadian Business, Sept. 2011, Derek Wong http://www.carbon49.com/2011/09/12-ways-to-turn-green-intentions-into-green-actions/

CHAPTER 4 – Greenhouse Gas Emissions
. . . .

29 **The Coming Climate Crash, Lessons for Climate Change in the 2008 Recession**, New York Times, Sunday Review, June 2014, Henry Paulson Jr. http://www.nytimes.com/2014/06/22/opinion/sunday/lessons-for-climate-change-in-the-2008-recession.html

30 **Lessons Offered by Emerging Carbon Trading Markets**, Duke Sanford School of Public Policy, March 2014, Margaret Lillard http://news.sanford.duke.edu/news-type/news/2014/lessons-offered-emerging-carbon-trading-markets

31 **Lessons Offered by Emerging Carbon Trading Markets**, Policy Forum article in Science magazine, March 2014, Richard Newell, William Pizer and Daniel Raimi http://www.sciencemag.org/content/343/6177/1316.full

32 **Corporates that Lead on Climate – such as Philips and HP Perform Better Financially, CDP shows**, The Climate Group, Sept. 2013, http://www.theclimategroup.org/what-we-do/news-and-blogs/corporates-that-lead-on-climate-perform-better-financially-cdp-report-shows/

33 **Sector Insights: What is Driving Climate Change Action in the World's Largest Companies? Global 500 Climate Change Report 2013**, Price Waterhouse Cooper, https://www.cdp.net/CDPResults/CDP-Global-500-Climate-Change-Report-2013.pdf?utm_content=bufferc3376&utm_source=buffer&utm_medium=twitter&utm_campaign=Buffer

34 **Report Shows Companies Still Don't Take Climate Change Seriously – CDP Analysis Reveal Lack of Action on Emissions by Top FTSE Global 500 Corporations**, Guardian Sustainable Business Blog, Sept. 2013, Joe Confino, http://www.theguardian.com/sustainable-business/blog/cdp-report-companies-emissions-failing

35 **Lessons Offered by Emerging Carbon Trading Markets**, Duke Sanford School of Public Policy, March 2014, Margaret Lillard, http://news.sanford.duke.edu/news-type/news/2014/lessons-offered-emerging-carbon-trading-markets; http://www.sciencemag.org/content/343/6177/1316.full

36 **CDP**, https://www.cdp.net/en-US/Pages/HomePage.aspx

37 **Why CDP, GRI, DJSI Stand Out among Sustainability Frameworks**, GreenBiz.com, Aug. 2013, John Daview, http://www.greenbiz.com/blog/2013/08/19/why-cdp-gri-djsi-stand-out-among-sustainability-frameworks

38 **CDP Reports and Data**, https://www.cdp.net/en-US/Results/Pages/overview.aspx

39 **Linking GRI and CDP: How are the Global Reporting Initiative Guidelines and the Carbon Disclosure Project Questions Aligned?** GI and CDP, https://www.cdp.net/en-US/Respond/Documents/Linking-up-GRI-and-CDP.pdf

40 **Dow Ones Sustainability Index**, Wikipedia, http://en.wikipedia.org/wiki/Dow_Jones_Sustainability_Index#cite_note-5

41 **Working 9 to 5 on Climate Change: An Office Guide**, World Resources Institute, Samantha Putt del Pino, http://www.ghgprotocol.org/files/ghgp/tools/working9-5.pdfPankaj Bhatia

42 **Sector Insights: What is Driving Climate Change Action in the World's Largest Companies? Global 500 Climate Change Report 2013**, Price Waterhouse Cooper, https://www.cdp.net/CDPResults/CDP-Global-500-Climate-Change-Report-2013.pdf?utm_content=bufferc3376&utm_source=buffer&utm_medium=twitter&utm_campaign=Buffer

43 **Report Shows Companies Still Don't Take Climate Change Seriously – CDP Analysis Reveal Lack of Action on Emissions by Top FTSE Global 500 Corporations**, Guardian Sustainable Business Blog, Sept. 2013, Joe Confino http://www.theguardian.com/sustainable-business/blog/cdp-report-companies-emissions-failing

CHAPTER 5 – Energy Management

44 **ACEEE Study Finds "Smart Meters" Not Smart Enough to Slash Residential Power Use and Significantly Reduce Consumer Electric Bills**, American Council for an Energy Efficient Economy, June 2010, Patrick Mitchell, http://www.aceee.org/press/2010/06/aceee-study-finds-smart-meters-not-smart-enough-slash-re

45 **The Energy Dashboard Delusion**, Greentech Grid, April 2012, John Pitcher, Rob Watson, http://www.greentechmedia.com/articles/read/Guest-Post-The-Energy-Dashboard-Delusion-Part-1

46 **Energy Efficiency Lease Guidance, Center for Market Innovation**, Nov. 2010, The Natural Resources Defense Council (NRDC) with input from Cycle-7 and HR&A Advisors http://www.nrdc.org/greenbusiness/cmi/files/CMI-FS-Energy.pdf

47 **High Performance Tenant Demonstration Project – Guide**, Natural Resources Defense Council, http://www.nrdc.org/business/cgi/guide.asp

CHAPTER 6 – Energy for Lighting, Plug load and Server Rooms

48 **Miscellaneous Energy Loads in Buildings**, June 2013, Report Number A133 American Council for an Energy -efficient Economy, Sameer Kwatra, Jennifer Amann, and Harvey Sachs, http://www.aceee.org/research-report/a133

49 **Delamping and Reduced Wattage Lamps,** Technology Information Sheet, Saskatchewan Energy Management Task Force, http://www.emtfsask.ca/pdfs/delampwattage.pdf

50 **Tapping into Commercial Office Plug Load Savings: How Can We Reduce Energy Consumption of Plug Load Devices Through Changes to Hardware, Software & Occupant Behavior?** 2010 Behavior, Energy & Climate Change Conference, Nov. 2010, Catherine Mercier

51 **Save money with ENERGY STAR – But Keep these Tips in Mind,** BC Hydro, https://www.bchydro.com/news/conservation/2014/energy-star-in-the-office.html

52 **Cloud Computing Saves Energy,** Scientific American, June 2013, Umair Irfan, http://www.scientificamerican.com/article/cloud-computing-saves-energy

53 **Cloud Computing Can Save Big Firms Billions in Energy Costs,** GreenBiz, July 2011, Tilde Herrera, http://www.greenbiz.com/news/2011/07/20/cloud-computing-can-save-big-firms-billions-energy-costs

54 **Companies Shifting to Cloud Computing Save Energy & Cut Waste,** GreenBiz, Dec. 2011, Matthew Wheeland http://www.greenbiz.com/news/2011/12/06/companies-shifting-cloud-computing-save-energy-cut-waste

CHAPTER 7 – Energy for Heating, Cooling and Ventilation
· ·

55 **FACT SHEET • Solar Control Window Film,** Pacific Gas and Electric Company, 2007, http://www.pge.com/includes/docs/pdfs/mybusiness/energysavingsrebates/incentivesbyindustry/fs_windowfilm.pdf

56 **Window-to-wall Ratios and Commercial Building Environmental Control in Cold Climates,** University of Calgary J. A. Love, W. Tian and Z. Tian http://sbrn.solarbuildings.ca/c/sbn/file_db/Doc_File_e/Window%20to%20wall%20ratios%20and%20commercial%20building%20energy.pdf

    Efficient Cooling in Hot Climates; A Thermodynamic Systems Approach to Quadrupling Average Efficiency, Masdar Institute of Science and Technology, Massachusetts Institute of Technology, Peter Armstrong, Les Norford, Leon Glicksman, http://web.mit.edu/mit-tdp/docs/projects/Armstrong_poster.pdf

57 **Reducing Wasted Energy in Commercial Buildings,** MIT Energy Initiative, Feb. 2013, Nancy W. Stauffer, http://newsoffice.mit.edu/2013 reducing-wasted-energy-in-commercial-buildings

58 **No Cost/Low Cost Ideas to Reduce Energy Use in Office Buildings,** World Energy Engineering Congress, Dec. 2010, Alfred B. Scaramelli, Ph.D., P.E., Senior Vice President Beacon Capital Partners, LLC; Robert Best, Executive Vice President, JLL, Inc.

CHAPTER 8 – Water
· · · · · · · · · · · · · ·

59 **The Case for Fixing the Leaks: America's Crumbling Water Infrastructure Wastes Billions of Gallons, Dollars,** The Center for Neighborhood Technology (CNT) , Ryan Kilpatrick, http://www.cnt.org/2013/11/18/the-case-for-fixing-the-leaks-release/

60 **Water and Wastewater Systems in Imperial Rome,** Roger D. Hansen, http://www.waterhistory.org/histories/rome/

61 **We Have Better Things to do with Clean Water than Flush it Down the Toilet**, Bill and Melinda Gates Foundation, Impatient Optimists, March 2013, Carl Hensman, http://www.impatientoptimists.org/Posts/2013/03/ We-have-better-things-to-do-with-clean-water-than-flush-it-down-the-toilet

62 **WaterSense An EPA Partnership Program**, http://www.epa.gov/WaterSense/commercial/types.html#tabs-office

CHAPTER 9 – Waste Management
. . . .

63 **China Puts up a Green Wall to US Trash**, Christian Science Monitor, June 2013, Peter Ford, http://www.csmonitor.com/World/Asia-Pacific/2013/0619/ China-puts-up-a-green-wall-to-US-trash

64 **Toxic 'e-waste' Dumped in Poor Nations, says United Nations**, The Guardian, The Observer, John Vidal, http://www.theguardian.com/global-development/2013/dec/14/ toxic-ewaste-illegal-dumping-developing-countries

65 **United States International Trade Commission Investigation No. 332-528**, USITC Publication 4379, Feb 2013, http://www.usitc.gov/publications/332/pub4379.pdf

66 **Tools for Environmentally Sound Management for an ISO Compliant Environmental Management System that includes OECD Core Performance Elements for the World's Recycling Industries**, Bureau of International Recycling (AISBL) http://www.bir.org/assets/ Documents/publications/brochures/GuideESM-English.pdf

67 **US and Canada Green City Index – Assessing the Environmental Performance of 27 Major US and Canadian Cities**, A research project conducted by the Economist Intelligence Unit, sponsored by Siemens, http://www.siemens.com/press/pool/de/events/2011/ corporate/2011-06-northamerican/northamerican-gci-report-e.pdf

PART 2 — Creating a Productive Workplace

CHAPTER 10
. . . .

1 Quotation from **Getting Engaged HR Magazine**, February 2004, by senior writer Steve Bates, http://www.shrm.org/publications/hrmagazine/editorialcontent/pages/0204covstory. aspx#sthash.MfPUoE0B.dpuf

2 **State of the American Workplace – Employee Engagement Insights for US Business Leaders 2013**, http://www.gallup.com/strategicconsulting/163007/state-american-workplace. aspx

3 **Employee Engagement Research (Master List of 32 Findings)** , Sept 2012 Kevin Kruse, http://kevinkruse.com/employee-engagement-research-master-list-of-29-studies

4 **Leveraging Employee Engagement for Competitive Advantage: HR's Strategic Role**, SHRM Research, 2007, Nancy R. Lockwood, http://www.shrm.org/research/articles/articles/ documents/07marresearchquarterly.pdf

5 **The Relationship Between Engagement at Work and Organizational Outcomes**, Gallup, Feb. 2013, James K. Harter, Frank L. Schmidt, Sangeeta Agrawal, Stephanie K. Plowman, http://www.gallup.com/strategicconsulting/126806/q12-meta-analysis.aspx

6 **Employee Engagement: How to Build A High Performance Workforce**, Gallup, 2003, cited in Melcrum (2005)

7 **Investors, Take Note: Engagement Boosts Earnings**, Gallup Business Journal, June 2007, Bryant Ott, http://businessjournal.gallup.com/content/27799/investors-take-note-engagement-boosts-earnings.aspx

8 **The Impact of Employee Engagement**, Kenexa, http://www.docsrush.net/1428568/the-impact-of-employee-engagement-kenexa.html

9 **Satisfied Employees Boost Your Stock Price**, Network for Business Sustainability, May 2013, Lindsey Williams, http://nbs.net/knowledge/satisfied-employees-boost-your-stock-price

10 **What Is Employee Engagement?** Forbes, June 2012, Kevin Kruse, http://www.forbes.com/sites/kevinkruse/2012/06/22/employee-engagement-what-and-why/

11 **Job Satisfaction vs. Employee Engagement**, Decisonwise, Charles Rogel, http://www.decision-wise.com/job-satisfaction-vs-employee-engagement/

12 **MAGIC: The Five Keys of Employee Engagement**, Decisonwise, Charles Rogel, http://www.decision-wise.com/white-paper/magic-five-keys-employee-engagement/

13 **When Engagement Replaces Satisfaction**, Decisonwise, Tracey Maylett, http://www.decision-wise.com/when-engagement-replaces-satisfaction/

14 **Health and Productivity Gains from Better Indoor Environments**, William J. Fisk, in The Role of Emerging Energy-Efficient Technology in Promoting Workplace Productivity and Health, a report by Lawrence Berkeley National Laboratory, February 2002, http://www.annualreviews.org/doi/abs/10.1146/annurev.energy.25.1.537?journalCode=energy.2

15 **How IEQ Affects Health, Productivity**, ASHRAE Journal 2002, William Fisk, http://doas.psu.edu/fisk.pdf

16 **A Method to Estimate the Cost Effectiveness of Indoor Environments in Office Work**, Clima 2005 Lausanne, 8th REHVA World Congress, Switzerland, Oct. 9-12, 2005.Olli Seppanen and William Fisk, "," Clima 2005 Lausanne, 8th REHVA World Congress, Switzerland, Oct. 9-12, 2005

17 **Linking Environmental Conditions to Productivity, Eastern Ergonomics**, Conference & Exposition, New York, June 2004, Alan Hedge, http://ergo.human.cornell.edu/Conferences/EECE_IEQ%20and%20Productivity_ABBR.pdf

18 **Productivity and Future HVAC**, Clima 2005 Lausanne, 8th REHVA World Congress, Switzerland, Oct. 9-12, 2005.Shin-Ichi Tanabe,

 Studies Relate IAQ and Productivity, FacilitiesNet, Nov. 2006, David Callan and Salah Nezar, http://www.facilitiesnet.com/green/article/Studies-Relate-IAQ-and-Productivity--5581

19 **Stop Wasting Your Money on Employee Satisfaction**, Decisonwise, Tracey Maylett, http://www.decision-wise.com/stop-wasting-your-money-on-employee-satisfaction/

 Do Bonuses Engage Employees? Decisonwise, Reese Haydon, http://www.decision-wise.com/do-bonuses-engage-employees/

CHAPTER 11 – Employee Surveys

· ·

20 **Managers: Your Strongest (or Weakest) Link in Driving Employee Engagement?** AON Hewitt, Jenny Merry, Jake Outram, Hugh Hawthorne, Jessica Everitt, http://www.aon.com/attachments/human-capital-consulting/Summary_AonHewitt-2011-European_Employee-Engagement.pdf

21 **How to Track the Team's Mood with a Niko-niko Calendar**, Agile Trail, Sept 2011, Bernd Schiffer, http: http://agiletrail.com/2011/09/12/how-to-track-the-teams-mood-with-a-niko-niko-calendar/

22 **Employee Engagement Surveys: Useless or Very Useless?** Macleans Magazine, Feb. 2013, Emily Senger, http://www.macleans.ca/economy/business/useless-or-very-useless/

23 **What Employee-Engagement Surveys Really Tell Us**, Executive Online, March 2013, Mark McGraw, http://www.hreonline.com/HRE/view/story.jhtml?id=534355097

CHAPTER 12 – Productivity and the Workplace Environment
· ·

24 **Employees Really Do Waste Time at Work**, Forbes, July 2012, Cheryl Conner, http://www.forbes.com/sites/cherylsnappconner/2012/07/17/employees-really-do-waste-time-at-work/

25 **World Cup Taking a Bite out of Worker Productivity**, ABC News, June 2014, Susanna Kim, http://abcnews.go.com/Business/2014-fifa-world-cup-soccer-tournament-taking-bite/story?id=24182230

26 **How an Exploding Freelance Economy Will Drive Change In 2014**, Nov. 2013, Jeff Wald, http://www.forbes.com/sites/groupthink/2013/11/25/how-an-exploding-freelance-economy-will-drive-change-in-2014/

27 **The Rise of the Millennial Workforce**, Wired, Aug 2013, Alastair Mitchell, http://www.wired.com/2013/08/the-rise-of-the-millennial-workforce/

28 **WELL BUILDING STANDARD**, http://delosliving.com/about/well-building-standard/

29 **How To Brandify Your Office Space**, Open Forum Dec. 2011, Ivana Taylor, https://www.americanexpress.com/us/small-business/openforum/articles/how-to-brandify-your-office-space/://www.americanexpress.com/us/small-business/openforum/articles/how-to-brandify-your-office-space/

30 **Why Customer Loyalty is Declining and What Companies Can Do About It**, Oct. 2013, Steven Van Belleghem, http://www.theconversationmanager.com/2013/10/10/why-customer-loyalty-is-declining-and-what-companies-can-do-about-it/

31 **They're Watching You at Work**, The Atlantic, Dec. 2013, Don Peck, http://www.theatlantic.com/magazine/archive/2013/12/theyre-watching-you-at-work/354681/

32 **Fitness Trackers Deliver Results, Raise Doubts**, Scott Wooldridge, April 2014, http://m.benefitspro.com/2014/04/14/fitness-trackers-deliver-results-raise-doubts

33 **Diagnosing and Changing Organizational Culture: Based on the Competing Values Framework**, 3rd edition, by Kim S. Cameron and Robert E. Quinn

CHAPTER 13 – Space Use Efficiency
· ·

34 **Gartner Research's 4 Basic Rules For IT Spending**, XCHANGE events, May 2013, Alicia Stein, http://www.xchange-events.com/newsletter-articles/gartner-researchs-4-basic-rules-for-it-spendinga/#author

35 **Why Change Now? Preparing for the Workplace of Tomorrow**, Deloitte, 2009, Seth Siegel, Naomi Leventhal, http://www.deloitte.com/assets/Dcom-UnitedStates/Local%20Assets/Documents/us_talent_PreparingfortheWorkplaceofTomorrow.pdf

36 **Making the Case for Place,. Studies showing that people prefer telecommuting,**
Global Workplace Analytics http://www.globalworkplaceanalytics.com/resources/costs-benefits

37 **Telework in the Federal Government**, Deloitte, 2010, Wendy Freeman Carr,
Naomi Leventhal, http://www.deloitte.com/assets/Dcom-UnitedStates/Local%20Assets/
Documents/Federal/us_fed_TeleworkintheFederalGovernment_Brochure_112410.pdf

38 **Workshifting Benefits: The Bottom Line**, TeleworkResearchNetwork.com, May 2010,
Kate Lister, http://www.workshifting.com/downloads/downloads/Workshifting%20Benefits-
The%20Bottom%20Line.pdf

39 **Costs and Benefits, Making a Case for Place**, Global Workplace Analytics,
http://www.globalworkplaceanalytics.com/resources/costs-benefits

40 **Q1 2013Mobile Workforce Report: BYOD and costs impact productivity**,
March 2013, Chris Witeck, Director Product Marketing, http://www.ipass.com/blog/
mobile-worker-byod-costs-impact-productivity/

41 **Nearly Half of Firms Supporting BYOD Report Data Breaches**, Computer
Weekly.com, Aug. 2011, Warwick Ashford, http://www.computerweekly.com/
news/2240161202/Nearly-half-of-firms-supporting-BYOD-report-data-breaches

42 **No BYOD Policy? Time to Grasp the Nettle**, CXP Unplugged, Jan 2013, Chris Gabriel
http://cxounplugged.com/2013/01/byod-policy/

43 **The Second Economy** , McKinsey Quarterly , October 2011, W. Brian Arthur,
http://www.mckinsey.com/insights/strategy/the_second_economy

CHAPTER 14 – Open Offices and Productivity
· ·

44 **Sophomore Blues: Big student Housing Player Slumps**, Breaking Commercial Real Estate
News, Sept 2013, http://www.bullockandassociatesinc.com/Pages/BreakingCRENews.aspx

45 **The Billionaire Boss with No Office**, New Zealand Herald, May 2014, Seth Stevenson,
http://www.nzherald.co.nz/business/news/article.cfm?c_id=3&objectid=11250576

46 **The Billionaire Boss with No Office**, New Zealand Herald, May 2014, Seth Stevenson,
http://www.nzherald.co.nz/business/news/article.cfm?c_id=3&objectid=11250576

47 **Changing Office Trends Hold Major Implications for Future Office
Demand**, March 2013, Mark Heschmeyer, http://www.costar.com/News/Article/
Changing-Office-Trends-Hold-Major-Implications-for-Future-Office-Demand/146580

48 **The Open-Office Trap**, The New Yorker, Jan 2014, Maria Konnikova,
http://www.newyorker.com/business/currency/the-open-office-trap

49 **The Open-Office Trap**, The New Yorker, Jan 2014, Maria Konnikova,
http://www.newyorker.com/business/currency/the-open-office-trap

50 **Sickness Absence Associated with Shared and Open-plan offices – a national cross
sectional questionnaire survey**, 2011, J.H, Pejtersen, H. Feveile, K.B. Christensen, H. Burr,
http://www.ncbi.nlm.nih.gov/pubmed/21528171

51 **The Open-Office Trap**, The New Yorker, Jan 2014, Maria Konnikova,
http://www.newyorker.com/business/currency/the-open-office-trap

52 **The Open-Office Trap**, The New Yorker, Jan 2014, Maria Konnikova,
http://www.newyorker.com/business/currency/the-open-office-trap

53 **Privacy at Work: Architectural Correlates of Job Satisfaction and Job Performance**, Academy of Management Journal, 1980, Eric Sundstrom, Robert Burt, Douglas Kamp, University of Tennessee at Knoxville, http://amj.aom.org/content/23/1/101

54 **Handbook of Health – Environmental Stress and Health** 2000, G.W. Evans

55 **A Problem is a Problem is a Benefit? Generation Y Perceptions of Open-plan Offices**, Property Management, 2012,Heidi Rasila (Aalto University, Espoo, Finland) Peggie Rothe (Aalto University, Espoo, Finland), http://www.emeraldinsight.com/doi/abs/10.1108/02637471211249506

56 **Who Wastes The Most Time At Work?** Forbes, Sept 2013, Cheryl Conner, http://www.forbes.com/sites/cherylsnappconner/2013/09/07/who-wastes-the-most-time-at-work/

57 **Individual Differences in Employee Reactions to Open-Plan Offices**, 2005 Alena Maher and Courtney von Hippel, http://senate.ucsf.edu/2013-2014/mb5-maher%20and%20von%20hippel%20article%20on%20open%20plan%20offices.pdf

58 **Cognitive Control in Media Multitaskers**, Proceedings of the National Academy of Sciences, Vol. 106 No. 33, August 25, 2009 , Eyal Ophira, Clifford Nass, and Anthony D. Wagner, http://www.pnas.org/content/106/37/15583

Multitasking Muddles Brains, Even When the Computer Is Off, Wired, Aug 2009, Brandom Keim, http://www.wired.com/2009/08/multitasking/

CHAPTER 15 – Designing a Productive Open Office
. . . .

59 **Furniture Forms and Their Influence on Our Emotional Responses Toward Interior Environments**, Oregon State University, Corvallis, 2011, S. Dazkir, and M.Read, http://eab.sagepub.com/content/44/5/722.short

60 **Looking for a Lesson in Google's Perks**, New York Times, 3/15/13. James B. Stewart, http://www.nytimes.com/2013/03/16/business/at-google-a-place-to-work-and-play.html?pagewanted=all&_r=0

61 **The Relative Merits of Lean, Enriched, and Empowered Offices: An Experimental Examination of the Impact of Workspace Management Strategies on Well-Being and Productivity**, University of Exeter, 2010, Craig Knight and S. Alexander Haslam, http://www.ncbi.nlm.nih.gov/pubmed/20565201

62 **Canadian Schools of Feng shui**, http://www.canadianfengshui.ca/corp.htm

63 **Impact of Contour on Aesthetic Judgments and Approach-avoidance Decisions in Architecture**, University of Toronto, Department of Psychology, 2013, Oshin Vartaniana, Gorka Navarreteb, Anjan Chatterjeed, Lars Brorson Fiche,Helmut Lederf,Cristián, Marcos Nadalf, Nicolai Rostruph, and Martin Skovi, http://www.pnas.org/content/110/Supplement_2/10446.abstract

64 **Blue or Red? Exploring the Effect of Color on Cognitive Task Performances** DOI: 10.1126/science.1169144, Feb. 2009, Ravi Mehta, and Rui (Juliet) Zhu, http://www.acrwebsite.org/volumes/v36/NAACR_vol36_25.pdf

CHAPTER 16 – Acoustic Comfort
• •

65   **We all Crave it, but Can you Stand the Silence? The Longest Anyone can Bear Earth's Quietest Place is 45 minutes**, Mail Online, Aug 2012. Ted Thornhill , http://www.dailymail.co.uk/sciencetech/article-2124581/The-worlds-quietest-place-chamber-Orfield-Laboratories.html#ixzz3C0iJgbA9

66   **Noise in multiple workstation open plan computer rooms: measures and annoyance**, Journal of Human Ergology 1992, A. Mital, J. McGlothlin and H. Faard

Productivity: Impacts of Ambient Noise, Speech Privacy & Acoustical Conditions on Worker Performance, A Review of Independent Research, 2004, David M. Sykes PhD, IAPP, HFES, https://www.speechprivacysystems.com/wp-content/uploads/2009/10/Productivity_Acoustics_Overview0805.pdf

67   **Curing the Noisy Office**, Occupational Hazards, 1995, W.E. Hemp, M Glowatz Jr., M. http://www.questia.com/magazine/1G1-17365947/curing-the-noisy-office

68   **Cognitive Performance and Restoration in Open-Plan Office Noise**, 2012, Helena Jahncke Lulea, University of Technology, https://pure.ltu.se/portal/files/40220521/Helena_Jahncke.Komplett.pdf

69   **Statutes of The Swedish Work Environment Authority**, The Swedish Work Environment authority Arbetsmiljoverket Arbetsmiljoverkets forfatthingsamling. Solna (Sweden): Arbetsmiljoverkets, Publikationsservice. (2005)

70   **Stress and Open Office Noise**, Journal of Applied Psychology, 2000, G.W. Evans and D. Johnson, http://www.ncbi.nlm.nih.gov/pubmed/11055149

71   **Handbook of Health — Environmental Stress and Health** 2000, G.W. Evans

72   **Stress and open office noise**, Journal of Applied Psychology, 2000, G.W. Evans and D. Johnson, http://www.ncbi.nlm.nih.gov/pubmed/11055149

73   **Too Many Interruptions at Work?** Gallup Business Journal (6/8/06) Jennifer Robison, http://businessjournal.gallup.com/content/23146/too-many-interruptions-work.aspx

74   **Unique Performance Advantages of a Quiet Technology™ Sound Masking System**, Cambridge Sound Management, Thomas Horrall FASA http://cambridgesound.com/wp-content/uploads/2013/02/Unique-Performance-Advantages.pdf

75   **From Cubicles, Cry for Quiet Pierces Office Buzz**, New York Times Science, May 2012, John Tierney, http://www.nytimes.com/2012/05/20/science/when-buzz-at-your-cubicle-is-too-loud-for-work.html?pagewanted=all&_r=0

76   **From Cubicles, Cry for Quiet Pierces Office Buzz**, New York Times Science, May 2012, John Tierney http://www.nytimes.com/2012/05/20/science/when-buzz-at-your-cubicle-is-too-loud-for-work.html?pagewanted=all&_r=0

77   **Headphones & Earphones Can Cause Permanent Hearing Loss: What You Need to Know**, posted by Stony Brook Surgery Aug. 2012 http://medicine.stonybrookmedicine.edu/surgery/blog/headphones-and-earphones-can-cause-permanent-hearing-loss-what-you-need-to-know

78   **How Noise-canceling Headphones Work**, How Stuff Works, William Harris http://electronics.howstuffworks.com/gadgets/audio-music/noise-canceling-headphone3.htm

79 **Mental arithmetic and non-speech office noise: An exploration of interference-by-content**, Noise & Health (Volume 15, Issue 62, 2013), 73-78. Nick Perham, http://www.noiseandhealth.org/article.asp?issn=1463-1741;year=2013;volume=15;issue=62;spage=73;epage=78;aulast=Perham

80 **More than Food: Engineering Quiet in Restaurants**, The Rare Republic, http://rarerepublic.com/features/food-engineering-quiet-restaurants.html

CHAPTER 17 – Visual Comfort
• • • • • • • • • • • • • • • • • •

81 **Cornell University Lighting the Computerized Office, 1989** Alan Hedge, William R. Sims Jr. , Franklin D. Becker

82 **Case History: Federal Building and Courthouse Save Taxpayers Money**, National Lighting Bureau, http://www.nlb.org/index.cfm?cdid=10374

83 **Daylighting and Productivity in the Retail Sector**, Report for Heschong Mahone Group, 2004 Ramona Peet, Lisa Heschong, Roger Wright, and Don Aumann, 7-284, http://www.eceee.org/library/conference_proceedings/ACEEE_buildings/2004/Panel_7/p7_24

84 **Your Circadian Clock is Critical to Your Memory**, Nov 2008, Mercola.com http://articles.mercola.com/sites/articles/archive/2008/11/01/your-circadian-clock-is-critical-to-your-memory.aspx

85 **Coping With Excessive Sleepiness; The Sleep-Diabetes Connection**, Denise Mann, WebMD http://www.webmd.com/sleep-disorders/excessive-sleepiness-10/diabetes-lack-of-sleep

Obesity Prevention Source, Waking Up to Sleep's Role in Weight Control, Harvard School of Public Health; http://www.hsph.harvard.edu/obesity-prevention-source/obesity-causes/sleep-and-obesity/

86 **Melatonin, Sleep Disturbance and Cancer Risk**. Sleep Med Rev. Aug. 2009 Aug;13 D.E. Blask https://www.ncbi.nlm.nih.gov/pubmed/19095474

87 **Exposure to Natural Light Improves Workplace Performance**, Psychology Today, June 2013, Christopher Bergland, http://www.psychologytoday.com/blog/the-athletes-way/201306/exposure-natural-light-improves-workplace-performance

(Abstract) in Journal of Sleep and Sleep Disorders Research, Volume 36, 2013 http://www.journalsleep.org/Resources/Documents/2013AbstractSupplement.pdf

Exposure to Natural Light Improves Workplace Performance, The Athlete's Way – Psychology Today, 6/5/13, Christopher Bergland, http://www.psychologytoday.com/blog/the-athletes-way/201306/exposure-natural-light-improves-workplace-performance

88 **Windows and Offices, A Study of Office Worker Performance and the Indoor Environment**, CEC PIER 2003, Study by California Energy Commission and Heschong Mahone Group

89 **Windows and Classrooms: A Study of Student Performance and the Indoor Environment**, CEC PIER 2003, Study by California Energy Commission and Heschong Mahone Group, 2003.

90 **Daylighting Brightens up Energy Picture**, Logistics Management, 6/1/04. James Cooke

91 Chicago Tribune, 6/5/02, http://www.highbeam.com/doc/1G1-118745671.html

92 **Body Clocks, Light, Sleep and Health**, Spring 2011, Daylight Architecture Magazine by Velux, Russell G. Foster, Oxford University, http://www.velux.at/de-AT/Documents/PDF/Publikationen/DA15_Complete.pdf

93 **Indoor Exposure to Natural Bright Light Prevents Afternoon Sleepiness**, 2006 Sleep 29(4) K.Kaida, M. Takahshi, T. Haratani; Y. Otsuka, K. Fukawawa, and A.Nakata, http://www.journalsleep.org/Articles/290409.pdf

94 **Study: Office Daylighting Boosts Worker Health**, The Fifth Estate, 8/12/14. Cameron Jewell, http://www.thefifthestate.com.au/innovation/design/study-office-daylighting-boosts-worker-health/65642

95 **Light-scattering Nanoparticles Help LEDs Mimic Sunlight Like Never Before**, Digital Trends, April 2014, Drew Prindle, http://www.digitaltrends.com/home/new-led-panel-technology-uses-nanoparticles-accurately-mimic-daylight/ http://www.digitaltrends.com/home/new-led-panel-technology-uses-nanoparticles-accurately-mimic-daylight/#ixzz3CuktzTp3

96 **Why We Want a House With a Great View**, July 2013 Houzz, Mitchell Parker http://www.houzz.com/ideabooks/15071371/list/why-we-want-a-house-with-a-great-view

97 Lighting – Computer Ergonomics, Ontario Ministry of Labour, Nov. 2010 http://www.labour.gov.on.ca/english/hs/pubs/comp_erg/gl_comp_erg_3.php

   Eliminating Computer Eyestrain – a eBook Resource http://www.ehs.iastate.edu/publications/ebooks/Eyestrain.pdf

98 **Task Lighting Solutions: Their Economic and Ergonomic Benefits**, Humanscale, Karin Tetlow, http://www.humanscale.com/userfiles/file/tasklightingsolutions.pdf

100 **Fluorescent lighting, Headaches and Eye-strain**, Lighting Research and Technology, Vol. 21, 11-18, 1989, A. J. Wilkins, I. Nimmo-Smith, I., A. Slater & L. Bedocs, http://lrt.sagepub.com/content/21/1/11.abstract

100 **Canadian Centre for Occupational Health and Safety**, http://www.ccohs.ca/oshanswers/ergonomics/lighting_flicker.html

CHAPTER 18 – Thermal Comfort and Indoor Air Quality
. . . .

101 **Energy Saving System to Remove Volatile Organic Compounds (VOCs) from Indoor Air**, IB-2970, Lawrence Berkeley National Laboratory, http://www2.lbl.gov/tt/techs/lbnl2970.html

102 **Air Quality and Thermal Comfort in Office Buildings: Results of a Large Indoor Environmental Quality Survey**, Berkeley Center for the Built Environment, University of California, C. Huizenga, http://escholarship.org/uc/item/7897g2f8#

103 **Impacts of Indoor Environments on Human Performance and Productivity**, Lawrence Berkeley National Laboratory, http://www.iaqscience.lbl.gov/performance-info.html#self-est

104 **Using Cell phones to Negotiate Energy-efficient Settings in Office Buildings**, MIT Technology Review, Burcin Becerik-Gerber, 2013, http://www2.technologyreview.com/tr35/profile.aspx?trid=1315

CHAPTER 19 – Health, Work-Life Balance & Productivity
• •

105 **WELL Building Standard Executive Summary** http://nowinteractive.net/delos-downloads/ WBS-Executive%20Summary-Apr2014.pdf

106 **The Effects of Indoor Air Quality on Performance and Productivity**, International Centre for Indoor Environment and Energy, Technical University of Denmark, published in Indoor Air, 2004,http://www.ncbi.nlm.nih.gov/pubmed/15330777

107 Website to calculate a walk score http://www.walkscore.com/

108 **How to Build a Better Call Centre**, Canadian Business, April 2012, Jeff Beer, www.canadinabusiness.com/business-strategy/how-to-build-a-better-call-centre/

109 **Not A Happy Accident: How Google Deliberately Designs Workplace Satisfaction**, Fast Company, March 2013, Mark C. Crowley, http:// www.fastcompany.com/3007268/where-are-they-now/ not-happy-accident-how-google-deliberately-designs-workplace-satisfaction

110 **Employee Incentives – 5 Companies That Go the Extra Mile**, Wagepoint, Feb. 2013, Brandy Davis, http://wagepoint.com/blog/5-companies-that-go-the-extra-mile-for-employees

CHAPTER 20: Is Your Portfolio Green & Productive? You Can Measure It – Really.
• •

111 **The State of Telework in the U.S. – How Individuals, Business, and Government Benefit**, June 2011, Kate Lister & Tom Harnish, http://www.workshifting.com/downloads/downloads/ Telework-Trends-US.pdf

112 **The Workplace Of The Future Is Still The Office**, Rawn Shah, Sept. 2014, http://www.forbes.com/sites/rawnshah/

113 **Marissa Mayer Breaks her Silence on Yahoo's Telecommuting Policy**, Fortune, April 2013, Christopher Tkaczyk, http://fortune.com/2013/04/19/ marissa-mayer-breaks-her-silence-on-yahoos-telecommuting-policy/

114 **Using Workplace Data Analytics to Match Corporate Real Estate Supply and Demand**, Realcomm, July2014, John Hampton, Senior VP, Corporate Solutions, JLL, http://www. realcomm.com/advisory/advisory.asp?AdvisoryID=648

115 **Eight Metrics Every Facility Manager Should Track**, *i*-office, Dec. 2013, www.iofficecorp.com

116 **Global Workforce Study 2012, Towers Watson**, http://www.towerswatson.com/assets/ pdf/2012-Towers-Watson-Global-Workforce-Study.pdf

117 **Productivity: Impacts of Ambient Noise, Speech Privacy & Acoustical Conditions on Worker Performance – A Review of Independent Research**, 2004David M. Sykes PhD, IAPP, HFES, https://www.speechprivacysystems.com/wp-content/uploads/2009/10/ Productivity_Acoustics_Overview0805.pdf

118 **How Social Networks Network Best**, Harvard Business Review, 2009, Alex Pentland, http://hbr.org/web/2009/hbr-list/how-social-networks-work-best